EXISTENCE, EXPERIENCE AND ETHICS

Prof. S.A. Shaida

EXISTENCE, EXPERIENCE AND ETHICS

— Essays for S.A. Shaida —

Editor
A. Raghuramaraju

D.K.Printworld(P)Ltd.
NEW DELHI - 110 015

Cataloging in Publication Data — DK

Existence, experience and ethics :
essays for S.A. Shaida / editor,
A. Raghuramaraju.
Includes bibliographical references.
Includes index.

1. Existentialism. 2. Self. 3. Experience.
4. Ethics. 5. Philosophy. I. Shaida, S. A.
(Sultan Ali). II. Raghuramaraju, A., 1957 –

ISBN 81-246-0138-0

First published in India in 2000

Published and printed by :
D.K. Printworld (P) Ltd.
Regd. office : *'Sri Kunj'*, F-52, Bali Nagar
New Delhi - 110015
Phone: (011) 545-3975, 546-6019; *Fax*: (011) 546-5926
E-Mail: dkprint@4mis.com

Preface

To his innumerable students, friends and admirers, Professor Sultan Ali Shaida is a personification of 'Sweetness and Light.' They have found in him a flower of liberal education at its best that spreads its fragrance wherever it goes. This volume is a token of affection and gratitude they feel towards him for not only his pedagogical abilities and academic competance but also for the values he stands for as a socially sensitive individual. It is my pleasant task to say a few words both about the volume and the towering personality to whom it is dedicated.

Professor Shaida is a keen student of philosophy as well as literature and has published in these areas books and papers both in English and Urdu. An active student leader at Aligarh Muslim University with sympathy towards the Left movement in politics, he was later inducted into the Communist Party of India as a party member (a 'ticket holder' in common parlance). Subsequently, his social and political commitments and preferences moved him towards philosophers such as Sartre and Marcel. After his studies at AMU, he started teaching at Zakir Hussain College (formerly, Delhi College) of Delhi University and completed his Ph.D., in Ethics under the guidance of Professor S.S. Barlingay on Naturalistic Fallacy. In 1975, he shifted to IIT-Kanpur. Interaction with the students and teachers of science and technology apart from those of Humanities and the vibrant academic activities at IIT-Kanpur, made him overcome his nostalgia for Delhi. He got used to this new ambiance. He has earned the respect of all who have come into contact with him. The ever-increasing circle of friends and students has found in him an embodiment of sobriety and warmth.

He was a U.G.C. National Lecturer in Philosophy during 1984-85. He is on the editorial board of *Indian Philosophical Quarterly* and *Aligarh Journal of Islamic Thought*. Professor Shaida was also in the panel of Taraqqi-e-Urdu Board and Bureau for Promotion of Urdu, Ministry of Education, New Delhi.

In his official capacities, he has always been patient, polite and accommodative. At IIT-Kanpur, he held several posts. He was the senate nominee on the Board of Governors; Head, Department of Humanities and Social Sciences; Chairman, Council of Wardens. While in service he went to Malaysia where he held the post of Professor at the International Islamic University, Kuala Lumpur, from February 1989 to December 1992. Professor Shaida superanuated from IIT-Kanpur on June 30, 1996.

Professor Shaida's major philosophical concerns have been in the areas of Existentialism, Aesthetics, Literature and Ethics. The volume concerns the themes of his abiding academic interests. As he always argued for inter-religious dialogue, the volume has in its Section IV three special essays on this subject.

It may be pertinent here to recall the academic space inhabited by Professor Shaida, and in the process to broaden the context of the volume. The Indian Institutes of Technology have played an important role in education in the post-Independent India. IIT- Kanpur has the unique distinction of having a large faculty of Humanities and Social Sciences (HSS) from its inception. In India, perhaps, it is only in the IITs that the humanities and technology departments are situated very close to each other. The Department of HSS at IIT-Kanpur continues to have an ambivalent relation with the dominant technological ethos of the IITs. The two important components that have shaped this ambivalence are: (i) the point of view which accepted the physical science methodology and, following positivism, oriented the humanities and social science courses along the lines of physical sciences; and (ii) the point of view which highlighted the fundamental differences between physical sciences and humanistic studies. This latter stream quite often implied a forceful critique of positivism both within natural and humanist studies. Those belonging to this stream offered courses such as sociology of knowledge, Indian Philosophy, Political Philosophy, Marxism, Gandhism, Phenomenology and Existentialism. This stream has largely remained non-positivist, even anti-postitivist and brought into the discussion more complex issues surrounding both individual and collective existences. Professor Shaida belongs to this non-positivist stream and the essays in this volume too share his perspective.

On Professor Shaida's superannuation, it was decided by his friends and students to bring out a volume. A venture of this kind could not have succeeded without the constant support and encouragement of many. I would like to acknowledge Professor Shaida, who played a role of a catalyst — remaining outside yet facilitating — for his help whenever I needed. The contributors to this volume have not only positively responded to my request to contribute an essay but also promptly sent them making it easier for me to process this volume for publication. For this, I am indebted to them in more than one way. I particularly want to express my sense of gratitude to P.R. Bhat, Bhargavi V. Davar, Sasheej Hegde and K.S. Prasad, for their valuable suggestions in preparing this volume. They have carefully read some of the papers and suggested modifications. They were always available to me whenever I needed help.

I also thank Margaret Chatterjee, Bijoy Boruah, A. Ramamurthy, Amitabha Das Gupta, S.G. Kulkarni, Nizar Ahmed, Dinesh Srivastava, Goutam Biswas, M.A. Moid and many others who extended their help and made important contributions. I cannot forget the help that my students — Gautam Satapathy, Bala Ganapati — extended to me in typing and proof reading the manuscript. Finally, I thank D.K. Printworld (P) Ltd., New Delhi particularly its Director Sri Susheel K. Mittal for publishing this festschrift.

It was a pleasure editing this volume. Never feeling alone, I found myself in the company of friends whose cordiality and concern were reminiscent of Professor Shaida. I join my contributors in wishing Mrs. Zeb Shaida and Professor Shaida a life of joy and bliss.

Aug. 1999 **Raghuramaraju**

Contents

PART II
EXPERIENCE

PART III
ETHICS

PART IV
ETHICS APPLIED TO RELIGION

Introduction

A. Raghuramaraju

THE sheer diversity of topics represented in this volume to honour Professor S.A. Shaida, present a challenge for any editor to grasp the reach (and the limitation) of the discussions. Though the essays can be organised in different combinations, I shall present here, by way of introduction, one such possible combination. In doing this, I have extracted internal patterns available amongst the various essays; and also have at times and when necessary brought extraneous relations to hold the diversity of the material in this volume together. The larger philosophical context of this volume is its attempt to implicate critically the horizon of modernity. The postulation of an autonomous individual marked the beginning of the project of modernity. This project initiated by Rene Descartes has two fundamental features, namely, what it excluded and what it included. Yet another important feature of this process is the logic of exclusion and inclusion. This project, at least in its initial stage, excluded from its domain all that is given in culture and society, thus inaugurating a discontinuity between modernity and the pre-modern. It accepted the notion of individual defined as exclusively constituted by (and constituting) the cognitive elements, instrumental rationality, objectivity and universality. This acceptance seems bereft of any reference to the non-cognitive aspects, such as emotions, context, history, culture and tradition.

The essays in this volume present:

(i) Different critiques of this autonomous individual's existence, its notion of agency, and suggest alternatives by highlighting other aspects, namely, existence as 'you' and as 'we'.

(ii) They highlight the place of experience, particularly the aesthetic experience.

(iii) Further, they critique, within the ethical domain, the notion of rationality, objectivity and universality. They also present other modes of justification, such as context-laden justification, and argue for the possibility of a dialogue between different contexts.

(iv) And lastly, they bring back into discussion the religious domain in a revised form, particularly highlighting the need and the imperative for setting the terms of inter-religious dialogue.

The volume is divided into four sections.

Section I, entitled ***Existence: 'I', 'You' and 'We'***, represents different interrogations of the autonomous individual existence postulated by modernity. Each of the essays attempt to broaden the ground of existence by highlighting aspects of its 'underside': the mental, the 'insane' aspects of mind, the experience of pre-self-conscious self, the history of autonomous individual before its invention in modern Europe, and such other forms of existence as 'you' and 'we'.

The project of modernity has championed the establishment of an autonomous 'I', the self. The 'cognitive self' postulated by Descartes reduced everything to the self. This reduction is both the strength and the weakness of this formulation. The essays in this section, while critiquing the attendant reductionism, point out the other important aspects within 'self'. Margaret Chatterjee's essay provides a comprehensive introduction to the section by presenting three forms of human existence, existence as 'I', as 'you' and as 'we'. The recognition of existence as 'you' alongside existence as 'I', enlarged the field of existence; positively facilitated a better understanding of existence as 'I';

and further helped in avoiding the possible danger of 'I' from relapsing into solipsism. However, this recognition and the acceptance of inter-subjective domain didn't pay enough attention to another important form of existence, that is, existence as 'we'. The author, drawing insights from the Jewish texts, argues for the need to recognise the importance of 'we' and its corollary the cultural and communitarian social space to facilitate a more realistic grounding of 'I' and 'you'.

Amitabha Das Gupta argues against the contemporary approach to mind especially the physicalists' who reduce mind, i.e., the 'subjective conscious mental states' to mere neurological states. In this context he seeks to arrive at a conception of **what mental states are** through the study of what **mental states are not.** While Das Gupta discusses the reductionism from outside, Bhargavi V. Davar in her essay explicates the internal reductionism within the contemporary philosophy of mind where mind is reduced to rationality, health and sanity, thus discarding the socially constructed 'mental illness' as an aberration.

The fourth essay by Sasheej Hegde accepts the fact that self is the agent of knowledge and representation, and even the critique of knowledge. He, however, argues that

> any discourse about 'self' which does not ask critical questions about its own representation of history remain radically acritical.

Informed by this criticism of self by itself, Hegde lays bare different episodes of self: experience of self before the emergence of a self-conscious subject of experience; delineation of a philosophy of reflection, and so on. While Hegde points out the need to look at the history of self, critical of itself, A. Raghuramaraju in his essay points out a more distant place in history. He highlights the contribution of the medieval period to the emergence of modern self and its rights. He concedes that rights are born in the modern period. However, the author highlights the medieval period's contribution to human rights.

From these critiques of the reductionistic notion of an autonomous self, 'I', we move to another related theme, namely, the need to have the notion of 'you'. The two essays discuss the need to recognise 'you' in our understanding of 'I'. Ahmed Nizar in his essay discusses how the self, 'defined as interiority is inconceivable without something exterior with which it is conceptually coupled'. Arguing along the same lines, Prasenjit Biswas elucidates the philosophy of Emmanuel Levinas. Levinas makes the understanding of 'you' as a necessity for the understanding of 'I'. The author situates this inquiry beyond the Husserlian attempt to arrive at unifying consciousness and the Heideggerian project of transcendental being.

Section II, entitled **Experience**, discusses the experiential domain; more specifically the artistic experience which constitutes an important facet of human existence. There are two essays that reject the two extreme positions in aesthetics, namely, that of purists and realists. Purists argue for the autonomy of art and the realists reduce art to facts. Bijoy H. Boruahs' essay instead advocates an alternative and suggests that,

> perhaps the mimetic virtue of art in the scheme of human life is such that neither pure aestheticism . . . nor documentary didacticism, . . . truly determines the connection between art-life and real-life.

The essay by Rekha Jhanji too draws our attention to the interdependence between life and art, particularly to the fact that artists draw sustenance from the experience of life situations, and by creating works of art they help others "to understand life and to come to terms with its manifold dimensions".

While the above two essays discuss the relation between art and reality, the following essay by B.N. Patnaik rejects the popular view that miscommunication is the 'reverse of communication'. The author explicates some of the essential aspects of the concept and analyses two stories of Milan Kundera, *The Hitchhiking Game* and *Edward and God*.

The other two essays in this section discuss aesthetics in Marxism and in the philosophy of G.E. Moore, respectively. S.S. Barlingay in his essay argues that the aesthetic notions such as 'good' are invariant across different theories. He asserts that "aesthetic problems will not be different if Marxism is accepted". For Barlingay, at most, these differences are merely in emphasis or in degree and not in kind. The other essay by Hasna Begum highlights the much neglected normative aspect in the writings of G.E. Moore. In this context, Begum explicates a special notion of spiritual existence often characterised by him only negatively, and discusses the relation between good and beauty, ethics and aesthetics. From an aesthetics that is concerned with the heightened level of experience, the next section deals with ethics, which is largely about the disciplining experience.

Section III, entitled **Ethics**, critically rallies around the ethical and methodological issues related to the modern concept of the autonomous individual. Universalizability and universality are the two important ideas associated with the modern concept of man. This eventually meant the rejection of any significance to 'context', particularly to the varying social contexts. There are two essays that contest this eventuality. The first essay by P.R. Bhat criticises the theory of absolute universalism and even the modified version by A. Gewirth, namely, the 'principle of generic consistency'. Instead, Bhat argues for the need to accept the universalism (of Kant and not Kantians) which "does not deny the social groups their rights." He calls this as 'linguistic universalizability'. The second essay by Satya P. Gautam concedes the contribution of liberalism in liberating the Western societies from the control of tyrants and priests. However, he argues that the universalistic stance adopted in the liberal political theory fails to take into account the concrete conditions such as gender, class, race, and ethnicity, conditions that produce and reproduce the privileges and oppressions. This failure, Gautam alleges, has grossly widened the gap between ideal principles and their actual practices.

Along with universality, the concepts such as rationality and objectivity form the cluster with important over-lappings, which again rally around the modern concept of the autonomous individual. The essay by Jagat Pal feeds off an interesting instance in R.M. Hare's ethical philosophy. Hare does not derive rationality from objectivity, which he rejects, but derives it from universalizability. Universality, defined as resting on the notion of consistency, is related in Hare to *phrastic* elements and not to the *neustic* elements. *Phrastic* elements, unlike *neustic* elements, don't determine by themselves the rightness or the wrongness of any contradictory judgements. Discussing a related issue, Vanlalnghak, in his essay rejects the view that value can be derived from the fact. Without claiming that facts are divorced from values, he argues that there is a link between the two but that it is not of a logical kind. As morality deals with real life situations, the author recommends the need to adopt analogical reasoning, where we move from fact to fact and draw some moral conclusions.

Deviating from the critique of context-free universalism, and the rejection of using deductive logical models in discussing real life moral issues highlighted in this section so far, the following two essays take us away from this framework. The first essay by V.T. Sebastian rejects the location of values either as objective or as subjective. He, working within the phenomenological framework, argues for the need to locate value within the life-world context in which 'I' turns to the 'thou', and 'I' and 'thou' joined together as 'we' become the originator of all social and cultural values. This life-world is not merely an objective world but it is accessible for interpretation. The culturally constituted value, according to the author, provides a better understanding of morality. The second essay in this direction by Pabitrakumar Roy takes us further away from the modern framework (in which even phenomenology is a non-reductionistic part) and towards two non-modern thinkers, namely, Plato and Gandhi. Roy distinguishes the two modern schools, Kantians and Utilitarians, who accepted 'act-centred' ethical theories against the 'agent-centred' ethical theories of both Plato and Gandhi. He lists the limitations of 'act-centred' ethical theories and highlights the importance of 'agent-centred' ethical theories.

Section IV, entitled **Ethics Applied to Religion**, has three essays, each discussing different aspects of inter-religious interaction. The first essay by Asghar Ali Engineer rejects the view of the rationalists who associate religion with dogmas. While accepting the presence of dogmas in religion, Engineer, however, maintains that these are contingent and constitute aberrations of the religious discourse. He, through the use of the distinction between 'norm' and 'context', explains away various historical aberrations and dogmas as contextual, hence contingent, and not normative. For him, normatively all religions, though they may highlight different virtues — Hinduism—Non-violence; Christianity—Love; Islam—Justice; Buddhism-Compassion - are all complementary to each other. He specifically analyses the developments within Islam and Hinduism, and shows how communalism between these communities is politically motivated and not originally founded. The second essay by Syed Vahiduddin too highlights the importance of diversity, particularly religious diversity, and suggests that

> the plurality of faith [is] not . . . a curse but . . . a necessity born of the human situation.

He adds:

> One-sidedness in religion leads to fanaticism .... [and] only a superficial view can see in the encounter of religions irreconcilable hostility.

While Engineer clears the ground for a dogmaless religious discourse and inter-religious complementarity, Vahiduddin highlights the importance of religious diversity and inter-religious interaction. The last essay of the volume by Goutam Biswas provides a clear methodology to implement inter-religious dialogue. In this context, Biswas closely analyses the very concept of dialogue. This clarified notion of dialogue proceeds and 'over passes' language: it starts from experience, proceeds through the language, and reaches beyond language. Biswas asks, "How is inter-religious or intra-religious dialogue possible?" He examines the three approaches of — Phillips, Hick and Friedman — and concludes that Friedman's idea of 'touch stone reality' rightly answers the dilemma of religious particularism verses religious universalism.

Thus, the volume relates the three main topics, existence, experience and ethics. In this context, the essays identify the limitations of the major definitions of the modern self, the enlightenment notions such as rationality, objectivity and universality. Different alternatives are suggested to overcome these limitations. The uniqueness of this volume lies in its multi-disciplinary space of articulation. Further, I think the methodological ground cleared by most of the papers could lend a further critical edge to contemporary studies of the modern disciplines.

Part I

EXISTENCE: 'I', 'YOU' AND 'WE'

1

'I', 'You', and 'We': An Exploration*

Margaret Chatterjee

WHAT I shall venture to explore centres on the German contribution to the analysis of inter-subjectivity. If I am asked why this particular bit of intellectual history should have any relevance today I can only indicate in signpost fashion that I think that Kant's difficulty over relating the transcendental, empirical and noumenal has not yet been overcome, nor has a problem arising from the Hegelian legacy, that of relating history as such to personal histories, been solved either. The subtext brings in the consideration that the main contributors to the story were Jewish, heirs not only to Kant and Hegel, but no less to Maimonides, Kabbalah, Hasidism and the imperatives of community. To recognise in "inter-subjectivity" a misnomer for an interpersonal situating whose fulfilment lies in *hevrutah* or community provides an insight worth pondering over in our *fin de siècle* times when solitude may appear as the only alternative to extreme gregariousness and the herd mentality.

So let us recall what is set us as a task. How does the "We" establish itself through the tantalising boundaries of skin, words, cultures, time gaps (then and now), intermittency of communication, the recoil from togetherness in aid of self-preservation, the natural pendulum between the towards and the away from. Or is the "We" primary, an undifferentiated

---

* Part of a keynote address presented at a Personalist Conference at Oriel College, Oxford, August, 1995.

matrix out of which emerges/develops the "I" and the "You". Epistemology has served us ill in opening up this particular area. At most, subject/object language could be paralleled by subject/subject language. But this presupposed the centrality of the individual self and its world, so that a subject/subject relation only seemed feasible if one subject succumbed to the other and sunk into the condition of object. In other words an implicit dominance-submission model would prevail, reversible perhaps between the parties concerned but scarcely yielding a "We".

Where should one begin? Kant's Transcendental Ego, which is no one's ego in particular but the condition of the possibility of experience, might serve as a starting point. The associated notions of *denken überhaupt* and the synthetic unity of apperception likewise are fertile, were it not for their strictly intellectual character. This brings to mind a comment made by Feuerbach in his graduate thesis of 1828 on "On reason, one, universal, infinite."[1] It reads as a panegyric to reason, and yet there is a sting in the tail: "In thinking I am thus mankind not the individual, but no-one in particular". The Hegelian *Geist* in comparison is far denser, thicker, with transcendental logic left behind. The master/slave analysis is an alternative treatment of *recognition* to Kant's third moment of synthesis (i.e., synthesis of recognition in a concept), providing a "We" grounded in reciprocal recognition but pegged in terms of inequality. It is this inherent lack of parity that Sartre struggles with and that issues in his rather skew-eyed analysis of love. While Kant's opus sparked off this train of thought in epistemology it must be admitted that the import of his ethical writings leads in a different direction. Following through the advice of the Paralogisms, the soul provides a useful regulative idea *vis a vis* our commerce with *others.* The "end" idea (the advice not to treat others as means) likewise is to be applied to others rather than to oneself. The *telos* of a kingdom of ends serves as a reminder of the dignity of persons. No existentialist could put it better. This image prevails until he

1. Henri Arvon, *Ludwig Feuerbach ou la Transformation du sacré*, Presses Universitaires de France, Paris, 1957, p. 9.

reflects in his old age not so much on theodicy as on the radical evil within man himself. There can be no surer subverter of the "We" than this. The "We" is utterly mocked in the barbarities of the torture chamber and the concentration camp. Kant's original confidence in the "We" (I am reading this into his oeuvre as an Enlightenment thinker) was founded on the capacity of reason, as he thought, to be practical. In other words it is an ethical "We" that he talks about. It is spelt out in the kind of discourse generated by moral reflection, and which, for him, was intimately connected with the possibility of civil society. We are at a considerable remove from what I call the negotiated "We" which stemmed from British philosophical sources and may well have had as one of its roots a longer history of parliamentarianism than prevailed on the continent. That is as may be.

The Hegelian "We" is of such gigantic proportions that it is no wonder that liberal thinkers boggled at it. However other possibilities were available in the basket of ideas in the 1840s. Feuerbach surfaces with two which could reveal a dilemma, man's awareness of himself as a species and the distinction between I and Thou, for the former is at a level of high generality and the latter shows itself in specific dyadic relations. But Feuerbach saw these as two sides of the same coin[2]. He writes:

> The single man for himself possesses the essence of man neither in himself as a moral being nor in himself as a thinking being. The essence of man is contained only in the community and unity of man with man; it is a unity, however, which rests only on the reality of the distinction between I and Thou.

The discourse of alienation as proffered by several writers of the time can be seen as specifying the various ways in which what one could call the primitive "We" is ruptured. Moses Hess's article on "The Essence of Money" (1843-4) shows how the money economy subverts the concept of humanity, and Marx's

2. *Principles of the Philosophy of the Future,* 1843, pp. 859 and 860.

well-known chapter on "The Mystery of the Fetishistic Character of Commodities" in *Das Kapital* works out a similar point with reference to the capitalistic mode of production. The discourse of rights also seems to teeter on the edge of an associated dilemma. The concept of rights is four-squarely based on the implications of individuality. But the rights of one coexist with the rights of another. This situation provides both the ground for conflicts of rights and the possibility of a joint affirmation of rights as in the case of co-ordinated action on class lines. This is but one example which points up the fact that matters concerning "We" are more likely to centre round issues in morals and politics than in epistemology. As such the "We" is seen as polarised not only to the "I" but to the "They". Political pamphleteering at a more popular level often notoriously invests the "They" with an aura of sinister plurality. But does all this suggest that with the mention of plural terms we have virtually abandoned talk of "persons"? I do not think that this is the case.

If the language of 'alienation' (*Entfremdung*) uncovered the problematic of "We" in a philosophical way there was another concept which focused on it in a context which spanned literature and philosophy. I refer to *Bildung,* a kind of ego-centered *paideia* which, paradigmatically in Wilhelm v. Humboldt, follows through individual *enteleché* in a single-minded manner, with others involved only in a quasi-instrumental capacity. We encounter here the agonies of romantic love portrayed in the literature of the times and especially in *Faust*. The Romantic theme of the wandered (cf. Werther) and the theme of unrequited love or at least of relationships which start in ecstasy and end in disillusion provide evidence of the problematic of the "We" which the philosopher should not neglect. Interestingly enough, both the romantics and Marx and Engels wrestle with a "We" broken loose from familial relationships. Romantic lovers are usually doomed thanks to the operation of contrary powers or, even more unkindly, the inability of passion to sustain itself. But what about the class idea? This is built on a commonality of *interest* and as such not entirely free of an element of negotiation. Having lost their chains the primal "We" of the workers would presumably shine forth, or so the theory went.

But whether we can properly speak of a primal "We" remains a question to haunt us. It certainly haunts all discussions of man's species being, precisely that form of being which for Marx and Engels is ruptured through the private ownership of the means of production. For all the economic terms in which the argument is cast the social analysis remains grounded, it seems to me, in the deepest moral reflection. What is advocated is a radical change in the socio-economic structure of society so that man can recover his humanity and enjoy the "We" of membership of a just social order. The simplifications of the 1844 manuscripts have to be seen for what they are, part of a critique of an existing situation rather than a blueprint for tomorrow. That the "We" of class affiliation could collapse thanks to the subversive effect of wage differentials and other seductions could not be anticipated. Romantic lovers and social revolutionaries no less seemed fated to succumb to a 'world' with which yet another set of contemporaries were contending — the evangelicals across the Channel. The myths of perfect love, a perfect society, and a heavenly kingdom no doubt sprang out of diverse fermentations of thought. In each, however, it may not be too far-fetched to say, lay unpearled and unfulfilled the quest of a paradigmatic "We".

I wish to say a little about Husserl next which means moving forwards in time although backwards to Kant insofar as Husserl keeps as close as he can to a transcendental approach. Or one can put it this way. Marx and Engels at bottom set their sights on *Gemeinschaft,* believing that the obstacles to it are at the level of *Gesellschaft.* Husserl was very aware of the currency of relationships since he came to phenomenology via psychology, but seeks an enabling condition for our multiple strategies, the onion skin which is neither kernel nor root. Whatever is said in his *Cartesian Meditation V,* which provides the relevant text for this whole area of enquiry, presupposes an important point carried over from his earlier work, which amounts to a telling rebuttal of any charge of formalism as far as the Transcendental Ego is concerned. This, unlike Kant's cognitive subject, bears traces of the sedimented layers of personal history and this means that Husserl makes room for a very queer fish indeed, a kind of material *a priori.* I believe that in his excursus into the possibility of a transcendental "We" something very similar can be found. The Fifth Meditation bears the rather unfortunate heading of "Intersubjective Monadology". No doubt this is symptomatic of what seems to dog almost any attempt to establish intersubjectivity transcendentally, namely, a magnetic pull towards the Aristotelian concept of *enteleché* which after all, whether in Leibniz or elsewhere, has its locus in particularity. Apart from this Leibnizian cargo Husserl also carried another weighty piece of baggage, a Cartesian set of terms which he saw fit to utilise for his French audience. He speaks of the transcendental "We" as the 'subject' of the objective world, which might, I suppose, throw some light on the commonality of the world investigated by the sciences. Husserl's problem, within the terms of his own philosophical system is first of all how what is itself a centre of constituting can also itself be constituted, and then, translating this into the plural, what kind of bridge-building operation can link one centre of constituting activities with another. Otherness and commonality at the level of consciousness is not easy to reconcile. For example, he says, and I paraphrase, that the liaison with others is *sui generis,* an effective communion which is, to be precise, the transcendental condition of the existence of a world of men and things. This is reckoned to come about through what he calls 'pairing', which might mean, *inter alia,* that the other plays the role of counter-part *vis á vis* me and *vice versa.* This brings in the question of reciprocity, a concept used by some other writers too, for example Maurice de Nédoncelle and Martin Buber. But how we could ever *know,* within the framework of separate consciousnesses (behaviour being an unsure guide since we can pretend) about the other side, remains problematic. In fact, it may be more easy to identify situations when reciprocity is absent. Maybe this is why he says (the translation is mine):

> . . . each man is for another a physical, psycho-physical and psychic being constituting an open and infinite world which one can approach but which on the whole one never penetrates.[3]

He also utilises empathy and analogy as tools for trying to unlock a door which it seems hard to open. His most fruitful strategy however, is his invocation of the horizon idea:

> The 'secondary' world is necessarily given in the form of a horizon, that is to say it is accessible in taking off from the primordial world in an orderly series of acts and experiences.

Whether a horizon can be properly said to be *given* is a further matter I cannot go into here. But there is much to be said, after all, in favour of the *approximative* character of the "We". Bearing in mind the separate 'lived times' of the parties concerned, their discrete lifeworlds, the inherent perspectivism of all single standpoints, to say nothing of masking strategies and discontinuities at the dyadic level, and the snakepit of conflicting interests in collectivities, the "We" seems more like a *telos* than a starting point or presupposition. Husserl never really seems to abandon Augustinian rootedness in the subjective. That such a view of subjectivity has much to do with Christian reckoning of salvation in highly individualistic terms give us pause. Husserl is heir to a mainstream European tradition. To 'experience' another intentionally (i.e. as a content of consciousness) is probably impossible, and in any case would not amount to 'meeting'. To prune away all transcendental elements from the interlocking of empirical selves or histories where each is a loose and shifting nexus integrated more or less in certain relatively stable patterns would be, for Husserl, to succumb to what he dubs the standpoint of the "positive sciences". Why not only Husserl but some other philosophers too thought this to be an undesirable alternative can only be briefly indicated here. Not only Max Scheler, but G.E. Moore whose philosophical affiliations were vastly different,

3. *Cartesian Meditations,* Fr. Ed. J. Vrin, 1953, p. iii.

regarded the interpersonal realm as a locus of *value*. If there were to be a place for value in a world of fact it was surely here. To grant the thinness of the fabric[4] of human relations — its sheer contingency and incompleteness, the painfulness of the erection and demolition of defences — is yet not to deny a transparency uniquely able to allow the breaking in of the transempirical. Husserl takes us thus far. That successors who drew on his thinking were able to go beyond this by removing his methodological *epoché* shows that his attempt to articulate a *framework* for interpersonal relations could bear fruit.

At about the same time that Husserl developed some of Kant's ideas in a phenomenological direction, Hermann Cohen was drawing on the Kantian insight that the relation between man and man was essentially a moral rather than an epistemic one. Cohen takes into account Kant's thinking on the concept of mankind (which he echoed in his own discussion of *Menschheit/Humanität)* plumbing moreover for his working out of the religion of reason the rich Judaic sources which deal with the concepts of otherness (the concepts of stranger, brother, neighbour, foreigner). Mending of relations with others is made the vehicle of mending relations with God through the very structuring of the Yom Kippur ritual. The message pinpoints that there is no "We" without forgiveness, a category which surely straddles the ethical/religious divide.

The stages in Cohen's understanding of the meaning of "We" can be traced from the 1904 work *Ethik des reinen Willens* which reads as a response to Kant's *Tugendlehre,* i.e., the second part of his *Metaphysic of Morals* (1797) which deals with his doctrine of virtue. Cohen maintains that honour (*Ehre*) is derived from the "You" which is the source of the "We". Honour involves seeing myself in the other, whereas love, he says, involves seeing the other in myself. To say that totality inhabits each you — a linguistic usage which sounds awkward in English — seeks to convey, I believe, the peculiar relation of universality and

4. I borrow this phrase from Rowan Williams who uses it in another context.

peculiarity which the interpersonal situation embodies. Each "you" I address is a different you when the yous are successive separate persons. But the same might be said of this apparently single "you" before me from moment to moment. A few moments ago your smile spoke of content. But now a different mood sweeps over your face much as clouds sweep over the sky. Is there an *allgemeine Du* or an *allgemeine Wir,* a you in general or a we in general? Cohen comes near to inheriting a Kantian transcendentalism at this point. But in the work under discussion he still keeps to the language of virtues derived from the *Tugendlehre* and the totality referred to is the totality of the human condition of man as a moral being. The other person is the human in its particularity and finiteness. Or, put in another way, humanity is both the goal of human endeavour, a state of being where all treat each other as ends, and what is instantiated in each particular individual. This view was also held by Franz Rosenzweig for whom man inheres in mankind and mankind is "a kind of *telos* that has to be recognised in every human individual"[5]. Awareness of both aspects of this situation invests our actions towards the other with that universality which, following Kant, he identifies with the ethical.

The treatment becomes less formalistic in a work on the ethics of Maimonides published in 1908 (*Characteristik der Ethik Maimunis*). He writes:

> . . . there exists no I without a Thou. *Reah* means 'the other', the one who is like you. He is the Thou of the I. Selfhood is the result of an unending relation of I and Thou as well as its abiding ideal. . . . In short, selfhood ensues from the interaction between I and Thou.
>
> — *Ibid.,* III

He does not mention the "We" in this passage but the stance taken suggests that the I and the Thou are internal to the We.

---

5. Quoted by Nathan Rotenstreich in *The Philosophy of Franz Rosenzweig* (ed.), P. Mendes-Flohr, University Press of New England, Hanover and London, 1988.

After all the We is not only grammatically plural but ontologically such. Some circularities may not be vicious.

But Cohen does not stop here. His maturest thought came after he became a *baal teshuvah,* that is after his return from assimilation when he had discovered the insights of eastern Jewry. These insights took their first shape in the Berlin lectures of 1913 and 1914 and then in *Die Religion der Vernunft* which appeared posthumously in 1919. What earlier veers between postulate and goal now can be seen as *promise*. It is in fact the prophetic element which enables Cohen's treatment of the We to move from its transcendental moorings. It is in this work that his concept of correlation is introduced, a concept already utilised by Kant in one way and to be adopted for quite a different purpose later by Paul Tillich. The wineskins of Kantian critical idealism are no longer able to contain Cohen's ideas. The idiom henceforth will be Biblical, and, as Leo Strauss notes, also political. The key concept now is the fellowman (*Mitmensch)*. He writes:

> The correlation of man and God cannot be actualised if the correlation of man and man is not first included.

The category of personhood now becomes explicit. *Nephesh* or concrete embodied existence is presupposed. I often think that the whole discourse of persons would not have been needed if the concept of *nephesh* had been adopted by the gentile world. But Hellenism dies hard.

The individual is he who stands before God, and standing in this context connotes the stance of worship. The others that stand *with* me constitute the 'we' of the covenantal community. Cohen does not arrive at this position all at once. It is worked out through an elucidation of concepts in two languages — *Nebenmensch* (the next man), and *Mitmensch* (fellowman) and *ger* (stranger), *nokri* (foreigner) and *reah* (the other). What springs to notice in its topicality is the role given to pity in bringing about the transition from regarding another as 'next to' or 'near' and regarding him or her as 'fellow' or 'with'. Pity first arises for the stranger ("For ye were strangers in a strange land") and so the stranger should claim attention along with the orphan and the widow. Put philosophically rather than Biblically the 'we' takes birth in the discovery that the other is as you are, once a stranger. Put religiously this finds expression in the words of Rabbi Akiba: "Thou shalt love your other (*Reaḥ*), he is as you". To do otherwise is not so much to treat Thou as It as to treat You as He, the neutral term which connotes indifference. Put into the plural this is the 'they' of those with whom we do not concern ourselves, the 'they' and 'them', refugees, minorities, the marginalised. Cohen goes on to identify poverty, unrestricted property and war as the abrogation of 'we'. From this we can gauge how 'we' indicates not only the dyadic relation of man and man but the relation between peoples, between nations. Truth or faithfulness (the word *emeth* means both) lies at the heart of the 'we' of persons and the 'we' of nations.

With this Cohen's thinking echoes messianic motifs which he found fully in keeping with the Kantian-style conception of what is set as a task, a new era and a united mankind. The route indicated is one of suffering and compassion, a rediscovery of the 'I' purged of selfishness, a rejoicing in the Thou and an affirmation of the 'we' of common humanity. A further emphasis can be found in Rosenzweig's development of the theme of love of the neighbour in that such a love converts my personal time into the time of responsibility. A strong thread of ideas can be traced from this to Levinas' treatment of responsibility for the other. Love of the neighbour for Rosenzweig redeems the other from tragic self-enclosure, and presumably serves to redeem oneself also from the same tragedy. The question that might suggest itself over this syllabus of ideas is whether what might well be a non-symmetrical relation can properly be described by the term 'we'. There seems no inherent objection to such an ascription unless 'we' is to be reserved for paradigmatically mutual situations. Oblique but highly interesting commentary on this can be found in contemporary discussion among halakhists on the subject of Amalekites and Edomites and their more recent counterparts as identified by some in Israel today.

At first sight there would seem to be some link between Hermann Cohen and Martin Buber to whose ideas about 'we' I wish to turn next. The evidence, however, is inconclusive. His biographer Maurice Friedman writes that Buber began his first draft of *I and Thou* in 1916 and completed it by the autumn of 1919, the year in which Cohen's *Religion der Vernunft* appeared posthumously. Buber's own comment was that he had read it too late for the book to have influenced his own thought.[6] They had disagreed about the war and also about Zionism to which Cohen was opposed. Cohen never gave up his faith in the state and yet failed to see the need for a state for the Jewish people. Philosophically Cohen's orientation remained rationalist in the Kantian manner while Buber had been a pupil of Simmel and Dilthey. Buber denied not only the influence of Cohen, but also that of Rosenzweig to whom he had been very close indeed, and that of Ebner. It is in fact necessary to note the particular route by which Buber moved from a form of mysticism to his own characteristic insights into the interpersonal realm and then more specifically to the horizon of the 'we' which for him is eventually found in *hagshamah* or community, especially after his move to Israel. I only sketch this in barest outline.

For German scholars the difference between *Erfahrung* and *Erlebnis* pinpointed a distinction masked by the English word 'experience'. The experience of things, i.e., observation, was different from the interiority of lived experience. The latter notion no doubt owed much to Kant's treatment of inner sense, that is to say, to the temporal dimension of inner life. But as far interiority was concerned a much earlier stream of thought found in the discourse of religious mysticism purported to provide access to the *non-temporal.* If this had not been so the corpus of mystical writing would have been purely of psychological interest. So when Buber undertook doctoral work on Nicholas of Cusa and Jacob Boehme, he found that the whole concept of *Erlebnis* or lived experience needed rethinking. The thing to emphasise now was not the contrast with knowledge of objects but the capacity

6. *Vide* Afterword to *Das Dialogische Prinzip* written in 1954.

which mystics appeared to have to have entry into a special kind of *Erlebnis* through which unity could be attained 'with the world spirit'. What the latter phrase might mean in post-Hegelian times was of course a moot point. While Buber was a student at the University of Berlin he used to attend a club called the *Neue Gemeinschaft* where all such high-flying was tempered by at least three other sorts of intellectual enquiry. The first centred on the empirical interests of the psychologists who were exploring diverse methodologies for their own researches (whether psychology deals with *Erfahrung* or *Erlebnis* or something else is after all a vital matter if one is deciding how 'positive' a science psychology can be). The second took up the question posed by Simmel — how can subjective minds interact socially? The third trend, under the inspiration of Dilthey, posed questions about life and life-worlds, something which was not to be conflated with *Geist* in the Hegelian sense. The problem was that the notion of the 'lived through' was scarcely adequate to express either the mystical experience or the relation between one person and another. The three trends had as their origin the diverging interests of the disciplines involved, a divergence which throws light on the very different approaches of psychologists, sociologists and philosophers to this day. Psychologists became engaged with diverse data derivable from behaviour and speech, retaining the term 'personality' largely in the context of the analysis of development; sociologists turned to human interactive structures; and philosophers were left with the task of finding a via media between *Geist* and *Leben.* I still refer to the situation at this early stage of Buber's thinking. His move away from the *Erlebnismystik* presented in his book *Daniel: Dialogues on Realization* (1913) is significantly different from the move taken by those who found in the notion of *Existenz* the key to avoiding historicism on the one hand and biologism on the other. The German sources of his thought, including in this the work of Nietzsche, are not difficult to trace.

Not to be forgotten, however, is the rich Hasidic strand which relates intensities of experience, especially religious experience, to everyday life, finds springs of action in non-intellectual powers, and locates the proper employment of all human endowments in the micro community. The environing of human activity which at about the same time the scientifically minded were identifying in *Umwelt* (a concept derived from animal studies) Buber found, via Hasidism, in the human world, resulting in what he called *"die Ontologie des Zwischenmenschen"* (the ontology of between man and man). All this finds expression in his *I and Thou,* the book by which he became known in the English-speaking world. His treatment of 'meeting' provided a rallying point for personalist critiques of objectivism, and within theology, additional grist to the mill of those deriving personalist analogies either way, from God to man or man to God in lie of the analogies from nature prevalent in classical cosmological thinking. The impact on German Protestant theology was enormous — a theme for another occasion. Buber's work could be hailed by sympathizers in England who were out of tune with the prevailing mood of British philosophy in the thirties and forties. This mood was characterised by its almost obsessive interest in perception, no doubt in reaction to the questions of high generality treated by Bradley and other idealist philosophers. And yet the problematic of 'we' does not really feature in *I and Thou,* the main thrust of the work being the phenomenological elucidation of a realm distinct from that of the I/It relation.

What I now wish to suggest is that Buber was able to move out of his *Erlebnismystik* stage, into the analysis of I and Thou and beyond into *hagshamah* in ways which owe a great deal to his relation to A.D. Gordon, founder of the first *kvutza* (commune) formed in 1909 at Deganiyah. Gordon's "Letters from the Land of Israel" were published in *Der Jude* in 1916 and this was the year in which Buber started work on *I and Thou.* Descriptions applied by admirers to Gordon were always regarded as an embarrassment by him, and this includes both the use of the word 'mystic' and the phrase 'the religion of labour'. If mysticism involves a flight from the real world, from the bodily and from responsibility then Gordon was not a mystic. Labour, hard manual labour, involves the 'we' in harsh relation to nature. The possibility of this was grounded in his understanding of human consciousness. Two concepts in particular elucidate this, *ḥavvayah* (experience) and *hakarah* (consciousness). Each individual embodies the expanding energies of nature and this means that man is firmly *rooted* in nature. This is the source of experience. It is also the source of creativity. The human being gradually develops an expanded sense of personality, gaining sustenance from an environing world which includes parents, family, organic and inorganic nature. What Gordon calls consciousness is a kind of awakening, the emergence of 'I' within the flow of experience. This self-affirming capacity gives rise both to the development of personality and to a sense of loneliness. Ruptures of creativity occur both within the individual and in society when consciousness breaks away from experience in acts of self-assertion and claims to power which Gordon sees typified in the aggressive forms of totalitarian collectivity. Since what he indicates by the word experience is an outward-looking flow of the inner towards the environment including society we have here a way of thinking that has much in common with what more recently is described as open-mindedness. When experience flows through consciousness creative energies deploy themselves outward in an non-exploitative manner. This is the life of expansion in which the energies and labours of all can be enlisted and it is here that the 'we' shows itself. The prophetic nature of Gordon's writings derives much from Kabbalistic ideas, using them with a new import. Expansion (otherwise a characteristic of the divine) becomes the key to man's own nature and likewise his overflow of energies. Human creativity is seen as drawing the divine into the earthly, enabling man to ascend to the divine, but an ascent made in community. Eliezer Schweid speaks of this as an "inverted version of the Kabbalistic doctrine of flow and emanation"[7].

---

7. Eliezer Schweid, "Prophetic Mysticism" in twentieth century Jewish thought, *Modern Judaism,* 14 (1994), the Johns Hopkins University Press, p. 166. I am also grateful for an opportunity to discuss the relation between the two thinkers with him.

Gordon, it seems to me enables Buber to work out to the fullest extent how the *Verwirklichung* (realisation) foreshadowed in his early work must be cashed in terms of the world of human relations, and via the I/Thou nexus be embodied in *hevrutah* or community. This pulls together the many issues that occupied Buber throughout a long life of thought and action — spirit and life, *Gemeinschaft* and *Gesellschaft,* state and society, the teacher/pupil relation, the relation, the Jewish people and the nation — all of which involved the 'we' in various ways. Reality can be hallowed through work, not the mechanical work of the wage-slave but the kind of work Buber eventually saw for himself in the *kibbutzim* of Israel. He did not idealise work as some social theorists had done, but rather in his many involvements with a variety of social issues which included Arab-Jewish relations and his serious questioning of the ethics of the Eichmann trial he in fact explored the *hazards* in the face of which the 'we' concretises itself in fact.

Buber's explicit discourse on the 'we' falls within the inaugural course of lectures he gave as Professor of Social Philosophy at the Hebrew University of Jerusalem in 1938. In those lectures, *inter alia,* he had occasion to provide a critique of Heidegger's *Mitsein* which, on Heidegger's own showing, belongs to the level of the inauthentic since, *pace* Heidegger, the fundamental ontological question is not man's relation to others but his relation to himself. In other words Heidegger's treatment is monological. We have now to see why Buber should have hesitated to use the term 'we'. The analysis of distance and relation[8] which he gives identifies the difficulty of how to reconcile the quiddity of persons and the circumstance that their very being is a function of their relation to others. To tackle this almost involves assigning a greater weightage to the Thou than to the I. There is something very contemporary about Buber's perception of what he calls "the polyphony of the person's existence" if we recast this in terms of a nexus between themes

8. "Distance and Relation", first published in English in *The Hibbert Journal,* Vol. XLIX, 1951.

which constantly meet, collide, and yet gather together in a recognisable pattern. Could there be in this an echo of the reference Dilthey's (Buber's teacher) once made to the tonality of the day, finding *in* time and *over* time the development of themes which at any vertical cross section of counterpoint sound like a painful dissonance? It is almost as if, because of the dialogical analysis which is the nerve of his thinking, he is *wary* of speaking of 'we', and this because of the dynamic fluidity of any particular I/Thou relation. He does, however, in his inaugural lectures speak of an essential 'we' parallel to the 'essential Thou'. This is the basis of any particular 'we' that may arise. He writes:

> By *We* I mean a community of several independent persons, who have reached a self and self-responsibility, the community resting on the basis of this self and self-responsibility, and being made possible by them.[9]

He further says:

> Only men who are capable of truly saying *Thou* to one another can truly say *We* with one another.[10]

Since the 'we' for Buber is not conceivable without the I/Thou relation it is realisable *par excellence* in small communities. The way in which he saw nationhood in terms of a 'community of communities' was spelt out by him in his addresses to *kibbutzniks* once he was in Israel and his consultations with educators on a host of occasions in different countries. Living through the terrors of the thirties and forties on the continent as he had he always distrusted the 'we' which was based in any measure on power. The collectivisms of the times had an ugly face. Extreme individualism no less amounted to an opting out of the interpersonal realm. Buber had studied psychiatry in Leipzig, Berlin and *Zürich* and although he did not analyse the maladies

---

9. Martin Buber, *Between Man and Man*, Beacon Press, Boston, 1955, p. 175.

10. *Ibid.*, p. 176.

of the times through the lens of psychopathology to the extent that Karl Jaspers did he was too interested in human nature to ignore what psychologists were saying about it. Such concerns led him to dialogue with Carl Rogers in April 1957. The meeting was of interest for the way in which Buber detected a 'power' element in Rogers' techniques which were otherwise reckoned to be non-directive. It was on this occasion, moreover, that Buber characterised dialogue by mentioning three elements – surprise, the prizing of otherness, and acceptance of the other as he is, confirming him in his potentiality. This would seem to imply a holding back from any attempt to change the other.

To return to the discourse of 'we', Buber's later expositions of the dialogic relation throw further light on the role of speech in communication. Speech presupposes distance since speech occurs *between* persons. Through speech there can come into being a mutuality of 'making present'. What is clear, however, is that the 'we' does not express fusion, but rather, as John Macmurray puts it in his Gifford Lectures, a rhythm of withdrawal and return. This, however, Buber believed, could lead to a growth in selfhood, not a monadic selfhood but one held in the openness of relationship. Buber always denied that he was seeing dialogic relations in ideal terms although Levinas, for example, thinks he ignores the pathos of proximity and duality. Community perhaps was freer from the tension-fraught 'transactions' that dyadic relations can be heir to. At any rate the extent of the diffusion of the notion of I/Thou and of dialogue suggests that Buber's identification of a personal realm distinct from that of objects met a response among those who sought a way out of the positivist alternative no less than among those anxious to find a bridge between man and God through the dimension of personal relations. It is also interesting to note that no less a philosopher than William James anticipated Buber's terminology when he wrote: "The universe is no longer a mere It to us, but a Thou, if we are religious"[11].

---

11. *Essays in Pragmatism*, ed. by Alburey Castell, Hafner publishing Co. New York, 1949, p. 106f. First published as *Pragmatism*, 1907.

As for what he has to say about speech Buber is one with Gabriel Marcel in stressing the ontological weight of language. If such a phrase seems opaque one could illustrate the *loss* of the ontological weight of language from Chekov's *The Cherry Orchard* where in a near claustrophobic set, with the orchard visible outside, the family members talk past each other. In contrast to this the dialogue in Marcel's plays goes beyond mere conversation in a most painful probing of the wounds the characters have inflicted on each other. As dramatist and music critic Marcel had unique access to the two art forms which most of all present dissonant voices on the move, a working out in sound which may have no resolution. Moreover in both he is alive to the ontological weight of the unsaid, the unvoiced, gaps, rhythms continuing across pauses, the silence of refusal and the silence of rapport. There is also in both drama and music a puzzle about beginnings and endings. Why should the play/ musical composition begin here and end there rather than anywhere else. Both Buber and Marcel would bring as an answer to such a question the kind of interpretation they give of apparently chance encounters. The key lies in 'mystery' for both, but not in mysticism. The kind of verbal communication appropriate to mystery Marcel finds in invocation and Buber in addressal, each akin to prayer and very different from the current discourse of multiple narratives beating their wings in empty space.

I have had little to say about religion in these reflections and this may leave unsatisfied those for whom the Divine Being provides a paradigm of personhood. But the theme of the intersubjective seems wide enough. Moreover as the theist's concept of the Divine sets up an image of a thoroughly non-symmetrical relation with finite persons it seems to be unhelpful if one is trying to elucidate 'we'. The main theme in Buber's best known work is that of *presence* of each to the other, thereby confirming the other, something which is *familiar* in the human world although so often *lacking.* Since this is his focus he starts not with the relation to God but with the I/Thou relation which later provides a *simile*, as he tells us himself, for talking about

God. The 'turning' of which both A.D. Gordon and Buber speak is a turning in response and responsibility to the other. Neither could identify with the orthodox of their own community. Was it not perhaps an advantage to speak of the Centre,[12] of spirit, or as for Marcel, of Being, without necessarily mentioning the name of God? This is fully in consonance with his reference to each religion as an exile into which man has been driven. To erect boundaries between what is religious and what is not, between the holy and the profane, is to try to delimit what in reality is a plenum accessible in many ways, not excluding nature and art, but most of all in human relations. The last sentence of "Distance and relation" reads:[13] "It is from one man to another that the heavenly bread of self-being is passed." Passing would not be possible without distance. The 'we' does not require a cancelling of individuality but rather presupposes it. To conclude, of all writers attempting the difficult task of elucidating the 'we' Buber after all seems able to do what Levinas thinks he cannot do except in the rarefied air of 'spiritual friendship' — reconcile proximity and duality, individuality and community, identifying the subtle textures of horizontal relationships in the homespun fabric of everyday life.

---

12. *Werke*, I, p. 156.

13. *The Knowledge of Man*, tr. from the German by Maurice Friedman and Ronald Gregor Smith, George Allen & Unwin, Ltd., London, 1965, p. 71

2

What Mental States are Not

Amitabha Das Gupta

The Conflicting Scenario

THE scenario of the contemporary philosophy of mind does not present a coherent picture. It has failed to be coherent because of the presence of the two conflicting intuitions regarding what mental states are and are not. The two intuitions have been posed as mutually exclusive because each negates the other and thus a compromise between the two has been ruled out. The two conflicting intuitions are:

> *First*: Mental phenomena are really a species of the physical. This has been said in view of the explanation provided by the biological science regarding the constitution of our mental life. The philosophical view that mental is physical is thus the result of the scientific study of mind.
>
> *Second*: It is absurd to hold that mental phenomena are physical. By definition it cannot be other than physical. The reason is, to be non-physical is the essential property of the mental phenomena.

The two are the conflicting intuitions which give rise to two different traditions in philosophy of mind. The first may be characterised as the materialist/physicalist tradition whereas the second may be characterised as the essentialist tradition. In the contemporary scenario the intuition expressed in the essentialist tradition has been completely suppressed and instead physicalism has been celebrated as a ruling doctrine of the philosophy of mind. This has been done in favour of the scientific approach to mind.

The point to be noted here is that by suppressing the intuition of the essentialist tradition you are not overcoming the conflict. In fact by doing this you are suppressing the intrinsic feature of the mental phenomena. The conflict thus remains the same. The denial of the intrinsic feature of mental phenomena cannot lead to a satisfactory approach to mind. The outcome of this approach will be inevitably reductionistic. In behaviourism, we find mental states are reduced to dispositions to behaviour, whereas in physicalism mental states are reduced to certain neurophysiological mechanisms. Functionalism, of course, came as a much better alternative than the other two in terms of its approach to mental states, because mental states are defined by their causal relations. All these approaches within the tradition of the materialistic conception of mind deny the intrinsic nature of the mental phenomena i.e., the idea of having subjective conscious mental state.

If scientific reductionism is not an alternative, can essentialism be the alternative? I think this will be a wrong way of confronting the conflict. The issue is not that of confronting an either/or situation. The essentialist alternative is equally problematic. It involves an unwarranted metaphysics of mind which has been discarded long ago both on scientific and epistemological grounds. The situation thus demands resolving the conflict. But how to do it? This is particularly relevant if we accept that there should be a scientific study of mind. At this stage, a crucial question comes regarding what constitutes the scientific study of mind. One must have clear conception of this in order to undertake a scientific study of mind. This will itself resolve the conflict because a clear conception of a scientific study of mind cannot ignore the essential properties of mind, i.e. the subjective conscious mental states. This fact must be recognised and accordingly a new framework must be invoked for the study of mind. Reductionism arises because of the physicalists' refusal to see that mental states have essential properties which cannot be reduced to physical/neural state. As said earlier this does not imply to go back to Cartesian metaphysics. On the contrary, it suggests that the scientific study of mind instead of being reductionistic must take into account of the relationship between body and mind. In view of this, the basic strategy adopted in this article is to arrive at a conception of what mental states are through the study of what mental states are not.

There are three problems to which this article has addressed. Accordingly, they form the three sections of the article. The first section is on physicalism and the reductionistic programme that it initiates. The second section is on the critique of physicalism where my main concern will be to show the logical and the epistemological ground on which physicalism fails. The thrust of the entire objection will be to reestablish that mental states have non reducible properties. In the final section my attempt will be to show the necessity of accepting consciousness as forming the part of the scientific study of mind.

I

Physicalism: The Reductionism of the Mental

Physicalism assumes a distinction between a basic science like, physics and special sciences, such as, economics, sociology, psychology, etc. These special sciences in spite of their distinctive characteristics are governed by the laws of the basic sciences, particularly, of physics. In this respect, the crux of the argument is that the events of the special sciences can be all shown to be physical events on the ground that the laws under which they fall are laws of physics. Accordingly, in the context of psychology it implies that psychological attributes are no way different from physical attributes and they do not have separate existence apart from body. The description of various mental phenomena, such as, pain, desire, belief, etc. can be translated into the language of physics. This shows the centrality of physics while we try to describe the nature of mental phenomena. If the language of psychology is taken to be the language of physics then the subject matter of the former may be placed as the part of the subject matter of the latter. In brief, this is the general standpoint of physicalism expressed in the context of the study of mind.

The specific aspect of this physicalist thesis which has a crucial importance in philosophy of mind is the identity thesis. It is the identity about the two classes of events, namely , the mental and the physical. The proposal that mental and physical events are identical with each other is not an innocent proposal. It has a far reaching consequences. In fact, its scientific importance cannot be denied and that is why a description about what mental states are cannot be given without taking event identity thesis into consideration. If you want your description to be scientific you have to accept physicalism at some level. But what will be the nature of this physicalism has to be decided carefully if we don't want your theory to be reductionistic. On the basis of event identity thesis the two kinds of physicalism is distinguished. They are called type and token physicalism respectively. The former takes mental events in the sense of universals whereas the latter takes it in the sense of particulars. I shall now offer a brief description of the two kinds of physicalism characterised by the two versions of event identity thesis with an explicit aim to show their reductionistic nature.

TYPE -TYPE IDENTITY THESIS

As mentioned earlier, type physicalism advocates type-type identity thesis which essentially implies that the property of a certain kind of mental state is identical with the property of a certain kind of physical state. Thus, to use the familiar example of the physicalist, having pain is a mental property which is identical with C-fibre firing expressing a neural property of a physical type occurring within the brain or central nervous system. As we can see, identity involved here is between the two types and further the nature of this identity is so strong that there is an inseparable relation between the two. Churchland (1988: 26), thus, characterises it as numerically identical. As types, they are conceived as universals and since they are universals they are capable of instantiations. 'Pain' for example, is a particular type of mental state which is instantiated in different individuals.

There is a common sense objection to the thesis that mental events should be treated as neural events. The precise nature of the objection is that the nature of these two types of events are not same. Speaking purely from the point of view of common sense, mental states are normally thought of in terms of objects of experience. These objects are intentional objects or sense data. As a result, mental states are characterised by certain phenomenal features which do not have any spatial locations. Neural states, on the other hand, do not have any phenomenal characteristics but they do not lack spatial locations. Though these are obvious differences they are, nevertheless, fundamental to the constitution of the mental and the neural state. These differences suggest that identity between these two states cannot be obtained without involving into contradiction. Contradiction arises because that which is not mental is claimed to be identical with mental. Type physicalism commits such a contradiction.

The objection raised from common sense has been answered by the physicalists. As pointed out, the difficulty in connection with the identity thesis arises because of not defining what mental states are in scientific terms. Mental states are defined as objects of one's experience and thus the difference between mental states and neural states become apparent. But in actual terms, as the physicalist argue, there is no difference. J.J.C. Smart (1970: 67), for example, argues that mental states cannot be defined in terms of intentional objects or sense data. To say, for example, I have the experience of seeing yellow-orange is not to say that experience itself is yellow-orange. To speak alternatively, there is nothing called yellow-orange brain process. This clearly implies that the physicalist when they talk about identity they do not mean that it is the identity between intentional objects and brain processes. The notion of identity, on the other hand, implies the identity of mental events, such as, having the experience of yellow-orange image with a neural event in the brain. The common sense objection that type-type identity thesis involves contradiction may be thus over-ruled on the ground that the basis of this objection is spurious. However, one cannot fail to see the reductionism involved in the whole thesis. The thesis derives its entire strength from the fact of scientific reductionism — a fact which dismisses the Cartesian myth about the mind.

The next important point is that it is due to this scientific thrust, the identity thesis has been always posed by the type physicalist as a scientific hypothesis and not as a philosophical theory. The reasons provided for this are as follows. First, the identity between the two events, namely, the mental and the physical is a nomological claim. That means their identity is nomologically necessary where the event 'e' satisfying a psychological property is identical with the event 'e_n', satisfying a neurological property. The scientific nature of the claim further shows that identity among events is a matter of empirical discovery and hence all propositions concerning event identities turn out to be contingent in nature. As contingent propositions they are subject to refutation in the face of contrary evidence. This possibility allows the physicalists to accept that we can always conceive of pain without the corresponding neural state consisting of C-fibre firing. If this is so, the statement "Pain is not C-fibre firing" will not be taken as contradiction. The identity thesis involving the mind-brain identity is thus an expression of contingent but not of logical truth. It's truth is to be established not on any logical ground, but on an empirical ground. This shows that identity thesis has a nature which can be best characterised as a scientific hypothesis which provides justification for the reduction of the mental.

TOKEN PHYSICALISM: MULTIPLE REALISABILITY OF THE MENTAL

We have seen that type physicalism while talking about the identity of the mental with the physical relies on the lawful connection existing between the events of the two type. The idea of lawful connection supports whole scale reduction of the mental to the physical. Subsequently, it is felt that reductionism of this sort is neither attainable nor is it desirable. It is not attainable because the whole idea of lawful connection which provides basis to the reductionism is itself questionable. It is pointed out that there are no clear cut laws which connect the two domains unambiguously. It is not desirable because such a reductionism destroys the uniqueness of the mental. Token physicalism came as a consequence to these thoughts. As said earlier, the major concern of token physicalism is with mental particulars. In view of this major concern the formulation of token physicalism may be stated in the following terms. There are three statements involved in this formulation: First, my pain at time *t* is a mental token. Second, corresponding to this pain there is C-fibre firing in my body at time *t* which is a physical event. Third, hence my pain at time *t* is identical with the C-fibre firing in my body at time *t*. This is called token identity thesis where identity is ascertained not on the basis of any law because there is no law in clear sense of the term. Identity in this context thus implies that a particular mental event (my pain at time *t*) is identical with some physical events, such as, C-fibre firing. An important point to be noted here is that the notion of event in the domain of the physical is used in the heterogeneous sense. The essential implication of this point is that a particular realisation of a mental event is possible due to the operation of different physical mechanisms.

We find token identity thesis is figured prominently in the works of some of the leading philosophers of mind. Davidson (1980: 117-18) is one of such authors in whose writings we find an insightful argument in favour of token identity thesis. There are two important ideas of Davidson. First, events are classified as physical or mental on the basis of their descriptions.

An event is called mental because it involves mental description where as it is called physical when it involves physical description. This forms the two domains namely, the mental and the physical. Second, since the events are description dependent so are the laws which are also description dependent. There are laws governing the events of the physical domain and there are laws governing the events of the mental domain. In the domain of the physical there are causal laws by which events are explained whereas in the domain of the mental there is a rationality principle by which we explain the things like coherence or consistency of mental events, such as, beliefs, desires or intentions of the agent. From this, it evidently follows that the descriptions involving physical and mental events are bound to be different because the very nature of these two classes of events are different. As a result, as Davidson pointed out, there cannot be any causal law which can connect the events of the two domains. However, as Davidson insists, this does not rule out the possibility of having interaction between the events of the two domains. Causal laws may not be applicable to physical events in the same way as they are applicable to mental events. But, Davidson's point is that causal relation or interaction between the two classes of events is always there. As an evidence to this we find that a mental event may cause a physical event and at the same time, a mental event may be found to be produced by some physical events. On the consideration of this causal relationship, Davidson argues that mental events are identical with physical events. But this identity cannot be ascertained on the basis of a causal law, nor this causal relationship can be taken as the expression of a causal law. Davidson describes this situation as psycho-physical anamolism which arises due to causal anamolism associated with the two domains. Thus, I may know that a particular mental event is identical with a physical event without knowing what is the law binding these two events. In view of this, Davidson argues that identity of the mental with the physical does not imply reduction of the former to the latter.

A similar statement is found in the writings of Jerry Fodor (1980: 125) and Richard Boyd (1980: 87) Fodor's position is similar to the position held by Davidson. The central idea of Fodor is: A psychological event is identical with neurological event. But there is no lawful connection between the two. Psychological predicates and neurological predicates are different in nature and thus the former cannot be paired with the latter. This means that there cannot be any correlation between the two and as a result we cannot think of a law which could be the basis of this identity. Fodor's move is against reductionism with a view to keep a separate place for mental states. However, that does not make him to go against physicalism and that is the reason why we find Foder holding the position that each mental event is identical with some physical event.

The above description suggests that due to the absence of the explicit connection between the mental type and the physical type there could be different physical mechanisms which are responsible for the realisation of a particular mental kind. If this is so then it allows the possibility of a mental event or state to be realised in more than one way. Richard Boyd calls it the plasticity of an event which means that it is the part of the capacity of an event to be realised in more than one way. In the literature this is known as the multiple realisability thesis of token physicalism. In fact, this thesis leads to a consequence according to which a mental event can be realised in a non-physical way. Boyd, of course, makes it clear that it is a logical possibility implying, thereby, that it does not actually happen in the real world. However, the important point is that this possibility allows us to conceive of a mental event being realised in a non-physical way which implies rejection of physicalism. This is the ultimate fate of token physicalism which results into multiple realisability thesis.

I shall now go into the second section where I shall argue what is wrong with physicalism. While doing this, I shall not consider type and token physicalism separately. This requires justification and they are as follows: First, in spite of its differences, token physicalism presupposes type physicalism. In fact, without the support of the latter, token physicalism could not stand on its own. Davidson's argument that there is no explicit lawful connection to be found between the two types of events or Fodor's argument regarding the difficulty of pairing mental predicates with neurological predicates all point out the practical difficulties of type physicalism. They assume that there is a lawful connection but they don't assert it due to these practical difficulties. Hence, there is no qualitative difference between these two kinds of physicalism. Second, multiple realisability thesis has two implications. At one level, while it projects multiple realisability of the mental it assumes that there must be some physical mechanisms which allow such phenomena to be possible. The primacy of the physical has been never denied and, therefore, the thrust of type physicalism has been never minimised, without being reductionistic in its obvious sense. But it is equally important to note that some sense of reductionism is bound to enter into the very notion of token physicalism mainly on the ground that it fails to take account of the essential properties of mental state. The second implication of multiple realisability thesis is that it allows the possibility of a separate existence between body and mind. If this is so the entire ground on which token physicalism stands does no longer exist. The thesis suggests that for mind to exist it is not necessary that there should be a human body. A computer can thus have a mind and can feel pain. If this is the logical outcome of token physicalism a question may be now raised: In what sense does token physicalism exist? With these words I shall now go to the critique of physicalism.

II

Essentialism: The Objection from Qualia

The anxiety has been expressed at the beginning that the essentialist intuition regarding the nature of mental state cannot be rejected on the ground that it is not scientific or it leads to the acceptance of Descartes' dualism. The issues with which we are concerned here are: Do the mental states have essential properties or not? and, are they reducible to the properties of brain? According to the essentialist intuition, mental states have certain intrinsic properties. The properties which are essential to it are the phenomenological characteristics or qualitative aspects of mental states. Since these properties are intrinsic to mental states it is always possible that they may occur without the corresponding physical state. In short, this objection may be termed as qualia objection which states that phenomenal characteristics are intrinsic to mental states and, therefore, mental states cannot be identical to physical states. This speaks for the refutation of reductionism — a scientific programme initiated by physicalism.

Our next problem is how could we establish that mental states have essential properties? and, how could we form qualia objection in order to direct it against physicalism? This is where we find the celebrated answer given by Saul Kripke (1972: 332-42) which is directed against the type identity thesis of physicalism. On the basis of this theory of reference, necessity and essential properties, Kripke shows the untenability of type-type identity thesis. Kripke argues that natural kind terms, such as, water, heat, cold or pain are rigid designators. The reason for calling them regid designators is that they refer to the same kind of entity in all possible world. But why do they do so? This is where essentialism enters. By virtue of certain essential properties these terms behave in this particular fashion. It is important to clarify here that these essential properties do not belong to the descriptions that we attach to these substances. On the other hand, these properties are essential because they are intrinsic to these substances. That means they are the part of the very nature of these substances. Now given this perspective, take the example of water. As we all know, the essential property of water is consisting of one Oxygen and two Hydrogen atoms. 'Water' is thus defined as 'H_2O' and accordingly we say 'Water = H_2O'. If water is a rigid designator, so also is H_2O. The next argument of essentialism is: To say Water = H_2O is true is to say that it is necessarily true. This necessity follows from the fact that the sentence 'Water = H_2O' refers to the same kind of thing both in actual and possible world. It is evident that this statement expresses a necessary truth which we have come to know not through *a priori* analysis of the meaning of the expressions, namely, 'water' and 'H_2O'. On the contrary, we have come to know this truth *a posteriori* since the truth of this statement is established by scientific investigation. This is a case which goes against the traditional conception of necessity where to say that something is necessarily true is to say that it must be *a priori*. Both of them coincide. Kripke argues that this equation does not hold. A statement expressing necessary truth, such as, 'Water = H_2O' is determined *a posteriori*. As he points out, we cannot simply argue that it is a contingent statement on the ground that the truth it express is determined *a posteriori*. The identity statement 'Water = H_2O' is necessary.

However, as Kripke points out, the existing common tendency is, of course, different. We normally treat these sentences as contingent. Now this tendency though found to be common is an expression of a dogmatic belief which does not have any rational basis. This is Kripke's argument which calls for a total rejection of the dogmatic view. He worked out a strategy to expose this traditional error. His strategy consist of two steps. First, we have to find a genuinely contingent identity statement. Second, this may be obtained by replacing the rigid designator of the necessary statement by description. 'Water = H_2O' may be thus replaced by the definite descriptions: "The cooling tasteless, odourless, wetting liquid that quenches thirst = H_2O". As we can see this statement has now become genuinely contingent statement on the ground that the definite description replacing 'water by "the cooling tasteless . . . liquid that quenches thirst" may not refer to H_2O' but to some other chemical compound which Hilary Putnam calls XYZ. This possibility shows that there may be a chemical compound other than H_2O to which we apply the same description that we apply to 'water'. On the basis of this Kripke argues that the common tendency to consider the statement 'Water = H_2O' as contingent can be now explained in the light of the result obtained by applying the strategy. The statement 'water is H_2O' is treated as contingent because of our failure to see that the meaning of this statement is different from the meaning of the corresponding contingent statement obtained by replacing the expression 'water' by the definite description. We cannot distinguish the meaning of the two statements because we confuse the meaning of the former with the latter.

Kirpke claims that the similar kind of argument from the point of view of rigid designator can be applied to mental state terms. Mental state terms are like natural kind terms and as natural kind terms they behave like rigid designator. On the same consideration neural kind terms are also rigid designators. On Kripke's argument, identity statement like 'pain = C-fibre firing' must be a necessary statement like 'water = H_2O' and on the same consideration it must be also an aposteriori statement. Thus, 'Pain = C-fibre firing' as Kripke observes is an aposteriori statement.

However, like the earlier case involving the statement 'Water = H_2O' here also the common tendency is to treat the statement 'Pain = C-fibre firing' as contingent. There may be a world — a possible world where pain may not be necessarily identical to C-fibre firing. Thus, we can think of two possible worlds representing two different situations. In one case (PW_1) pain is felt in the same as we do in the actual world but it is felt without C-fibre firing. In the other case (PW_2) the situation is opposite, where there is C-fibre firing but there is no feeling of pain. Now the point is that these doubts are to be removed in order to establish that 'Pain = C-fibre firing'. Kripke points out that to do this the strategy that has been earlier adopted cannot be applied in the present case. The main problem is with the rigid designator 'pain'. In order to get a genuinely contingent statement the expression 'pain' has to be replaced by descriptions stated in terms of sensible properties. But this is not possible because 'pain' cannot be replaced by any such analogous expressions without involving absurdities. Let me explain this with reference to the counter instances of 'Pain = C-fibre firing' as cited in the possible world example. In the case of possible world, PW_1 the situation is that there are pains but they are not C-fibre firings and, therefore, they are not pains. Whereas in the possible world, PW_2 there are C-fibre firings but they do not feel like pain though according to the definition they are pains. It requires hardly any justification to say that this whole scenario is absurd. Sensible qualities are, on the other hand, not contingently related to pain. They are essential to pain. If something feels like a pain it must be a pain. Similarly, if there is a pain it must be felt as painful. There cannot be a possible world where pain fails to be felt as painful. The only way to identify pain is by feeling it. If there is a C-fibre stimulation without resulting the feeling of pain then the only natural conclusion will be that C-fibre stimulation occurred "without there being any pain" (Kripke). This goes against the necessity of the identity statement: 'Pain = C-fibre firing'. As Kripke concludes: "For a sensation to be *felt* as pain is for it to *be* pain."

The above considerations show that it is possible to defend such identities like 'water = H_2O'. But the same is not possible with 'Pain = C-fibre firing'. The main problem is that the contingency associated with this statement cannot be removed. The physicalist thesis that pain is identical with C-fibre firing is thus to be rejected. It significantly shows that mental states have essential properties which may not be reducible to physical properties. Kripke argues that the same essentialist objection holds true of token physicalism. The essentialist challenge makes it evident that there is something essentially wrong with physicalism. Without the qualitative aspects of the mental states there cannot be any true picture of the mind.

ESSENTIALISM AND CONSCIOUSNESS: THE EPISTEMOLOGICAL OBJECTION

From Kripke's argument we can reasonably infer the existence of a subjective conscious mental state. In fact, the former presupposes the latter. To accept that there are properties which are intrinsic to mental states is to grant that mental states are conscious. Thomas Nagel (1980: 159-68) calls it the subjective point of view which is analogous to the position defended by Kripke. I see Nagel's argument for consciousness as a culmination of essentialist intuition. With this idea in my mind, I shall now briefly discuss Nagel's argument. This will give a completion to the essentialist attack on physicalism.

Kripke opposes physicalism by showing that there cannot be any identity between the physical and the mental on a logical ground. Nagel, on the other hand, opposes physicalism by posing an epistemological barrier which says why the knowledge of objective facts regarding body can not give us the knowledge of mind. Identity is not possible on an epistemological ground. The basic barrier to this is the existence of consciousness. An organism may be said to have conscious mental states by virtue of a quality that is intrinsic to the organism itself. As Nagel says "an organism has conscious mental states if and only if there is something that it is like to be that organism — something it is like for the organism." For him this intrinsic aspect of mental states consist of "the subjective character of experience". Nagel points out that this feature of the mental has not been captured by the reductive analysis of the mental as found in the various scientific approaches to mind. A reductionstic programme in order to be successful must have a clear conception of that which is to be reduced. In this respect, as Nagel argues, mental phenomena and their subjective character have an inseparable relationship and, therefore, there cannot be any analysis of the former without adequately recognising the latter. Physicalism typically suffers from this defect. Let me explain this. In order to be scientific, physicalism seeks to give a physical account of the phenomenological features of the mental states. But Nagel rules out this possibility. The main ground of his rejection lies on the subjective character of mental states which are essentially associated with a singular point of view. Physicalism which is an expression of an objective physical theory rejects such a point of view. One may think that this subjective/singular point of view is concerned only with individual's point of view. But this is not so. It refers to what Nagel calls species specific point of view and thereby, it rules out the subjective point of view to be utterly individualistic in nature. Nagel, further points out, that there are not one but many such species specific points of view existing. They determine the character of respective species. Thus, just as what it is like to be human is determined by a particular species specific point of view similarly what it is like to be a bat or a martian is determined by the respective species specific point of view.

The major thrust of Nagel's work is that along with these subjective/species specific points of view he accepts that there is an objective point of view. The objective point of view is shared by the different subjective points of view but as such it is independent of the subjective point of view. They represent two different standpoints and, thus, as contrasts to physicalists, Nagel argues that the subjective point of view cannot be translated into the objective point of view which is commonly shared by the different species. The impossibility of translating the former to the latter leads to an extremely revealing insight — it reveals that only humans can know what it is like to be human or only martians can know what it is like to be martians. If this is so then there is no way I can explain, for example, to a martian what it is like to be a human and similarly I cannot explain to a human what it is like to be a martian. They are like incommensurable systems where incommensurability arises due to the impossibility of translation of the subjective point of view into the objective point of view. Nagel explains this fact of incommensurability with reference to a concrete case i.e., the case of bat. Bat's perceptual processes can be explained with reference to some objective facts expressing neurophysiological processes responsible for bat's perception. At this point Nagel argues that we can very well have the knowledge of the neurophysiological constitution of a bat, but this will not give us the knowledge of what it is like to be a bat. This means that the knowledge of objective point of view will not give us the knowledge of subjective point of view. This leads to the final conclusion of Nagel. The epistemological barrier posed by the subjective-objective distinction leads to the crux of the physicalist problem. The issue that may be raised here is whether or not the knowledge of the physical processes of the brain (objective stand-point) leads to the knowledge of the subjective stand-point of the species concerned? Nagel's point is same as what he said in connection with bat. The knowledge of the objective standpoint, namely, the neurological constitution of the brain will not help us to know the conscious content of our experience. The knowledge of the former will not lead to the latter, hence reductionism will be of no use. This is the epistemological barrier which comes due to the fact that mental states have essential properties expressing conscious subjective states.

III

Consciousness: Towards a New Framework

The earlier discussion on the essentialist attack on physicalism shows that mental states have essential properties. This speaks for the subjective conscious nature of mental states which are not reducible to physical processes. However, this does not suggest to go back to the essentialist metaphysics of the past. The most challenging task before philosophy of mind is how to develop a scientific approach to mind without negating the essentialist intuition. This means how to place consciousness within the range of scientific approach to mind. To do this, we require a new framework. John Searle (1984: 1-13) in his work on philosophy of mind, developed a framework which is able to place consciousness within the scientific study of mind. I shall now give a rough indication (not even a description) of the suggested framework.

Instead of defining what is consciousness, I think the best strategy will be to make explicit the basic features or constituents of consciousness. Accordingly, we can identify that there are three features of consciousness. First is intentionality. Mental states are intentional i.e., they are directed to objects or events in the outside world. Second, mental states are subjective i.e., the way I feel my pain, you can't feel in the same way. Third is mental causation. Our thoughts and feelings guide our behaviour in a definite way. In this sense they may be said to have causal effects on the physical world e.g., I decide to raise my arm and my arm goes up. Consciousness may be broadly defined in terms of these features. To accept that mental states are conscious subjective states is to accept that they have these features.

The basic problem now is how to have a scientific study of the phenomenon of consciousness along with these features? The difficult question to be answered here is: How a neurological system represented in my brain have consciousness? How could the matter inside my skull be conscious? The similar question may be asked with respect to the three features of consciousness. First, how can the physical matter in my head be about anything or refer to anything? Second, how can we relate subjective mental states with scientific conception of reality which is objective? Third, how could thoughts or feelings affect anything physical? These questions are to be answered if we think that scientific approach to mind is possible without being reductionistic.

I shall now give an idea of Searle's framework within which such a study can be conceived. The greatest obstacle to the scientific study of mind is the mechanical conception of causality whose application is found in physical sciences. Traditionally, to say *A* causes *B* is to imply that they are two different events where one is identified as cause and the other as effect. In the context of mind the same idea of causality has been applied where the interaction between mind and body is seen in terms of cause-effect relationship. Searle questioned this relationship. His argument consists of the two following propositions:

1. Brains cause minds
2. and, Minds are features of brain.

Now the crucial question here is: If mind and brain have a causal relationship, how can one be the feature (and not effect) of the other? That means you are treating mind and brain at the same level. But how can then it be a causal relationship? This is where we came to the essence of Searle's framework.

Searle makes a distinction between micro and macro properties of systems. Objects have both micro and macro properties. Macro properties may be described as the surface features of physical systems, e.g., solidity of the table or liquidity of water. These properties are explained at the micro level i.e., at the level of atoms and molecules. The liquidity of water, for example, may be explained by the interaction of H_2O molecules. True that the liquidity of water is caused by the molecules of certain nature. But strictly speaking the liquidity of water is not effect. It is a higher level feature of the system. The two are not different events. The surface or macro features are realised in the micro system.

We can apply the same micro-macro distinction to the mind-brain relationship. Mental phenomena are caused by the brain processes but they are not effects. They are the events realised in the central nervous system. A particular intentional mental state like thirst — the desire to drink, for example, is caused by certain biological processes. But this particular mental state is realised in the biological system. The objective conception of science cannot exclude the subjectivity of mental state. In the context of the study of mind subjectivity is an objective fact. The definition of the signs of mind requires redefinition. In view of this, it may be argued reductionism in philosophy of mind is a false move. In physical sciences causal reduction leads to ontological reduction. Whereas this is not true of consciousness which refuses ontological reduction. As Searle say, consciousness is the emergent property of the brain and thus reduction of it is not possible. Scientific reductionism is possible on the basis of the appearance-reality distinction. In the context of consciousness, this distinction does not hold. The reason is, in the case of consciousness, to quote Searle, "its reality is the appearance". Irreducibility thus follows from the very definition of consciousness. This is how one can talk about consciousness or the subjective mental states without either being essentialistic or reductionistic. In view of this the two intuitions may not be seen as conflicting but as complementary.

References

Block, Ned (ed.), 1980, *Readings in Philosophical Psychology*, Vol. I, Cambridge, Harvard University Press.

Boyd, R., 1980, "Materialism without Reductionism: What Physicalism Does not Entail", in: *Block*, 1980.

Brost, C.V. , 1970, *The Mind/Brain Identity Theory*, London, the Macmillan.

Churchland, P., 1988, *Matter and Consciousness, A Contemporary Introduction to the Philosophy of Mind*, Cambridge, Mass., M.I.T. Press.

Davidson, D., 1980. "Mental Events", in: *Block*, 1980.

Davidson, D., and G. Harmon (eds), 1972, *Semantics of Natural Language*, Dordrecht, D. Reidel.

Davis, S. (ed.), 1983, *Causal Theories of Mind: Action, Knowledge, Memory, Perception and Reference*, Berlin, de Gruyter.

Fodor, J., 1980, "Special Sciences or The Disunity of Science as a Working Hypothesis", in: Block, 1980.

Kripke, S., 1972, "Naming and Necessity", in Davidson, D. and G. Harman, eds.

———, 1983, "Identity and Necessity," in S. Davis, edn., 1983.

Nagel, T., 1980, "What Is It Like To Be a Bat?", in Block 1980.

Searle, J., 1984, *Mind, Brain and Science*, Cambridge, Mass: Harvard University Press.

Smart, J., 1970, "Sensation and Brain Processes", in Brost, C.V. edn., 1970.

3

Writing Phenomenology of Mental Illness

Extending the Universe of Ordinary Discourse

Bhargavi V. Davar

THIS article is about writing phenomenologies of mental illness in the Indian socio-cultural context. I discuss the phenomenology of mental illness, first and foremost, as a philosophical problem; secondly, I propose it as a necessary research programme. Writing phenomenologies of mental illness raises a number of philosophical issues about rationality, subjectivity and competence, for mental illness, as a disease category, is supposed to be contradictory to a rational experience. I argue that these problems are often not as indomitable as claimed, and that attempting such phenomenologies will provide the much required natural life settings for discoursing about the mentally ill. While such phenomenologies are available in the West, we have few such writings in the Indian context. The contemporary relevance of initiating a research programme in this area is argued for.

I

The idea of writing a phenomenology of mental illness seems to be paradoxical. Vincent Van Gogh's paintings are exemplary phenomenologies of his insanity. The tragic genealogy of his madness is paradoxically written with the brilliant logic of colour and stroke on the walls of the museum dedicated to him in

Amsterdam. It is ironical that Vincent's madness should require the highly rational and institutionalised setting for its exhibition, complete with stiff security arrangements and a popular stores that merchandises duplicates of the marks of his insanity. The contradictions of being a "Marxist manic-depressive" are written, apparently with little existentialist sensibility, in Louis Althusser's recent memoir, *The Future Lasts Forever.* Both Vincent and Louis were writing the seemingly impossible and they wrote it so very well: The phenomenologies of those intensely personal experiences which "of all the realms of experience . . . broke the bounds of ordered understanding through narrative, description, and analysis. . . ."[1] Mental illness is a human experience, but it seems that we cannot find the right words to describe it using an experiential language. What could be the epistemological status of the works, written in the first-person, of these psychotic men who were, by all known social and scientific understandings of mental illness, non-persons? Can these madmen, who are supposed to be without selves, be allowed to speak for themselves? Are they allowed to have a privileged access to their primary self-experiences?

For a historian or a collector of Western art, for the average citizenry of the Netherlands which has deified Vincent, for an aspiring "modern" artist, the question about the rationality in Vincent's works is silly. The works of Vincent and Louis cannot be easily debugged for the "true" and the "delusional", the "lucid" and the "incoherent", the "inspirational" and the "insane". Attempting such epistemological demarcations among a whole range of cognitive representations would at best be messy, and at worst, irrelevant. Their definitive place in the rational unfolding of a historical (aesthetic or Marxist) consciousness is unquestionable. Their instrumentality (or agency) in effecting radical changes in thinking about art or about man, consciousness and history, immortalises them in the history of ideas. The phenomenologies will have been an intimately personal tragedy,

---

1. N. Jackson, 1996, p. 144.

perhaps wrought in despair, in manic ecstasy and confusion, or perhaps in a recess of clarity. Yet, they are equally an ideological overcoming, a rational, radical reconstruction, even a moral rejuvenation, for the Western thought.

Even though some philosophy and art have rationalised and accommodated madness within social discourse, the average "insane" person attending a mental health clinic anywhere in the world will not receive the adoration that Vincent receives. Nor will the method in his or her madness, be applauded. An "insane" person is under-privileged within all social-communicative practices, including psychiatry, social praxis and law. He or she has little negotiating power within all these discourses. Contemporary law, the pride of Enlightenment, deletes the insane from the universe of "persons".[2] Even Vincent's glory came only after his suicide. He died poor, alone and unknown, just another madman dying within the solitary confines of a mental hospital. A major proportion of the homeless and the wandering, many of them women, are severely mentally ill.[3] Within a mental health discourse and equally, within social, legal discourse, some human behaviour is certainly considered "irrational" and excluded from the realm of the "human". Psychiatrists do not necessarily or always describe insanity in terms of rationality/irrationality. Macklin writes that "Despite the efforts made by philosophers and others to develop and refine the concept of rationality, the application of that concept to a number of practical concerns in psychiatry remains problematic",[4] especially so in legal contexts. But the mental health professionals do often use 'operationalised' constructs such as 'motivation', 'competence', 'adjustment', 'ability',

---

2. For an enduring critique of the present mental health Bill and its inadequacy in preserving the rights of the mentally ill, see works by A. Dhanda 1984, 1987.

3. Bachrach and Nadelson, 1989.

4. R. Macklin, p. 205.

'interest', 'drive', etc., which are supposed to be marks of rational behaviour. The categorical[5] definitions of madness, such as found in the American *Diagnostic and Statistical Manual*[6] or the WHO's *International Classification of Diseases*[7], deploy irrationality [including emotions unbridled by reason] as definitive of madness. These diagnostic manuals resonate with the Enlightenment ideals of Reason and have been subjected to critical scrutiny from multi-perspectives.

The philosophical approach of diagnostics within psychiatric and in general, medical practice has been referred to as "diagnostic" or "taxonomic realism".[8] The medical discourse addresses the following philosophical problem: "Are classifications of disease conventions of labeling or the result of discovering some fact of the matter in nature?".[9] In medicine, disease is the (observable) quality of a human object. Within psychiatry, mental illness is a natural kind. Insanity belongs in the realm of nature and can be named as an item, similar and

---

5. The diagnostic manuals for diagnosing mental illness, such as the DSM or the ICD, use what is called the "categorical" system of diagnosis (as opposed to the multi-axial system). There are recent debates about this categorical system, which classifies the types of mental illness as discrete, well-defined symptom clusters, stable in time, with no overlap or mutations. However, the commonly experienced forms of mental illness such as depression, anxiety and neuroses, do not seem to fit these classifications, and other classificatory systems are being proposed. For discussions on the merits and demerits of available systems of psychiatric classification, see Goldberg and Huxley, 1992.

6. *Diagnostic and Statistical Manual*-IV, 1994. Henceforth referred to as DSM-IV.

7. *International Classification of Diseases* - 10. Henceforth referred to as ICD-10.

8. In a paper examining Lawrie Reznek's book, *The Nature of Disease,* D'Amico (1995) questions Reznek's position that the "taxonomic realism" adopted by some thinkers on health and disease is philosophically unjustifiable.

9. D'Amico, 1995, p. 551.

different, from other kinds among human mental things. Mind is a natural object and can have qualities of health and sickness.[10] A scientific discourse about insanity uses the same natural science philosophy of type/token; primary/secondary; universal/particular; similar/different; essence/accident; and other categories often resourced in the realm of objects. The diagnostic manuals, or the classification systems used in the clinic, present symptom inventories of different "types" of insanity. Recent debates in the area of diagnostics point out that inventories should also mark the type of insanity for gender, race and culture.[11] As in the case of all inventories of natural kinds, such a disease inventory can never be complete, and so, the diagnostic manuals go through many revisions.[12, 13] The latest revision of the DSM, spurred on by the amazing developments in the brain sciences, privileges the view that mental illness is biological.[14] With this perspective, psychiatry has been properly installed within the observable foundations of knowledge about disease kinds, that is, anatomy and physiology.

The "disease model" of human distress is most arguably founded upon the nature of intervention with the physical body. Despite many decades of questioning by anti-psychiatrists,[15] this

10. I have no quarrel with conceiving of the mind as an object. In fact Davar and Bhat (1995) argued for a realistic conception of mind.

11. The literature in these areas are vast, but very recent examples are : Busfield, 1996; Jhadhav, 1997.

12. For a recent questioning about the DSM from cross-cultural perspectives, see Good, 1996 and Lewis-Fernandez, 1996.

13. The actual negotiations over diagnostic classifications are dependent on complex organisational, administrative and normative procedures, standardised by institutions such as the World Health Organisation and the American Psychiatric Association. The diagnostic entries are made to keep time with the ongoing research in the mental sciences, but the ideal match between research and diagnostics is often not realised.

14. Andreason, 1984.

15. Szasz, T., 1974.

model is still primary in modelling mental illness. The epistemology of the "disease model" is justifiable in a way that other models, for example, the "metaphor model"[16] is not. It is the disease model, rather than other supposedly "humanistic" models, which have obtained service benefits (such as insurance) for the mentally ill. It is now increasingly acceptable that mental illness is a disease, similar to and also different from bodily disease, rather than just "a myth" or a metaphor. This is not to say that the mind is just body (or brain) matter, but rather that, mind and body are not neatly territorialised, and that the so-called "dualism" can be — and indeed, have been — questioned both ways even within a natural kinds philosophy. That is, neither mind nor body, and consequently, the disease of either, is just matter.

In this article, I argue that a phenomenology of mental distress, that is, a self-referential, experiential discourse about mental illness in natural life contexts is both philosophically possible as well as practically required. I am not questioning the "disease model" within the medical or the psychiatric discourse. It has been argued elsewhere that a mental science requires categorical assumptions about health and disease.[17] However, the clinical diagnostic system is an artificial language, enough for the purposes of the science, but not enough for humanistic practice. The natural kinds language is not enough for a philosophy of care. A mediating natural language, or languages, about mental illness is required for the clinic to perform optimally in its caring function. Throughout this article, I use "phenomenology" as equivalent to "natural" language. By "phenomenology", I do not mean the classical study of essences or eidetic intuitions, but rather the spoken discourse of a self-expressive, experiential and personal — and untreated by analysis.

A philosophy of care for the diseased requires the insight that illness, including mental illness, is not just a matter of the

16. Sontag, S., 1979.

17. Davar and Bhat, 1995 argued for a realistic epistemology in the mind-related sciences.

formal classification of 'kinds'. Having scientific information about the disease kind one is suffering from is important, but not enough. Illness is an existentialist condition: an intra-personal, inter-subjective experience, lived out in natural life settings, using an ordinary language and enacted within the realities of a common social experience. Phenomenologies of mental illness describe mental illness as it is lived out. Such phenomenologies give 'voice' to what is left unsaid in ordinary language, and bring the mentally ill back within the universe of social discourse. The phenomenologies render mental illness proximal to our natural settings and natural types of communications, bringing the designated 'mad' person back to her life-world. Certain realms of human mental experience, such as the play of emotions in inter-subjective contexts, are best described by phenomenologies of mental illness. Such phenomenologies are also therapeutic, in that, they provide an occasion for someone suffering from a mental illness to textualise that suffering, distance herself from it and deal with it as if it was an object. Phenomenologies gives back to the mentally ill a sense of her own history, a possibility that is denied by the heuristics of diagnosis. Rare examples of such phenomenologies, other than the eminent ones discussed above, are autobiographies, art and other personal aesthetic expressions, written narratives by patients who are ill or who have been diagnosed,[18] and sometimes, even a clinician's case records, if he or she is sensitive to the problems of practising in inter-subjective settings. Freud's case-studies, whatever the merits and demerits of his science,[19] are exemplary phenomenologies. Such phenomenologies of mental illness find words, faltering and personal, perhaps in folk idiom and cultural imagery, even better, if in the vernacular, for describing those experiences. They record personal associations, threads of meanings, one's life of metaphors and expressions, one's own

18. Examples of such personal accounts of depression and manic-depression are Gilman (1973); Jamison (1995); Styron (1990).

19. Accounts of the "foundations" of psychoanalysis are found in Grunbaum (1984) and more recently, Davar and Bhat (1995).

way of coping with subjective distress, in a way that an illness discourse does not. I elaborate some of these ideas in this article.

I propose this article as a contribution to a philosophy of psychiatry: the study of the epistemological and ethical problems determining a psychiatric[20] discourse. The overall framework is phenomenological psychology. The article concerns itself with intervention issues in philosophy, that is, about strengthening the community-based, inter-personal, linguistic and the ethical basis of the practice of care for the mentally ill, rather than about issues of scientificity, justification, evidence, etc. Though not directly, the article is linked to contemporary concerns in community psychiatry in India and medical anthropology and the relevant literature is noted.

II

Medical diagnostics, like in many positivistic and applied sciences, is an artificial language. From the perspective of the diagnostic manuals such as the DSM-IV or the ICD-10, words need not be found in the ordinary language for describing the experience of mental illness, only symptoms and states. A typical diagnostic interview, conducted by using the many standardised questionnaires such as the MSE, GHQ, or other schedules, reduce the scope of human experience to a broad list of human behaviours common to types of mental illness as they appear in the clinic. Interviewees, usually junior clinical psychologists in service settings that provide complete care, are trained in deleting the selves-subjects from the interview context, and present questions and elicit answers as if mental illness had a separate, objective existence, unattached to an experiencing self. As Corin

20. The mental health discourse in contemporary society, goes beyond just psychiatry. The relationship between medicine, psychiatry, psychology, social work and sociology are complex and nuanced. Contemporary mental health practice is inter-disciplinary, atleast in the ideal treatment settings. However, to keep the canvas simple, I assume that psychiatry is the presiding mental health science.

writes:

> [T]he disease is seen as a reality outside individual experience, a reality that has it's own dynamics. This is not accidental. This perspective echoes the general medicalisation of psychiatry that is also reflected in the DSM-III system of diagnosis. The process of externalisation that is involved in the diagnostic system is shown by its explicit bracketing of any subjective involvement in diagnosis. . . .[21]

Donnelly shows that diagnostics reduces experiences to 'occurrences' and 'events', so that causal attributions can be made and feeling states and thinking subjects can be eliminated.[22] Diagnostics convert what Heinz Kohut called the 'experience-near' vocabulary of human distress, to the 'experience-distant' illness vocabulary. Thus, a distress experience, requiring inter-personal understanding in natural contexts, is transformed into a situation of classification given by an expert system in artificial contexts.

The classification system is linked in complex ways to the mental sciences and to issues about causation and prediction. The transformation of human suffering into the language of clinical heuristics is a necessary one if the knowledge representations of the mental health sciences are to be deployed at all in the service settings such as the clinic. The benefits of science cannot be disbursed on the assumption that a folk idiom alone is enough. But contrarily, the artificial language institutionalised through the artifices of the clinics, alone is also not enough for a clinician to be caring. An ordinary language for talking about mental disease is required, just as such a language is available for talking about diabetes or blood pressure. In ordinary, folk psychology, sited in everyday settings, we do have ways of talking about and dealing with experiences of

---

21. Corin, 1990, p. 156.

22. Donnelly, 1988.

subjective distress and illness. It is naive to think that psychiatric disease or therapy are inventions of modernity. In the medical anthropological discourse, this folk language has been popularly called 'idioms of distress',[23] referring to the metaphors by which human societies enact and cope with their distress experiences. The culturally specific idioms of distress, for example, possession and trancing found in many Indian communities, are often complete with an explanatory cosmology, a 'treatment' regimen as well as an intense inter-personal and emotional engagement with the distress experiences. Within this folk language, mental distress is meaningful in a natural life setting, and is dealt with using the commonly spoken language of the community. No special language is deemed necessary. But in urban, medicalised settings, this naturalness is lost. Personal narratives of mental distress, or writing phenomenologies of distress, gives us back the ability to discourse about mental distress using a natural language. Such appeals have been made by medical anthropologists who argue the need for "ethnographies of experience".[24]

Health and illness, whether of the body or of the mind, are more than just medical diagnoses. Having causal knowledge does not equal the self-embodying and living in a state of dis-ease. Illness is equally a mental experience lived out by selves in inter-subjective situations, setting the emotional pace and the intensity of their lives. To someone diagnosed with 'leukemia', or 'diabetes', their bodies do not just enact the disease such as a machine. There is of course the 'etiology' and the predictable 'prognosis' of illness. But other than this, the mind experiences, perceives, understands, and interprets its state of dis-ease, to construct a discourse about a self-in-disease, effecting, as it were, a personal translation of the medical diagnosis. It is this personal translation of disease that often determines the *meanings* of one's life, agency and choices, even medical choices, rather than the sterile explanatory *truth* of the medical diagnosis.

23. Nichter, 1981.

24. Kleinman and Kleinman, 1991.

As Good writes:

> [T]he difficulties with the objectivist account are more immediately evident when we look closely at illness and its experience. For the person who is sick, as for the clinician, the disease is experienced as present in the body. But for the sufferer, the body is not simply a physical object or physiological state but an essential part of the self. The body is subject, the very grounds of subjectivity or experience in the world, and the body as 'physical object' cannot be neatly distinguished from 'states of consciousness'. Consciousness itself is inseparable from the conscious body. The diseased body is therefore not simply the object of cognition and knowledge, of representation in mental states and the works of medical science. It is at the same time a disordered agent of experience.[25]

Similarly, Mordacci writes:

> In phenomenological terms, health and illness are, in the first place, experiences of the *lived* body, which are described (by the patient himself) as changes in lived temporality, spatiality, self-perception, relation to the context, and only afterwards (and by the physician) through psycho-physiological dimensions"[26].

Perception about oneself, about the other, about one's body and mentality, etc. are determined, sometimes, in severe illness, to such a degree, that an 'alternative' world-view becomes installed through living in ill-health. This world-view describes the sufferer's personal and social life. Within the inter-personal situations in which we function, 'leukemia' and 'depression' are not just items aligned alongwith, say, breakfast or watching TV. A 'depressive' does not just enact the symptoms: weepiness, fatigue, loss of interest, loss of libido, suicidal ideation, eating

25. Good, 1994, p. 116.

26. Mordacci, 1995, p. 480.

and sleep abnormalities. She experiences the world differently. She constitutes the Other and the Other constitutes her differently. She uses language differently. She experiences emotions differently. In other words, her existence, her being-in-relationships, her relationship to herself, her body and her mental state of dis-ease, are altered in many ways. These experiences of ill-health determine the way we look at the world, and at ourselves. They are existentialist experiences which remain undocumented in clinical 'case-work'.

III

The much talked about 'stigma' surrounding the mentally ill is at some fundamental level, a problem about not having an ordinary, existential *language* for talking about mental distress experiences. Post-modern discourse, such as by Foucault, emphasises that power operates through discursive practices. Implicit in this discourse is the view that silence too can be oppressively powerful, and this is especially true of the mentally ill. The stigmatised identities of an "insane" person, such as a schizophrenic, is cultured by a silence, or inauthenticities of communication, about their condition in natural life contexts. A mad woman in the family cannot be the author or the subject of a conversation in the same way, for example, as a cousin who is getting married. While there may be nuanced subtexts about her which slowly erect the stigma, her mental illness will rarely be part of an authentic conversation. Perhaps the most traumatising experience for a schizophrenic woman in a family is the silence that befalls upon her entry into an 'episode' or about her 'states'. Families and friends seem to experience a 'perceptual blackout' about the episode as an episode of subjective distress. It is surprising how families can carry on without directly addressing the issue of mental illness even when a close relative is being treated. Naming mental distress invites the responsibility of care. Whereas silence about this distress allows the scope for evaluation, judgement and scapegoating. This can happen in the work sphere, as well, where a psychotically ill person may be the subtext of a company's social discourse, his behaviour judged and indexed ostensively, but his illness unnamed and untreated, until one day he will be handed a termination letter for his willfully bad behaviour. Whereas, an employee suffering from an appendicitis may elicit animated discussion and commiseration, given paid leave, and in the government or the corporate sector, even financial assistance for getting medical help.

We have, in our socio-communicative practices, sometimes highly ritualised languages of dealing with other instances of mental distress, such as death, grief and mourning. The patterns of interaction in group behaviours have been called cultural 'scripts', 'schemas', 'models' etc. by the cognitive anthropologists and cross-cultural psychologists.[27] For ordering our social world, such cultural epistemologies and folk knowledges are indispensable. These scripts cover not only social behaviour wrought by convention, such as prayer scripts, shopping scripts, teaching scripts, etc., but also the seemingly idiosyncratic patterns of personal interactions. Thus, each family may have its own 'language' for enacting scripts within the home, to effect social interactions. But, in the highly urbanised, modern contexts, ways of rationalising and dealing with a mentally ill person through such scripts seems unavailable.[28] We do not seem to know what to say or do in the presence of someone diagnosed for a mental illness. Afterall, diabetics move about in inter-subjective contexts without feeling excluded, because of the everyday familiarity of the disease. We have a

---

27. See, for example, the recent comprehensive study by Shore, 1996.

28. The cross-culturalists in psychiatry are fascinated by the "indigenous" expressions of distress. Cosmological explanations of trance states, possession states and other culturally specific distress behaviours are more acceptable to the community where they are enacted, because of the closeness of the language in which they are expressed. However, it is questionable whether the social life built around such behaviours constitutes realistic care.

'sickness' script to deal with common physical diseases ("Are you unwell today?"; "Can I fetch you something to drink?"; "Did you take your medicines on time?"; "Why don't you take the day off?"; "I brought you some fruits"; etc.). Unfortunately, for mental illness, we are unable to find the right ways to express concern or show care. For example, how many of us have said "I brought you some fruits" or "Don't drive today" to someone who we know is suffering from a manic depression? We do not know if bringing fruits is the right thing to do for someone so diagnosed. This is not just a matter of not having a social etiquette or the human graces regarding the mentally ill, but of not having a social language of care. To give yet another example, we will know how to carry on a meaningful conversation with someone who has just disclosed that he has lost his job. But how do we commiserate with a person who discloses that she has just been "released" from a mental hospital after being treated. Most of us will have had some experience of being a spectator to an exhibition of psychoses in public places without knowing what one can do about it, or whether one should do anything about it at all.[29] Frequently, among us,[30] the question of mental illness is brought up and we do not always know how to respond.

Phenomenologies of mental distress would try to provide

29. Many of the "wandering lunatics", thus ignored by the helpless and passing public, are eventually rounded up by the police and taken to jails (not the mental hospitals). Recently, there was a furore about the violation of human rights in Calcutta, and eventually in Assam, about the numerous "non-criminal insane", many of them women, needlessly locked up in the jails. The Supreme Court intervention resulted in a public inquiry (Murthy and Dhanda, 1993). The wandering psychotically ill finally end up in these jails partly due to a social indifference or apathy to their publicly exhibited distress.

30. The recent World Mental Health database (Desjarlais, Eisenberg, Good and Kleinman, 1995) gives astonishing figures of mental illness among men and women in the "South" countries, including India. The statistical predictions about increasing mental disorder when we cross the century, in the context of growing poverty, violence and displacement, are shocking.

these scripts, that is, they would bring the experiences of mental distress within the natural and the linguistic realm: within the inter-subjective, emotionally intense realm of what is sayable and share-able. At a time when the most influential philosophies of language and science decried a private language, mental illness has been only that, being denied a legitimacy within the domain of the public. Phenomenologies of mental illness make the private language, public.

A natural language of mental illness can provide a 'communicative setting'[31] within social units, such as the family, the school, the office or the community. A communicative setting is, in philosophical terms, a universe of discourse. It provides a natural language context for disclosing, discoursing about, sharing and constructing a consensual reality about painful human experiences. These settings have also been called contexts of 'disclosure' in therapy. Two women engaged in talking about their victimisation experiences are sharing a communicative setting, re-creating the reality of their experience and trying to cope with that experience through a personal language of distress and overcoming. They are producing new explanatory schemas for self-understanding. The intimacies of friendship, self-support groups and women's groups, provide examples of other communicative settings. Family life is usually organised around many communicative settings. Such communicative settings provide the space to deconstruct or construct, using one's own personal language, that is also shared within the social group, the personal meanings of one's life experiences. Such settings allow the private language to be *spoken*, however idiosyncratic the personal dialect may be. By recasting a diagnosable medical condition in a personal language through such communicative settings, a phenomenology makes the mental distress experience familiar and everyday. Such a possibility is required if the distress is to be negotiated, or "managed", at the inter-subjective level in the natural community settings.

---

31. Maranhão, 1986, p. 297.

All human encounters and communicative settings, including sexed and cross-cultural encounters, are sustained by the actors' sense of sameness and difference, of sharing certain human essences in social discourse, despite differences. Jonas[32] casts the problem of understanding between human beings as a matter of processing sameness as well as difference, change as well as permanence in each other. If we are all completely the same, then there can be no call for understanding; If entirely different, then, understanding is impossible. "That all who bear the form of man have something fundamental in common, without which we could not even speak of 'man', nor of human history either — let alone of man's historicity and, perhaps, even of 'his' radical mutability in history — should be evident".[33] On the other hand, "there is no denying the poverty and even boredom of an understanding which forever finds in all its objects nothing more than what it already knows, for which all the wealth of history reduces itself to the endlessly repeating *de capo* of a fixed repertoire — not to speak of the injustice which lies in the measuring of everything different by the standard of the one, acknowledged essence, assigning each its grade according as it conforms to it" (p. 106). An engaging human encounter, including empathy, understanding and sensuality, or "putting oneself in the Other's shoes", resources what is essential as well as differentiated among the human actors in that encounter. In such an engagement, the self/other boundaries are obliterated to some extent, to facilitate an embeddedness and a sense of sharing the same space.

However, the social-communicative practices involving the insane, in India as well as elsewhere in the world — inter-subjective and clinical encounters, social attitudes, and law — are not always encounters of engagement, but rather one of distancing, disengagement and exclusion. For example, we do not engage in a human encounter with a dead body, but rather mentally differentiate our 'selves' from 'it'. We do not try to put

32. Jonas, 1973.

33. Jonas, 1973, p. 106.

ourselves in the shoes of the dead body, that would indeed generate terrible existentialist anxieties and horrors. We ritualise death and condemn the body to a cremation ground. So also, in an encounter with insanity — say, sharing a communicative setting with a diagnosed person — we distance and disengage, placing ourselves in the imaginary "Us", the rational citizens, in opposition to "Them", the irrational non-citizens.[34] We are unable to "put ourselves in the shoes" of the insane. We do not allow ourselves to become diffuse and obliterated by co-mingling with the fractured self of the insane. We are not all that receptive to being "embedded" with the insane. The service settings, such as the clinic or the mental hospital, are artifices by which this estrangement is institutionalised. Writing phenomenologies of mental distress is to install a communicative setting where engagement with insanity is possible in natural settings. Phenomenologies of mental distress allow atleast a partial obliteration of the us/them divide and makes us ask, for example: What does it mean to 'be' a 'depressive'?

A phenomenology requires an inter-subjective context, a communicative setting, a language spoken, a personal story and a listening Other. A phenomenologist tells a story and a successful phenomenology requires the context and the abilities for story telling. The protagonists of the story of mental illness, the plot and the tools must be pre-designed. It could be said that precisely the possibility of this phenomenological language is at issue in the case of the mentally ill: Using a language competently requires that the linguistic and logical functions are performed satisfactorily. The possibility of narration requires that certain, fundamentally biological and cognitive abilities, especially speech related abilities, are not diseased or disabled. Notably, in the case of severe mental breakdown, aphasic,

34. This estrangement of the insane is true of all communities, whether traditional or modern. In all human encounters, there are conceptions of "normality" and "madness". It is these that facilitate exclusions. For the play of gendered power in marginalising distressed women in a healing temple of India, see Skultans, 1991.

echolalic, autistic, and other language and speech related anomalies make us suspect the competence of the person in distress. To take a seemingly analogous case, it would be impossible to write a phenomenology of death or of coma. One could write phenomenologies of "managing" coma or of dealing with impending death, but not the experiences of a comatose person. Somehow, there seems to be a hypocrisy here, for we do not think of a comatose 'person' as 'having' experiences, even less, being able to discourse about them. It would be difficult, though not impossible, to describe the personal worlds of someone suffering from dementia or brain damage. Schizophrenia may have speech related disability as a predominant symptom, rendering the narration incoherent. In catatonia, the very ability to speak is seemingly paralysed. As Jackson writes,[35] cleansing Althusser's text of psychotic delusion is no easy matter. But these are the glaring truisms of methodology, requiring practical attention in designing the writing of such phenomenologies. Obviously, one would devise criteria and contexts where such writing will be meaningful both for the narrator and his or her audience. Certain differences are necessarily made, for example, marking distinctions in mental distress experiences. Not all mental distress experiences are equally disabling.

Classical existentialist theorising about madness is based on the ontological difference between 'being' and 'nothingness',[36] between authenticity and alienation, and insanity is considered to be a state of non-being. The existentialist literature denies subjectivity and selfhood to experiences of insanity, and selves in this state are designated as "divided".[37] But it is not entirely true to say that the mentally ill have no sense of the "self", and that their sense of identity is completely vacuous. The number of diagnosed persons with completely divided selves is minuscule.

---

35. Jackson, 1996.

36. Sartre, 1956.

37. Laing, 1960.

The existentialist perspective homogenises experiences of insanity, as if all 'types' of insanity are the same, in fact, as if there is one type only. Therapies which deny selfhood to the mentally distressed reduce them to a stage of infancy, where they are not given an opportunity to come to grips with their own distress experiences and learn to deal with it. Ronald Laing's Kingsley Hall, a therapeutic community set up for the severely mentally ill, badly failed, as Jansen argues, because of the extreme infantilism of the residents wrought by a medical thinking which claimed that psychotic persons do not have a self-identity.[38] Existentialist therapies correctly emphasise the pre-linguistic, emotional realm of being, but a stress on the therapeutic function of a self-language is equally important if one is not to be reduced to a mentally regressive state of infancy through the distress experience.

Mental illness experiences, even of the more severe order, do not always, entirely, uniformly and thoroughly, confuse, divide or obliterate the self. The completely fractured self of madness is not necessarily an enduring experience, and "episodes" of such fractures are more representative of the common types of mental illness. A majority of the mentally ill do make self-referential statements, talk about themselves, relate to themselves and have a discourse about themselves just like anybody else. In fact, a pre-occupation with oneself, with one's past 'normal' identity and with one's changing 'mad' mentality may often be a significant part of one's experience of dis-ease and distress. Rather than losing one's sense of self, distress experiences often involves painful attempts at recuperation of the 'old' self and confusion, sometimes obsessional fear, about the present state of distress. The acute fear of losing one's 'self' and of becoming 'raving mad' is expressed by even persons living with a mental illness for many years, showing the ability of the distressed person to relate to a self, to make judgements about it and to see the process of change in that self. In other words, someone going through mental distress may often have

38. Jansen, 1980.

a self-identity that involves a coherent discourse, or a phenomenology, about that distress. It is possible to talk to oneself and to others about one's mental illness experiences. Jamison's repeated attempts in this area[39] are instantiative. To be able to 'write' about one's own 'madness' is to have a sense of one's own identity, even, to have marked oneself as a 'mad' subject. One can have a phenomenology about one's madness only if a sense of the self is sustained through that writing. Looking from the opposite side, having a phenomenology of mental illness will give us an understanding of the self that endured the madness.

Atleast a part of the confusion that the diagnosed person experiences about her-self can be explained by seeing the other socio-philosophical dimensions linking language and insanity. It is a truism in philosophy today, that the "self" is in language. Cognitivist epistemology and post-modern philosophy equally emphasise *that the self obtains*, in whatever personal or philosophical form, *through language*. We access our-selves through language. Mental distress, to some extent, is to lose the meaningful threads of the story about oneself; to lose touch with one's own idiom.

A mentally distressed person finds herself in the middle of many incommensurable languages institutionalised for different human purposes, among which making connections of truth and meaning about herself and her life experiences become complicated, if not impossible. A diagnosed person is often in circuit between different service settings where the highly artificial languages of medicine and therapy are used. Dealing with these languages are, to begin with, difficult. It has been noted that the incommensurability between the artificial languages and the patient's own natural language for expressing distress can be stressful for the patient. This is especially true in the Indian context where asking questions to obtain clinical knowledge is often considered to be an affront to expertise and

---

39. Jamison, 1995.

authority by the medical community. While few Indian users question the arrogance of expertise, many turn away dejected, stressed, and confused about the state of their bodies and minds. Jamie Saris writes:

> The subject at once acknowledges his (occasionally) profoundly altered phenomenological sense of himself and his surroundings, while struggling against his engulfment by a body of knowledge, psychiatry, which, in his eyes, sees little of him beyond an illness label.[40]

Donnelly[41] too urges 'righting the medical record', in order to assuage the patient's feeling of rejection and a perceived coldness of the medical system brought on by the heuristic methods adopted to cleanse the language of distress and to make it 'clinically' useful.

On the other hand, the person reached the service settings at the first instance, because her natural language failed in its performative functions within her own social domain. Mental illness has been characterised as a failure of folk psychology and natural language to deal with the day-to-day problems, then requiring an expert language.[42] Our natural sense of reality and common sense epistemology, which we do not ordinarily question, collapse in a situation of dis-ease. Corin writes about schizophrenia "as involving a loss of the 'natural evidence', that is a pre-conceptual understanding of the world and of oneself, on the basis of which people build more explicit meanings".[43] The person suffering distress sometimes literally loses her voice because of the many incommensurabilities between her personal language of distress, the institutionalised medical and therapeutic languages, and the social discourses about madness. Phenomenologies of mental illness record that lost voice, giving

40. Jamie Saris, 1995, p. 39.

41. Donnelley, 1988.

42. Davar and Bhat, 1995.

43. Corin, 1990, p. 159.

the chance for the person to see her own distress and to learn to deal with herself. Such phenomenologies are a restitution of the broken natural language, and through the language, of the self in distress.

A sense of self and agency was not necessarily extinguished in Vincent Van Gogh and Louis Althusser, both suffering from psychoses severe enough to require institutionalisation. In fact, both Vincent and Louis were writing with a consciousness of history, and of their own definitive role in changing it. A certain element of grandiosity, of their grand place in the cosmic plot, is evidenced, and this grandiosity is not entirely reducible to a psychotic delusion. But equally, they were writing with a subliminal denial — in the case of Althusser, it was amnesia — of the history of their own fractured consciousness and their personal tragedies of illness. In their own self-understanding, the tearing off of the ear or the strangulation of the wife were aberrations, freak incidents that they, perhaps, did not need to explain to themselves, even less, to others. Through their phenomenologies, they erected their sanity in order to speak the truth about themselves and their lives, despite the ever present risk of becoming inchoate, mute, or for that matter, garrulous.

At the personal, and the inter-subjective level, one intuitively devises ways of dealing with one's own state of mental illness. It is not only the case that one has a personal memory and language about one's normal and mad identity, it is also the case that often, in natural life settings, one attempts to cope with and "adjust" to this identity to live a moderately ordered life. The repeated attempts by ex-patients to live an ordered life and evolve a social circuit including a therapy regimen, and the possible contribution of such attempts in averting re-hospitalisation, has been discussed by Jamie Saris.[44] This possibility is obtained in the case of most common mental disorders, including depression and mood disorders, the obsessional and other neurotic disorders. Some sense of

44. Jamie Saris, 1995.

"handicap" is inevitable and residual to all types of ill-health and disease. Years after a minor surgery, one can still experience hangover effects. But a self-understanding of one's subjective experiences through phenomenologies, written or spoken, may facilitate obtaining that comfort level in dealing with one's own distress experiences.[45] A phenomenology is a type of disclosure, and the therapeutic value of disclosures *per se,* independent of other social or cognitive changes, is recently being positively appraised in interventions.[46]

Vincent and Louis, for example, 'adjusted' to their madness and devised methodologies to suit that madness, methodologies that forcefully subverted the dominant ideologies of their times and came to be eventually construed as revolutionary. The frenetic, frenzied haste of Vincent's brush, desiring to catch the momentary flood of light, the wind and the space, was a mechanism by which he "managed" a swift ego always in passage, a momentous self, a being repeatedly thrown into nothingness. Vincent's energetic efforts to catch up with himself brought him enormous fame: in history, his strokes were seen as a highly creative innovation, a representative of a radical genre, in which the art piece is not made, but, happens at the momentary existentialist conjunction of the artist's self with his reality. Althusser's madness was different — a manic depressive — but his career as an MDP required his Marxist career in order to sustain his sense of self. The threat of a complete disintegration of thought and vocabulary, of the incoherence of a raging, ecstatic insanity, of florid desires, delusions and fantasies, required the compensatory methodology of an inexorable, undaunted, stoic and materialist logic. No causal connections are proposed here, only interesting contingencies, between insanity and its sometimes creative compensations and methodological choices

45. Some of my manic-depressive friends are not only keenly aware of when they are having an episode, but also, what should be done about it whether by themselves (like taking drugs or visiting their psychiatrist) or by caring others.

46. Seshadri, 1996.

that somehow seem to carry the imprint of a reasoned decision-making. It is interesting that Althusser, diagnosed with MDP — a severe psychosis involving the very breakdown of the cognitive processes of thinking and reasoning — should have engaged in a highly evolved form of intellectual exercise, signifying rationality in its very essence. Equally interesting that Van Gogh, diagnosed with the fragmented ego of psychoses, should persevere in making that self cohere and finally, consume himself by the sheer exhaustion of keeping pace with those passing fragments, in an infinite number of brilliantly hurried, impressionistic brush strokes.

IV

The diagnostic classificatory systems of general as well as psychiatric medicine assume that subjects *have* madness, a type of objective biological condition, that has no relationship to history. The insane are not only considered to be without selves, but also without histories. Writing phenomenologies about one's distress re-installs the mentally ill as historical subjects, that is, as subjects with a sense of history. Writing the phenomenology of one's distress is writing one's own history. The phenomenology textualises and casts, in objective sequence, the unfolding of intimate and often tragic experiences, allowing one to see oneself from a distance as a "subject experiencing madness" and to deal with it. To the extent that phenomenology is a way of experiencing oneself as historical subjects, such phenomenologies carry the promise of being therapeutic.

The philosophical connections between history, as the epiphenomenal realm of collective human agency, and phenomenology, as the study of inter-personal lived experience are intimate. Sundararajan[47] pointed out that historiography is a type of phenomenology and that phenomenology is a type of historiography, thereby bridging a seeming conflict between the two. The continental existentialist and the critical-hermeneutic

47. Sundararajan, 1996.

understandings suggest that our sense of transcendental history and our sense of self, at some level, connect. Cultural history and the history of the self are not two mutually exclusive realms of knowledge representations. Individual memory and cultural memory are not disparate; they encounter and transcribe one another.

Sundararajan suggests that both history and phenomenology are about selves in time and about recuperating the sanity of our species. History and phenomenology are both the memory-organised principles, consolidating different "fictive identities" in different orders of time (individual time/civilisational time). The histories of cultures and the phenomenologies of selves, both, present and re-present human memory through cultural and individual scripts, so that the semblance of a human essence enduring through time can be repeatedly produced. We write and rewrite the histories of (man)kind and we repeatedly write phenomenologies of human individual experiences, both for the same type of human psychological compulsions: That is, to get a sense of ourselves through the passage of time, to make ourselves present, to render ourselves as pieces of curiosity, as objects, artifacts, or texts, so that we may gaze at ourselves, much as the accursed Narcissus did. Both history and phenomenology emplot the narrative, fictional unfolding of a self identity, embodied, structured and fractured as both subject and object, as experience and text, as sanity and insanity, enacted in time. Both history and phenomenology are ways by which "we respond to the fictional elements in our identity".[48] We cannot run out of fictions, ever. We repeat them, reproduce them, transform them into new linguistic, cognitive formations. History, therefore, like phenomenology, is not reflective, but constitutive.[49] In the writing of history and personal stories, we make ourselves present.

---

48. Sundararajan, 1996, p. 190.

49. Sundararajan (1996) writes: ". . . the hermeneutics of historiography is not a reflective but a constitutive one; language is not merely a device for communication, but is, in its own way, a formative force such that our practices are linguistically mediated forms of life", p. 188.

History, like phenomenology, is a mark of our sanity: The comfort derived is that we are, after all, not a senseless, irrational, amnesic, confused, or an incoherent species and are better than the other animal or life species. Writing phenomenologies/histories is a brave attempt to work through the fragments, the conflicts, the confusions and the breakdowns, to seek the rationality, the moments of clarity and choice in the evolution of the post-modern wo/man. We constitute and re-constitute ourselves as essentially the same, despite the madness and the idiosyncrasies: stable, moral, just, reasonable, logical beings (preferably male !). [Emotions are in fine print, if not omitted, from these narratives of the subject]. In history and in phenomenology, we state our choices about ourselves, as a human race and as individuals. This compulsion to reiterate the identity of humanness through historical and individual memory shows that the issue of madness, or irrationality, as much as the issue of death, and the very extinction of human rationality and existence, is a central existentialist worry. Our compulsions to repeatedly write our (rational) selves borders on madness. As Sundararajan writes:

> History is for self divided and divisive beings only. . . .

That we have to re-write ourselves through history and phenomenology shows that this sense of belonging is not a 'sustainable' state. History and phenomenology are endless vocations,[50] endless recuperations of our sanity, endless cures for our madness.

Writing the historical self through a phenomenology is the first step to understanding, if not, confronting or curing that madness. It is possible, even necessary, to own and rationalise a subjectivity (and aspects of human history) as 'mad' in order to be able to deal with that madness. To label the Other 'mad' is the beginning of a stigmatised identity; but to label oneself 'mad' is to engage with one's fractured identity and to begin the reconstitution, or the 'cure'. Writing the story of one's madness

50. Sundararajan, 1996, p. 194.

is to see oneself, through that writing, with the name of 'madness' that one has defined for oneself in private. It is to see oneself as a 'mad' subject in the artifact of the writing. It is then to engage with an intra-personal or inter-personal dialogue that can very often be therapeutic. Writing the phenomenology of one's madness is to find a name within oneself for experiences that otherwise eluded being named, or were lurking in the subconscious. Therapeutic settings, like the clinic, find an inventory and a semantics and provide a communicative setting for an objective engagement with this identity. Phenomenologies of mental distress can indeed have the same goals, but in a more intimate, inter-subjective and personal, if ordinary, language.

I do not expect that writing phenomenologies of mental illness will contribute to the inductively designed mental sciences, which come with somewhat different research expectations. For example, it may not be possible to infer the "proof" for a "law" from a phenomenological study. But it may be possible to generate some very interesting hypotheses. In any case, it would be required to enlist the methodological protocols of such writing, including the limitations one may want to place upon drawing broad-based conclusions from a phenomenological study. Whatever the contribution of such phenomenologies for the sciences, they will be of immense use in a clinical, community based philosophy of care for the mentally ill.

V

A number of contemporary problems before the mental health professionals in India, as well as elsewhere, has been the canvas for this article. I end the article by briefly listing the issues which will reach a greater degree of clarity with inputs from phenomenological psychology:

A. Within professional practice, it is increasingly clear that having scientific knowledge alone cannot ensure complete care, raising questions about ethics, rights, etc.

regarding the mentally ill. While the mental sciences are delivering the goods, service settings are deplorably inadequate in their caring functions. It is my belief that atleast a part of this problem can be resolved by creating the required ordinary languages for talking about mental illness in the community settings.

B. Contemporary policy changes across the globe, including India, emphasise a shift towards treating mental illness in the community. This policy change infact forces communities to evolve quasi-scientific, or folk epistemologies for dealing with their own mental illness experiences. Indian communities, which have hitherto expected expert knowledge to be disbursed from specialised institutions, now are engaging with mental distress in their homes, schools, and offices, without necessarily having the therapeutic language with them. Policy change alone is therefore not enough to "manage" mental illness in the community. It is also necessary to engage that community, encounter the available languages and mind-sets, and create new ways of talking about mental illness in the community.

C. We are more keenly aware of the limitations of the traditional social-scientific methodology in the case of mental distress experiences. Broad based epidemiological, and etiological research has given us information about causation and prediction. But still the individual variability of experiences as they appear in the clinic is far from clear, confounding issues about management. This is especially true in the case where gender is taken into consideration, for the history of psycho-therapy research has not necessarily been sensitive to gender differences in the experience of mental distress. It has also been strongly argued that the available quantitative research is simply not adequate to handle cross-cultural variations in the clinical settings. Given these (natural) limitations of the scientific paradigms, the quality of care one might receive in a clinic seems questionable. For an adequate theory of care within the clinic, many researchers appeal now to the phenomenological approaches.

References

Bachrach, L.L., and Nadelson, C.C., 1989, (eds.), *Treating Chronically Mentally Ill Women*, Washington: American Press.

Busfield, J., 1996, *Men, Women and Madness: Understanding Gender and Mental Disorder,* Hampshire, U.K: Macmillan.

Corin, E.E., 1990, "Facts and meaning in psychiatry. An anthropological approach to the life-world of schizophrenics", *Culture, Medicine and Psychiatry,* 14, pp. 153-88.

D'Amico, R., 1995, "Is disease a natural kind?", *The Journal of Medicine and Philosophy,* 20 (5), pp. 551-69.

Davar, B.V. and Bhat, P.R., 1995, *Psychoanalysis as a Human Science: Beyond Foundationalism*, New Delhi: Sage Publications.

Desjarlais, R., Eisenberg, L., Good, B. and Kleinman, A., 1995, *World mental health: Problems and Priorities in Low-income Countries,* New York: Oxford University Press.

Dhanda, A., 1982, "The Mental Health Bill of 1981 – A New Deal for the Mentally Ill", *SCC Journal,* 8, pp. 8-19.

———, 1987, "Rights of the Mentally Ill – A Forgotten Domain", in U. Baxi (ed.), *The Right to be Human,* New Delhi : Lancer International, pp. 147-160.

Donnelly, W.J., 1988, "Righting the Medical Record: Transforming Chronicle into Story", *Journal of the American Medical Association,* 260 (6), August 12, pp. 823-5.

DSM - IV, 1994, *Diagnostic and Statistical Manual of Mental Disorders.* 4th Revision. Washington, D.C.: American Psychiatric Association.

Gilman, C.P., 1973, (Original 1899), *The Yellow Wall Paper,* New York: Feminist Press.

Goldberg, D. and Huxley, P., 1992, *Common Mental Disorders,* London, Routledge and Kegan Paul.

Good, B.J., 1994, *Medicine, Rationality and Experience: An Anthropological Perspective*, Cambridge: Cambridge University Press.

———, 1996, "Culture and DSM-IV: Diagnosis, Knowledge and Power", *Culture, Medicine and Psychiatry,* 20, pp. 127-32.

Grunbaum, A., 1984, *The Foundations of Psychoanalysis: A Philosophical Critique,* Berkeley, University of California Press.

ICD-10, *International Classification of Diseases. Classification of Mental and Behavioural Disorder,* 10th Revision, Geneva: World Health Organisation.

Jackson, N., 1996, "The First Death of Louis Althusser or Totality's Revenge. A Review Essay", *History and Theory,* 35 (1): pp. 131-46.

Jadhav, S., 1996, "The Cultural Origins of Western Depression", *International Journal of Social Psychiatry,* 42(4), pp. 269-86.

Jamie Saris, A., 1995, "Telling stories: Life histories, illness narratives, and institutional landscapes", *Culture, Medicine and Psychiatry,* 19, pp. 39-72.

Jamison, K. R., 1995, *An Unquiet Mind,* New York : Alfred A. Knopf.

Jansen, E., 1980, "Therapeutic Community Models: The Richmond Fellowship", in *The Therapeutic Community: Outside the Hospital,* London: Croom Helm.

Jonas, H., 1973, "Change and Permanence: On the Possibility of Understanding History", in D. Carr & E.S. Casey (eds.), *Explorations in Phenomenology,* Martinus Nijhoff, The Hague, pp. 102-32.

Kleinman, A. and Kleinman, J., 1991, "Suffering and its Professional Transformation: Toward an Ethnography of Experience", *Culture, Medicine and Psychiatry,* 15, pp. 275-301.

Laing, R.D., 1960, *The Divided Self,* London: Tavistock.

Lewis-Fernandez, R., 1996, "Cultural Formulation of Psychiatric Diagnosis", *Culture, Medicine and Psychiatry,* 20, pp. 133-44.

Macklin, R., "Philosophical Conceptions of Rationality and Psychiatric Notions of Competency", *Synthese,* 57, pp. 205-24.

Maranhão, T., 1986, "The Hermeneutics of Participant Observation", *Dialectical Anthropology,* 10(3&4): pp. 291-309.

Mordacci, R., 1995, "Health as an Analogical Concept", *The Journal of Medicine and Philosophy,* 20 (5), pp. 475-97.

Murthy, R.S. and Dhanda, A., 1993, *Unlocking the Padlock: Mental Health Care in West Bengal,* Report of the Supreme Court Commission on the mentally ill in the jails of West Bengal, New Delhi.

Nichter, M., 1981, "Idioms of Distress. Alternatives in the Expression of Psychosocial Illness. A Case Study from South India", *Culture, Medicine and Psychiatry,* 5, pp. 379-408.

Sartre, J.P., 1956, *Being and Nothingness. A Phenomenological Essay on Ontology,* Washington: Pocket Books.

Seshadri, S., 1996, "Disclosure in Child Sexual Abuse", Paper presented at the National Seminar on Women in India and their Mental Health. Anveshi, Research Centre for Women's Studies, Hyderabad. February, 1996.

Shore, B., 1996, *Culture in Mind. Culture, Cognition and the Problem of Meaning,* New York: Oxford University Press.

Skultans, V., 1991, "Women and Affliction in Maharashtra: A Hydraulic Model of Health and Illness", *Culture, Medicine and Psychiatry,* 15, pp. 321-59.

Sontag, S., 1979, *Illness as Metaphor*, New York: Vintage.

Styron, W., 1990, *Darkness Visible: A Memoir of Madness,* New York: Random House.

Sundararajan, R., 1996, "Notes Towards a Phenomenology of Historiographies", *Journal of the Indian Council of Philosophical Research,* Special Issue, June, "Historiography of Civilizations". pp. 187-200.

Szasz, T., 1974, *The Myth of Mental Illness. Foundations of a Theory of Personal Conduct,* New York: Harper and Row.

4

Self, Identity and (Indian) Philosophy

Cross-Currents[1]

Sasheej Hegde

A theme, no less than a face, wears an expression.

— Wittgenstein

I

THE difference, or rather, the division, between a dynamic discourse and an energetic one, between that which speaks of a whole and of a whole which is only just — in part — a part, is never far away; and perhaps, this can be one way of engaging with our concerns here, glimpses of which can be had from a paper prior to this one (Hegde, 1992). The interest of that examination had consisted in an attempt to intervene in, and consolidate, the gains of a seminar answering to the theme 'Nature of Self in Indian Philosophies'. In focus was a certain movement, a passage through frames engaged in the persistent critique of what one *must* inhabit; and which had compelled me to enclose a series of near-programmatic statements about the axes along which much philosophical reflection on the self had been delivered. The research also led me, subsequently, into a

1. For Prof. S.A. Shaida, who is, is not. I have hardly known Prof. Shaida personally, having met him only once or twice. But I have known some of his students, Raghu, our editor, perhaps more intimately than others. In acceding to his request to write, I suppose, I *had* to choose a characteristically elusive theme, while also answering to Prof. Shaida/his students' concerns and taking a discussion forward. Hopefully, my contribution befits the occasion. Transliteration of terms from their Sanskrit forms have been retained.

range of problems — both spatial and temporal — concerning the question of "who and where 'we' are, and what the limits of an 'era' might be". In this my present article, I propose to both recall and retrace these investigations, pursuing them a little further, while also striving actively to redraw their frontier. Particularly, I wish to avoid here what my investigations hitherto had served to conflate, namely, (to echo, I think, Foucault) "the conditions of history itself in the density of the historic". It seems imperative to do so, since, from our point of view, any discourse about 'self' which does not ask critical questions in respect of its own representation of history remains radically acritical. Besides, what is more, such a gesture of avoidance, as a point of strategy (not of conviction), keeps open the possibility of translating rival, even apparently incommensurable, ideological universes into the terms of either.[2]

II

A characteristically striking — and at the same time symptomatically elusive — theme encountered by, and within, philosophical discourse is the idea of 'self'. *Institutionally*, and in terms of a past history from which it derives, the idea can be seen to resonate a hidden theme of exclusion and incarceration, of domination and subjectification, reminiscent, say, of the work of Foucault (1984). Alongside a more *moral* topography that, for instance, Charles Taylor (1989) has been concerned to inscribe, 'self' has been taken to embody the Cartesian project of self-mastery, while also including elements of (what Taylor has termed) 'expressivism', the Romantic and post-Romantic tradition of Western culture, that is, and uniquely non-Cartesian. There is also a wider, a more *socio-political* inscription that is facilitated

2. If I am permitted a further thought here: basically, I believe, nothing much is accomplished by denouncing an intellectual field as "Western", as a "colonial practice", as "dominating", and so on. That such denunciations are warranted by context and experience is perhaps undeniable. But the context, an experience, does not of itself establish a practice as 'colonial', 'dominating', etc.; rather, the problem demands a complex strategy. Indeed, engage the pages to follow.

by the question 'self', which brings us closer to some tasks of political philosophy and answers to what Paul Ricoeur (1984) has termed 'the political paradox': the double and paradoxical originality of 'polity'. Suggestive and wide-ranging as these modes of thought have been about the questions tackled, the narratives they provide and/or facilitate however seem to have, as their limit, a constriction of the space of problematisation. I am not of course implying that there can be a simple answer to the question of what the self is, and whether one is justified in describing it in some particular way; this is of course a highly contested issue to which I will refer later on in the text.

More important, I think, at least as a kind of epistemological detour is the logical space within which reflection on the 'self' has moved, and in terms of which different theories have been carved out. Broadly, this might be approached as incorporating and outlining moves in what has been termed *consciousness* philosophy (or again, perhaps more loosely, the relation between thought and reality). By way of a condensation of these moves, let me set up a model which, even if admittedly crude and perhaps even gesturing in all possible directions, is yet susceptible of tracking a trajectory in the reflection about 'self'. One need not bother with whatever refinement the model is capable of, since it is only meant to be strategic: it is a mere play of thought, meant to illustrate that on which a strictly epistemological reference on the question of 'self' could be drawn; as well as to facilitate a movement across. Recounted episodically, although not quite linearly, the model would comprise the following strands:

(a) metaphysical thinking (or thought) — the attempt broadly to explore what experience would be like before the emergence of a self-conscious subject of experience;

(b) the critique of metaphysics (or the theme of identity) — the forging, that is, of a self-conscious, morally responsible subject; or, what comes to the same thing, the delineation of a 'philosophy of reflection' privileging (i) the subject, the self-conscious subject of experience, and (ii) the synthesising function of the concept, of a consciousness imposing its order upon a disorderly manifold (the classifying gaze?) and thus transforming itself into a kind of (self-contained) theatre;

(c) the critique of consciousness — or (i) the denial of the ability of philosophical reflection to establish epistemological criteria, and (ii) the opposition to the rigidities of the concept, to the view of subjectivity as something self-contained, isolated from and standing over against the object of knowledge;

(d) the drives toward an idealism which argues that the structures of knowledge are entirely constitutive of the object;

(e) the insistence, broadly, that all consciousness should comprehend itself as perspectival and/or historical; and

(f) back towards a reinstatement of the distinction between appearance and reality, and/or the reinstating of the relation between knowledge and its object internal to consciousness.

We also have, within and in the context of these moves, the efforts to develop a critique of objectifying theory from the standpoint of an ontology of flux, as also the series of locutions against (we can say) the illusory autonomy of the modern subject and the attempt to attenuate the 'power of consciousness' *vide* the role of affectivity and the body.

The 'self', its logical lineaments, as thus outlined, is not exhaustive, to be sure; besides, to say the least, it can prove to be an ambiguous inheritance, in that, approached along the terms condensed above, one could be left wondering what the self is. And yet, it seems to me that a hypothesis has gone unacknowledged. Let me quickly turn to it, and in the section to follow elaborate.[3] If the interest which demands that the nature

---

3. I shall venture further into *our* problematic of self in section V of this article. The ensuing two sections are not, however, on that count a digression. Recall the imagery invoked by a part of our title, namely, 'Cross-Currents'. Rather than baldly state the problem, I am here concerned to prepare a way for it, into it.

of self be epistemologically articulated — in terms (say) of a specific structuring of the logical field — be made relative to traditions of philosophy, national or otherwise, and if this requirement is ultimately based upon the possibility that the self which accompanies all representation is an *embodied* self (not necessarily to be confused with a historically located actor), then it is this very possibility that must be examined (including, I might add, those others which emerge from that very possibility). Indeed, in a manner of speaking, it is the force of this lesson, rendered somewhat cross-culturally, that our summation above was meant to consolidate; but perhaps we ought to venture more culturally, and contextually.

III

One must here discount, at the very outset, that tendency to read philosophies *conjuncturally* — in terms, that is, often sounded in the literature, that philosophy in the East begins with the questions with which philosophy in the West has ended (or rather, finds itself to be ending): "How are we to know that which knows? How are we to know the knower?" Alternatively, one could ask the question that (for instance) J.N. Mohanty, at the end of his recent work laying out the conception of theoretical rationality with which the Indian tradition thought, is concerned to formulate, namely, "are Indian and Western philosophies radically different? That is to say, are they different as philosophies?" (1992: 283). As distinct from the conjunctural sort of reading that I just mentioned, if only to set aside, and which, it seems to me, amounts to constructing some perennial ground (even an abstract telos) for philosophy, Mohanty's question lends itself to a much more effective recontextualisation of *traditions* of philosophy. Against the abstract universality of the former, we are here, alongside Mohanty's question, engaging with the distinctive matrices of identity of both Indian and Western philosophy.

In proceeding to answer this question however, Mohanty is particularly interested to confront three "responses" —

emblematised by the figures of Husserl, Rorty and Heidegger — each given to drawing the limit between Indian and Western philosophy, but all, as a matter of fact, asserting the thesis that Indian philosophy is so radically different from Western philosophy that one should not call the former 'philosophy'. Mohanty of course is concerned to query the axes of these self-assertions, finding them inadequate on both factual and theoretical grounds, as also 'incoherent' when approached in terms of the totality of perspectives that each of these figures have been interested to generate (*ibid*.: pp. 283-90). According to him, "the crucial question is not, are the *darśanas* philosophies?", but rather: "Does the Indian *darśana*, by virtue of its subject-matter, its concerns, its methodology come under the purview of the concept 'philosophy'?"(*ibid*.: 297-8). In this connection, Mohanty dismisses two views, one 'relativistic', the other 'essentialistic', holding that both these options are mistaken, being a priori arguments incapable of refutation; and observes:

> I believe that there are enough similarities between Indian *darśanas* and the Western philosophies to justify translating *darśana* as 'philosophy' — enough differences erupting precisely where similarities first showed themselves to justify talk of *Indian* philosophy (*ibid*.: 298-9).

Mohanty's discourse makes it plain that, in defining the concept of 'philosophy', he is not quite under the sway of the manner in which that concept is ordinarily understood. Besides, his attempted demonstration that Indian philosophy has always been grappling with many of the issues which pre-occupy twentieth century philosophers (of both 'analytic' and 'phenomenological' persuasions) — as also the concomitant rejection of several "unhelpful cliches", of the "Indian philosophy is just so much intuition and mysticism" variety — could be received as a plea for attending to the Indian tradition itself. There is however a delicate balance to be maintained, especially when addressed in terms of the prospects for a genuine dialogue between Indian and Western philosophy:

> Make Indian philosophy sound too full of Eastern promise and it no longer engages with the Western tradition. Make it sound too much of a rehersal for Frege or Husserl, and, antiquarian interest aside, we may as well content ourselves with them (Cooper 1993: 26).[4]

At stake, then, is a certain nodal coiling up or interlacing which precipitates both the possibility and impossibility of a self-identity for *Indian* philosophy. Needless to add, Mohanty's discourse remains noncommital, even equivocating between issues bearing on the self-identity of Indian philosophy and coming unstuck upon the theme of a tradition's de-limitation.

IV

To join together, in a discourse, both possibility and impossibility, contextualisation and re-contextualisation, may seem to be a laborious artifice, as if, in order to economise, one sought to deal with many subjects at once. But that is in fact the case; and, in the immediate context here of rehabilitating a tradition's self-understanding, and bearing upon the theme of its identity/alterity, as it were, two questions seem to implicate themselves. One is the definitional problem of what is to count, for one's purposes, as rehabilitating a tradition's self-understanding — indeed the 'what' and the 'how' of this gesture of rehabilitation would require specification. The other, again definitional (although not quite in the sense inscribed by the first, as we shall see) relates to the problem of identity (or identification), of what is to count as the *identity* of a tradition or theme: indeed, how can one identify a tradition as such-and-such without already being familiar with it (that is to say, assimilated it into or as part of one's own)? But perhaps I may be allowed a further thought before venturing ahead. Let me combine the two questions just indicated, before proceeding to distinguish between them.

4. Note, Cooper is here reviewing, in the pages of the *Times Literary Supplement*, a series of arguments on Indian philosophy, incorporating the works of J.N. Mohanty, Ninian Smart, Daya Krishna and J.L. Mehta.

There is, it seems to me, a certain paradox about statements of identity, which, incidentally, has been the source of much philosophical perplexity down the ages, in Western thought, across Indian philosophy. Summarily stated, the paradox may be recounted thus. If a relation of identity holds between one thing and something else — say, for instance, as of May 1997 in India, the statement "The Prime Minister is identical with the leader of the BJP" — then it is necessarily false; but if it states that the relation holds between a thing and itself — say "The Prime Minister is identical with the leader of the United Front" — then it is the most trivial of tautologies. How, then, can such statements ever be informative, as they claim to be? The error here, clearly, has to do with viewing identity as a strange two-place relation between objects. A solution *could* lie in a more perspicuous formulation, replacing the paradoxical relation "is identical with" with the force, say, of an "exactly one": "There is exactly one person who both governs India and leads the United Front". But it is important to see that identity cannot be a relation; and, what is more, cannot be expressed by the old two-place relation view. Rather, identity amounts to an idea of self-sameness, and accordingly should be expressed by the operation of reflection. What the latter operation does is to exploit the idea of self-sameness, by turning identity statements and their illusory two-place predicates into statements with one-place predicates applied manifestly to one object: "*X* was angry with himself" is not about *X* and *X*, related by anger, but simply about *X*, who was angry reflexively, as it were.[5]

The foregoing, in freeing us from the image of two adjacent spaces, captures in a more suitable if enigmatic way the problems attendant upon acts of grounding traditions and themes *conjuncturally*, or even cross-culturally. To have shown that something *is* the case and/or that such-and-such a connection

5. To be sure, this is only a bare outline of what would require a much more carefully crafted series of considerations on the logic of identity. For some ideas that bear on the question, see Williams (1990). See also Footnote 7.

is expressed by a *given* case — or again, *vide* Mohanty, that the primacy of the logical in Western thought and of intuition in Indian philosophy is only apparent, that in fact "Western thought (has) constantly sought to go beyond logic to the foundations of logic in the structure of subjectivity that itself is only reflectively accessible" (1992: 293), while "the Indian philosopher *qua* philosopher exercises intuitive grasp and achieves intuitive experience no more and no less than his Western counter-part" (*ibid.*: 294) — is perhaps necessary, and even warranted by context and experience. But we have still not come so far as to prove *a priori* that there actually is an imperative of this kind. In order to discover this, one must take a step beyond it, into metaphysics, although into a region of it which is different from speculative philosophy, namely, into the logics of identity.[6]

V

To return to the questions themselves, let me take up the first, namely, the definitional problem of what is to count, for one's purposes, as rehabilitating a tradition's self-understanding. To formulate the issue in context, that is in relation to our theme of self: the definitional problem, when tacked on to this theme, only compounds the ambiguities and dilemmas that our summations above have sought to foreground. For one, we are left wondering whether the self is — an epistemology? an ontology? a critique of objectifying theory? the rudimentary movements of an experience? a body? a consciousness? an identity? a metaphysics of subjectivity? Likewise, the notion of 'selfsameness' that we have taken the idea of identity to express seems to gesture is all possible directions, and which unless

---

6. Cf. again the paragraph preceding this one, and the thoughts expressed therein that impinge on our conclusion here. Mohanty's locutions, I need reiterate, also bear on the self-identity and self-definition of the philosophical task. I shall dwell on this theme presently.

circumscribed cannot command assent.[7]

There is another course however, of rehabilitating a tradition's self-understanding, even as this gesture of rehabilitation comes to be tacked on to an extant and/or elusive theme. This has reference to a practice that is largely followed within much academic philosophy, as is taught and subjected to institutional protocols, namely, the dominant interpretation of the self as a "subject of mental states". That is to say, to what we would normally mean by the word 'person', 'man', or even 'living being', in so far as it designates a conscious experiencing entity. This rules out, as it were, a preoccupation with *ātman* as a metaphysical principle, an universal essence or law in the Upaniṣadic sense,[8] because we as individual experiencing entities are not aware of this universal essence, if it exists, and can become aware of it, according to the Upaniṣads, only by an act of deep spiritual insight, a kind of suprasensory or transcendental *gnosis*. In this way, the notion of *ātman* is more or less clearly defined in the narrow sense, and the question of the existence or non-existence of the *ātman* boils down to the problem of the nature of the individual, experiencing subject: whether it is illusory or real; temporary or permanent; phenomenal or numinal, or both. But what this amounts to is a whole denial of the *ātman* controversy, not simply its overwhelming importance in the Indian

7. William's account, in the work called attention to earlier (foot-note 5 above), stresses that through this formulation identity can be shown not to be a relation. But this does not, of itself, show how this yields a guarantee of the possibility of universalisability itself. (I am assuming, of course, that one of the logical properties of identity is universalisability, and that this criterion encompasses such other properties as symmetry, reflexiveness and transitivity.) Again, to shift the register somewhat: consider the idea that subjection to the law is not going to be a necessary condition of the real possibility of action in accord with law.

8. For this see generally Mohanty (1992), but more specifically chapters 2 and 6 therein. It seems to me significant that the word *ātman*, although figuring in the body of Mohanty's text, avoids systematically its motivated sense. On this, note also the arguments which follow.

philosophical tradition but also its relevance for the Western tradition, particularly for the latter's preoccupation with the question of the existence of a soul which in modern philosophical terminology reappears mostly as 'subject' or 'person'.[9]

Where, however, in the scholarship, the self is held as the equivalent of the term *ātman* — where clearly the self does not correspond to, is not equated with, the notion of a 'subject of mental states' — another set of problems announces itself. It is important to capitulate why, within the context of the Buddhist-Brahmanic controversy over the existence of the *ātman*, the arguments hardly ever took the form that the modern Western position took; in particular, the non-appearance in the Indian scene of the position which understands the notion of person as based on the experience of oneself as the *subject* of mental and other states.[10]

---

9. I owe this point and much else in this paragraph — as indeed the one to follow — to various sources, but principally to Karel Werner (1989) who, in the course of a short review, forces home these reminders. In contra-distinction to this, perhaps, one might weave Mohanty's *hypothesis* that "whereas in Indian thought the concept of the *subject* as the neutral disinterested knower occupies a decisive role, in Western thought the concept of the *person* as the active agent is more important, so much so that where the other concept emerges in either tradition, it is assimilated to the dominant concept" (1992, p. 4). Cf. also his point on pp. 193-4 relating to whether the Upanil]sadic *"atman* should be translated as 'self': "There is no doubt, however, that the *"atman*, even as it is the theme of (-) early discourses, has something to do with the human person — that, in other words, our access to the *"atman* is provided by the human person". It may perhaps be reiterated that the lineaments of self, as disclosed in section II above, do not seem to engage this ground whatsoever. However, for a certain revitalisation of the ground of the question, see the issues raised in Cadava *et al.* (1991), especially the introduction and the pieces by Balibar, Descombes and Derrida. One might yet have to contend with the currents of section II.

10. I think it would be most interesting to seek after specific Indian intuitions and conclusions about the word 'I', 'you', 'me' 'us', as also the usage of sentences with which a subject ascribes experiences to itself. The inference, if I might venture to add, is obvious: fieldwork *in* philosophy.

To turn now to that other question, namely, of what is to count as the *identity* of a tradition or theme, it can be maintained that aspects of the foregoing have already broached the issue. But, more specifically, we can ask: what is to count as *Indian* philosophy, as opposed to say *Western* philosophy? Or, again, what of Indian philosophies, the imperative, that is, to convey philosophy in the plural? This is without doubt a problem area into which I do not propose to enter — at least, not quite in the way in which the issue is often posed[11] — except to observe that the term poses peculiar problems of definition which are only magnified when considered in the context of 'self'. For it is not only a matter of defining the term's referential scope — here Karl Potter's (1989) effort to trace the development of *Advaita Vedānta* as a school of philosophy within a taxonomy of phases in the 'life' of a philosophical school is of particular interest[12] — its proper application is also subject to dispute, since what counts as 'Indian' will depend on where (and how) the boundaries between the real and the ideal, between the feasible and the merely possible, and between the 'indigenous' and the 'foreign' are drawn. And, if the lineaments explored in the burgeoning sociological and historical scholarship on India are any indication,[13] then it could be asserted that the marking of these lines is nearly impossible and/or futile. It has been claimed that the mark 'Indian' is doubly unrealisable, marking more the

---

11. But see, for a sensitive even if altogether brief appraisal, Chakrabarti (1987).

12. Interestingly, in all the commentary that has surrounded Potter's proposal, in the pages of the *Journal of Indian Council of Philosophical Research*, for instance, the axis of appraisal has hardly concerned the register I am inscribing here. To dwell on this question would take us too far afield, however.

13. The literature on this question is vast, but for one that bears on aspects of our problem, see Oberoi (1994), especially the introduction and the accompanying methodological reflections on religion and Indian historiography.

institution of identity and its associated politics of the late nineteenth and twentieth century India.[14]

Again, it is not as though the specific imperative of providing a necessary corrective to the standard picture of the Indian traditions (where metaphysics, theology and spirituality dominate, and ethics, politics and sociology are relegated to the background) has to be denied. But, it appears to me that the perspective from which most such attempts at correction are undertaken embody a concern less with the deliberations in the Indian thought about man, society and polity than with the intuitions and basic concepts that guide the design of the traditions itself. Thus, for instance, Daya Krishna, prefacing his attempt to foreground the socio-political matrix of Indian thought, observes:

> The question is not whether the understanding of a concept or a set of concepts is 'correct' in the light of what has been said in a particular text or a series of texts on the subject, but whether one is creatively using and developing it to understand one's own experience as did so many of the great thinkers in the past (1996: ix).

The problem with such a thematisation is that its terminology indicates a certain unclarity about what is in need of justification — the past, the present, Indian traditions, the thought about man, society, polity? And besides, one can even add that the metaphors 'using' and 'developing' — as indeed that turn of phrase "to understand one's own experience" — have their own history of expediency.

I take it, then, that the substantive question of what the identity of a tradition or a theme is would have to be posed — although it remains unclear just *what* question about the

---

14. For this see generally Kaviraj (1992), although I think Chakrabarti's formulations in that brief note alluded to above would necessitate a complication of the terms of this appraisal. Ponder yet again the points that follow.

possibility of any identity that that question (I mean the substantive question) is raising. The accompanying complications notwithstanding, what this enunciative position must entail is the imperative, so to speak, of going about individuating traditions, Indian, Hindu or otherwise, while also dealing more frontally with the question of a comprehensive *historical* inheritance.[15]

VI

The analysis this far has turned on the possibility of a prior definition of the self-relation, not quite as an existential analytics of the subject (consciousness, psyche or the self) — it is not a morals or a politics either — but as *reflection*. Or perhaps, more appropriately, as reconstructive appropriation. Philosophy's ideals of reflectiveness, of reconstructive appropriation, to be sure, I realise, do not present a homogeneous ensemble; but then, it cannot be denied that most philosophies/philosophers (and their figures of thought) do not deserve their historical legacy.[16] Accordingly, if one does not wish to deny to the concept of self all truth, and all possible relation to any possible object, then one cannot dispute that its *law* (as it were) must hold not merely contingently but also absolutely necessarily. The question now arises: how are all these imperatives possible, as also an associated thought about what they are meant to prefigure? Let me set up a passage, all over again, through Mohanty.

Mohanty's querying of the foundations of both the Western and Indian philosophical thinking bears, ultimately, on the question of the identity of philosophy. As he observes, passingly even if somewhat strikingly, in the course of an assessment of

---

15. Some suggestions — and an exemplification of this enunciative modality — can be had in my essay "Rules and Laws in the Indian Traditions: A Reconstructive Appropriation" (1998). This, my present article, could be seen to consolidate, in a more abstract logical vein, the insights (if any) of that negotiation.

16. See Williams (1996) for a short appraisal of this point.

the *alleged* primacy of intuition in Indian philosophy: "In my view, the task of philosophy ends with reflection" (1992, 294); and even mentions, early on, in his introduction, "(t)heoretical reason, as I see it, is best manifested in the way our beliefs are appraised as true, in the way our theories about what **is**, that is our sciences and ontologies, are substantiated" (*ibid.*: 5). In a work devoted to "bring(ing) into clear relief the nature of Indian philosophical thinking" (*ibid.*: 22), and given over to emphasising that "good phenomenology and good analysis are inseparable" — that indeed "the best of Indian philosophy is both phenomenological and analytical: it is both analysis of ordinary usage and description of how things are presented to the testimony of consciousness" (*ibid.*: 6) — I suppose this nexus of moves that Mohanty's text institutes is in order.[17] And yet, it seems to me that this gesture of identification — of self-relation, as it were — loads the allusion to philosophy, to the body of its institution that is in formation,[18] with a very specific ontological meaning. If it were a simple matter of concepts, it would come

17. That Mohanty's text lays claim to other ends as well — quite apart from bearing upon the self-identity of (Indian) philosophy — is perhaps only too obvious. We need only scan his introductory chapter, 'Indian philosophy: Between tradition and modernity' to bolster this inference. Particularly, I am struck by his suggestion that bringing into sharp relief the nature of Indian philosophical thinking "holds out the promise, not merely of studying Indian thought from the point of view of the Western philosophies, but also, by reversing that strategy, of critically studying the Western philosophies from the vantage points of the typically Indian modes of thinking" (1992: 22). Likewise, his suggestion that what are constituted as "lacks" in Indian thought "are not deficiencies, they are absences only in the context of comparative philosophy" (*ibid.*: 3) resonates a theme, for the comparative enterprise, that has to do with "deep structures". But of course the fecundity of these gestures are subject to the modalities of their inscription, self-relation, aspects I have been calling attention to in these pages.

18. This turn of phrase is advised, not traceable to Mohanty, of course, but offering content and perspective to his frequent allusions to the nature of *philosophical* thinking.

to an end as soon as an image were enclosed within its conceptual limits. But then, Mohanty's zone of problematisation often implicates a horizon quite other than that of the concept: indeed it seems less a question of describing forms than of weighing matter.[19]

Apparently Mohanty is not alone. There is a long tradition of theorising about philosophy, about *Indian* philosophy, which picks out epistemic access — a shorthand, I take it, for reflection and/or theoretical reason — as criterial of ontological meaning;[20] and, what is more, I have already alluded to some of the indeterminacies that could result from such a posturing (in the context of Daya Krishna perhaps, but could be directed towards Mohanty's project as well). Rather than dwell once again on these cross-currents, I want to disintricate aspects of the figure of *end* in relation to which Mohanty posits the identity of philosophy. What is special about this figure, one might ask? By way of an answer, I will single out briefly, and formulaically, four (significant) aspects of 'end':

(a) End (epistemically speaking) operates, more or less independently, either as something towards which we are all directed or even as an initiating circumstance.

(b) Clearly the notion implicates a sense, at once, spatial — in the sense of what is placed behind, motivational and/or directing — and temporal, of what comes after.

---

19. *Cf.* yet again Mohanty's insistence — presented interestingly as a "confession" — that the *phenomenological* and the *analytical* are, strictly, "inseparable" (1992:6). He speaks, repeatedly, of "degrees of emphasis", while also arraigning against the attitude that there is only one privileged sense of a text. Clearly something more is involved here than a description of forms: a weighing of matter?

20. A move which also underscores, I take it, the characterisation of Indian culture as, essentially, 'inward'. Thus, for instance, K.C. Bhattacharya, significantly in his article "Svaraj in Ideas" (1984) devoted to categorically rejecting the ideas of "a single universal reason", "a rootless universalism", "a patchwork of ideas of different cultures". But see, also, his "The Subject as Freedom" (1983).

(c) End also suggests a capacity for *tracking*, be it the properties of an object, or a determination over time. It can also imply, quite simply, a moving around, a lacing together (in short, a recoiling).

(d) Over-reaching itself, and not necessarily discounting each of the foregoing aspects, the figure also suggests a space of ontological commitments, at once moral and political.

Mohanty's counsel, writ large over the body of his text, clearly resonates aspects (a), (b) and (c), although, in my view, this sort of posit is 'happiest' (*sic*) when wedded to attempts at spatialisation as opposed to temporalisation. Not surprisingly, the chapter devoted to explicating the place of time in Indian thought weaves its account of the same with a series of near-programmatic, even heterological, thoughts about the thematisations of man, subject, person and nature as offered in (and by) the classical Hindu philosophies (1992: 184-226 *passim*). In sum, then: that a thinking of time requires a thought about its spacing.[21]

This fundamental assymetry — or symmetrisation, if you will — inflects the discourse (the gesture, really, of recuperation) in a specific direction, that is, *modally*. But where Mohanty is interested to traverse a course that lends itself to or keeps open the possibility of, at once, rehabilitating and developing a

21. Interestingly, Mohanty's "excursus" into the concept of time, in the chapter just alluded to, encapsulates this possibility from within Indian thought. Thus, having set aside the view that for Indian thought time is unreal, he observes: "The question on which the Indian philosophies differed were: Is time atomic or discrete, or is the continuity of time real? Is time inseparable from the changing events that fill time, or is it a separate entity in which finite entities have their places? Is time, however conceived, perceived or can it be known only by inference? It is these issues rather than the large question whether time is metaphysically real that occupied the bulk of the attention of the philosophers" (1992, p.185). And yet, I realise also that this is *hot* territory. Some aspects of my contemporary research have sought to traverse this ground; more work is imperative before these condensations are allowed to precipitate.

tradition's *self-understanding*,[22] we, in the spirit of a modal discourse, would be concerned to preserve the implication that before an idea, a philosophy, can be theoretically employed, it must be philosophically reconstructed.[23] This does not demand to know how the execution of a philosophy which the imperative commands can be conceived; but rather how the necessitation of a philosophy can be conceived which the imperative expresses in the task (which it sets).

VII

I would like to draw together, in my conclusion, all the insights into an *analytics* of self, identity and (Indian) philosophy that the foregoing examination gives us. These insights, in the final analysis, have great unity, and are, as we have spoken of them, a series of cross-currents. It is quite obvious that to understand a complex well one must participate in it oneself, although in the specific limited problem that I have treated of in this article there is no methodological obligation that forces me to get inside the characteristics of the discourse/ground I am exploring. Detached from everything related to a sociologically oriented thematisation, and again without dwelling far too ponderously on formal possibilities, I have tried to show especially that the problem of self is a decisive one for the judgement of philosophical values. Just as the idea of a figure enclosed within two straight lines does not prove its possibility, so too the possibility of a categorisation of philosophy must be attached to a question

22. Indeed, the entire disquisition is itself configured by the concept and theories of *pramāṇa*s as the decisive ontological axis for throwing light on the Indian concept of rationality.

23. See, for an overview of the issues involved, Marcus (1993), although one must yet contest the suggestion contained therein that *all* modal discourse is implicitly metalinguistic. We need to reiterate here, however, that this is a disputed terrain; even that Mohanty could insist that this is precisely what his work accomplishes. Perhaps, but consider the condensations offered in my final section. I am also not so sure that the best way to do this is to turn near-*pragmatist*, as does Krishna (or even Mohanty?).

about its self-relation; indeed, to a question about the imperatives from which, and in relation to which, a particular categorisation of philosophy draws.

As I am beginning to see and, in a sense, my foregoing account has presupposed, there are two different complications about the possibility of a philosophy that are to be answered. One is the question of how it is possible for a self-relation actually to *bind* a philosophy, that is to say, not just institute it but structure an act in compliance with it. However, before that question can be reached, there is a more general question about how it is possible for any self-relation to conceive of a philosophy at all that must be answered. I realise that this brief remark does not make very clear what the preliminary question is; but perhaps one could ponder here the effort inscribed in Ramchandra Gandhi — particularly his 'meditations' on what is termed "The Truth of India" (1984). What begins by being the querying of a subject turns out, inexorably, to be a celebration of him who queries in the first place: a pounding, an impounding, which exclaims "I am Thou". Henceforth, the entire project of constructing a foundation for self, of giving an unified ontology to (Indian) philosophy, comes to be focussed on this possibility of self-ascription of experience. The paradoxes of inscription, and combination, that this possibility encloses would have to be addressed, if only in order to avoid the postulation of a figure — an identity? — which comes with the assertion of autonomy.[24]

Should one say that this avoidance is modern? Or, traditional? Shall one say that it depoliticises a space of problematisation, that it displaces the nature of the political? Notwithstanding the infinite variety of forms which selfhood assumes, the desire to be one with self, to ground a philosophy of self-identity, seems

---

24. These self-same paradoxes could be read off other projects as well: for instance, in the figure of the 'subaltern' within a historiography that announces itself as Subaltern Studies (Guha and Spivak, 1988 is an overview); or even the effort to recover India's intellectual traditions *vide* Daya Krishna (1987).

to be quite straightforward; and the psychology of a discourse which masks itself thus seems consequently a simple matter to establish. The self, as it appears, makes possible instant dissimulation: it both founds and destabilises at the same time. Within this scheme — whose necessity I have sought to underscore in relation to the question of philosophical institution — I realise that striking a balance between *sensory* values and *sensual* ones seems a must. But that must await another time and place.

References

Bhattacharya, K.C., 1983, "The subject as freedom". *In* his *Studies in Philosophy*, Delhi, Motilal Banarsidass, pp.367-454. Second revised edition.

———, 1984, "Svaraj in ideas", *Indian Philosophical Quarterly* 11, pp. 383-93.

Cadava, E., P. Connor and J-L Nancy (eds.), 1991, *Who Comes After the Subject?*, New York, Routledge.

Chakrabarti, A., 1987, "What makes us Indian?" in R. Khan, (ed.), *Composite Culture of India and National Integration*, New Delhi, Allied, pp. 160-6.

Cooper, D.E., 1993, "The lost message: Indian philosophy re-examined," *Times Literary Supplement*, November 12: 26-7.

Foucault, M., 1984, *The Foucault Reader* (P. Rabinow ed.), New York, Pantheon.

Gandhi, R., 1984, *I am Thou: Meditations on the Truth of India*, Pune: I.P.Q. Publications.

Guha, R., and Spivak, G.C. (ed.), 1988, *Selected Subaltern Studies*, New York, Oxford University Press.

Hegde, S., 1992, "Of self/fragment: Other inquisitions, new (*sic*) beginnings". Paper presented at ICPR seminar on "The Nature of Self in Indian Philosophies", Goa.

———, 1998, "Rules and laws in Indian traditions: A reconstructive appropriation". In S. Saberwal and H. Sievers (eds.), *Rules, Laws, Constitutions*, New Delhi, Sage Publications, pp. 97-118.

Kaviraj, S., 1992, "The imaginary institution of India". In P. Chatterjee and

G. Pandey, (eds.), *Subaltern Studies VII: Writings on South Asian History and Society,* Delhi, Oxford University Press, pp. 1-39.

Krishna, D. (ed.), 1987, *India's Intellectual Traditions: Attempts at Conceptual Reconstructions,* Delhi, Motilal Banarsidass.

Krishna, D., 1996, *The Problematic and Conceptual Structure of Classical Indian Thought about Man, Society and Polity*, Delhi, Oxford University Press.

Marcus, R.B., 1993, *Modalities: Philosophical Essays,* New York, Oxford University Press.

Mohanty, J.N., 1992, *Reason and Tradition in Indian Thought: An Essay on the Nature of Indian Philosophical Thinking,* Oxford, Clarendon Press.

Oberoi, H., 1994, *The Construction of Religious Boundaries: Culture, Identity and Diversity in the Sikh Tradition,* Delhi, Oxford University Press.

Potter, K., 1989, "The Development of *Advaita Vedanta* as a school of philosophy." In, G. Parthasarathi and D.P. Chattopadhyaya, (eds.), *Radhakrishnan: Centenary Volume,* Delhi, Oxford University Press, pp. 71-99.

Ricoeur, P., 1984, "The political paradox". In W.Connolly, (ed.), *Legitimacy and the State,* Oxford, Basil Blackwell, pp. 250-72.

Taylor, C., 1989, *Sources of the Self: The Making of the Modern Identity*, Cambridge, Mass., Harvard University Press.

Werner, K., 1989, Review of *"Ich" und das Ich: Analytische Untersuchungen zur Buddhistisch-Brahmanischen Atmankontroverse* by Claus Oetke. *Journal of the royal Asiatic society*, No. 1, pp. 171-2.

Williams, B., 1996, "On hating and despising philosophy," *London Review of Books,* April 18, pp. 17-18.

Williams, C.J.F., 1990, *What is Identity?* Oxford, Clarendon Press.

5

The (Dark) Womb of Rights
An Exploration in Political Gynecology*

A. Raghuramaraju

Introduction

RIGHTS are generically related to human beings, making their relation to be a necessary one. More specifically, the birth of an autonomous human being postulated during the Enlightenment in the modern West almost dictated the nature and developments of rights discourse. Thus, this discourse is primarily dependent on the discourse of an autonomous human being. Though rights have their location in the modern West and are intrinsically related to man, this discourse continues to travel outside the West. Along with this geographical movement internal to the discourse of rights, we do come across instances where the purview of this discourse is conceptually extended to include non-human beings such as animals (Peter Singer), and even communities (Kymlicka, 1995). Thus, the discourse of rights is an expanding discourse. Normally, during the process of expansion, the discourse participating in the horizontal growth often loses sight of its origins. This essay using some important discussions from Richard Tuck's serious study on the background of rights entitled, *Natural Rights Theories: Their Origin and Development* (1979),

---

* Some parts of this essay are used as a lesson entitled "Human Rights: Their evolution from the ancient to the modern," in a P.G. Diploma in Human Rights, University of Hyderabad.

attempts to draw attention to both the birth and stages preceding the birth of rights.

Following an introduction to the birth of rights in the modern period, the essay draws attention to those developments in the womb, namely in the medieval period, preceding the birth of rights. The essay concludes by highlighting the medieval contribution to the rights discourse and thus argues for the need to have an active relation between the modern and the medieval, between the birth and the womb.

Birth of Rights

The discussions on human rights today generally begin with the birth of rights, of Thomas Hobbes or the notions of Social Contract or the declaration of rights. For instance, Kenneth Minogue declares that the "idea of human rights is as modern as the internal combustion engine" (1989: 3). More specifically he locates this in Hobbes and says:

> Hobbes was first to produce a genuinely philosophical account of something called 'natural rights'. . . . He was also the first philosopher . . . to locate the source of political authority in the people below, rather than in God alone. (1989: 7)

Even Leo Strauss implicitly endorses the practice of beginning the discussion of rights from the modern period. He in the context of clarifying that there are no human rights in the traditional natural law which is "primarily and mainly an objective 'rule and measure', a binding order prior to, and independent of, the human will," however, asserts that in contrast, "modern natural law is, or tends to be, primarily and mainly a series of `rights', of subjective claims, originating in the human will" (1966: vii-viii) These assertions either directly or indirectly, rightly locate the birth of the individual in the modern period; they, however, fail to give us the idea about the stages preceding the birth of individual and his rights. Granting that rights are born in the modern period, we can, however, rightly be curious about those developments preceeding the birth of rights.

So, the notion of right was not there in the classical period as the idea of an autonomous human being, crucial to the rights discourse, was not there. Metaphorically the classical period is a period of pre-puberty. Subsequently we are informed that rights are born in the modern period. How does one account for the period intermediating between the pre-puberty and the birth of rights? The preoccupation with the birth and the subsequent developments of the rights discourse did not enable us to recognise the contribution during the period preceeding the birth of rights.

One of the aims of this essay is to recall and lay bare the seminal contribution of the medieval period to the discourse of rights by using a biological metaphor. During this period, slowly but seriously, often unintentionally but effectively, man who was a mere part in the cosmic or natural order was taken out and made autonomous.

Womb of Rights

In this essay, the medieval period is metaphorically referred to as the womb of rights. Medieval period is popularly characterised as a Dark Age. While descriptively agreeing with this characterisation, I however use this in a positive sense and not in a pejorative sense. Rights preceding their birth in the modern period were in the womb, and womb cannot but be dark. The illuminated womb is a site of horror. The general readers often are preoccupied with the illuminated modernity and the birth of rights, and fail to have a peep at the developments in the dark room, in the womb, that is the medieval period. Here I am reminded of a parable from the famous Sūfī mystic Mullā Nasirudhin who was searching for the lost key under the light though he lost it in the dark space.

In highlighting the contributions of the medieval period in this essay, the intention is not to undermine the importance of the modern period. While the raw material for the development of full rights theory is made available by the thinkers prior to the theory of Social Contract, the philosophers holding the theory of Social Contract must be credited for cutting the umbilical cord and thus formalising the paradigm of rights. This involved getting rid off God who was lingering in their predecessor's works.

Without necessarily committing to the exact historical location, we can safely state that it is in the twelfth century that we first come across modern rights theory. In these theories the notion of right or *ius* is related to *dominium* or property, so the discussion of rights was in relation to property and property rights. Some of the significant developments that contributed to the language of rights can be shown to belong to two different periods, says Tuck. First is the period in which the language of rights appeared and developed. This is a period consisting of early and high middle ages. And the second is the period of the classical texts of rights theory. This stretches from Grotius to Locke. Tuck in his (1979) extensively discusses number of theories and thinkers who contributed to the origin and development of rights theory. Here I briefly recall only some important stages.

Stage 1: From the classical framework where man is a mere part within the cosmic whole, we come across in St. Thomas Aquinas a more direct relation amongst God, nature and man. He introduced a novel relation between man and nature by claiming that the material objects in nature have two aspects. One is about its nature and this does not lie within human power but rests with divine power. The other is concerning its use and here man does have natural *dominium* over material things. Man can use material objects for his own use. Within this framework of Aquinas, there is no provision for attributing rights to man, as only a limited *dominium* over nature was conceded to man. Though limited and provisional, this concession to man has turned out to be a seed from which the rights have grown and developed. Further, this interpretation of Aquinas coincides with the Franciscans who celebrated poverty. Franciscans argued that man is allowed by God to use all the commodities necessary for their daily lives without entailing property rights to man in the state of nature. Here it may be noted that this interpretation of the relation between man and nature by Aquinas was not intended for the development of rights, as it had its locale within the theological debate. However, this move was very significant as it facilitated a more direct relation, in contrast to earlier abstract relation, between man and nature.

Stage 2: This account of the natural state had angered the Papacy. Celebration of poverty implicitly undermined the authority of church, particularly their hold on the material possessions. It also meant that if it was possible for some men to live in an innocent way without owning property, then, it is possible for all men to do so. In 1392, under the apogee of John XXII *Quia vir reprobus*, was promulgated. In this, he met the Franciscan argument at its roots, by drawing parallels between God's *dominium* on earth and man's *dominium* on earth. John claimed that God's *dominium* over the earth was conceptually the same as man's *dominium* over his possessions. The promulgation also claimed that Adam 'in the state of innocence, before Eve was created, had by himself *dominium* over temporal things'. Thus, for John, all relationships between men and their material world were examples of *dominium* and *dominium* in this account has become natural having the consent of the divine law. This promulgation further established a more close relation between man and property, than the one, which is available in Aquinas or Franciscans. Here, it should be noted that while Aquinas conceded only use relation between man and nature, the papacy had argued for conceptual equality between man and God over *dominium* on earth. Further, both these views, i.e., the views of St. Aquinas and John XXII though were opposed to each other; they nevertheless indirectly contributed to the widening of the rights discourse. From a use relation conceded by God between man and nature to a conceptual equality between man and God is a significant development.

Stage 3: To the existing triangular between God-nature-man, another variable was added by William Ockham. That is,

Ockham brought the social realm into the discussions on rights. Ockham rejected Pope's argument that man has *dominium* over nature. He accepted the concept of nature but argued that natural man cannot have *dominium* over material things as *dominium* is a social fact, and is logically tied to human judicial institutions. By this intervention, he shifted the domain of rights from nature to society. Thus formulated, society as an important variable becomes a controversial matter within the ambit of the debate. So for Ockham, natural man cannot have *dominium*. He, however, conceded that natural man had active *iura* in them, *iura* over material world. The rights that had their genesis within the natural domain have been disconnected from their origin and have been attached to society. This intervention was significant because a new feature in the form of society was brought into the theological debate. Further, the notion of right that was accepted within the judicial discourse was the concept that was given by society through legal authority.

Stage 4: The renaissance humanist lawyers, such as Andrea Alciato, Mario Salamonio, Francois Connan and many others, had taken over the discussion from Ockham. They strongly held the view that rights are social. They rejected the very idea of a natural state, which was partly accepted by Ockham, and treated along the line of Roman law, all real human relations to be social relations.

This account of rights along with rejecting the idea of right as natural also posited a discontinuity between man and society. They looked down upon nature as a state belonging to animals. In contrast, the social state was treated to be a rational state. Hence, there was a tension between rights as natural, extended to man by God and rights as social. However, both these schools were not ready to see rights as belonging to human beings. This was not possible, for, man was seen either under the control of God or considered to be a product of society. An autonomous concept of human nature had not yet emerged. Nevertheless, it was the natural law theorists, who though keeping man within the control of God, in fact slowly contributed to man becoming more and more autonomous. The natural law theorists were ready to consider man as purely an isolated individual (this is the most important prerequisite for the development of subsequent human right theory), having control over their lives. In conceding to the view that it is the individual who has control over individual life, the natural law theorists treated individual's life for the individual as its property. In that, he has *dominium* over his own life. His life is not a product of social intercourse. This has provided the foundation for the classical rights theories of the seventeenth century. From this, let us turn to the other discussions in their theories.

Stage 5: In John's promulgation, man was almost lifted to the level of God. This resulted in undermining the importance of God. Richard Fitzralph corrected this in 1350, where he clarified the relation amongst God, man and nature. According to him, God in the beginning had full *ius* of possessing the world. God admitted man to share in his *dominium.* This move by God is governed by his grace. Man merely received God's grace and enjoyed the *dominium*. Hierarchy governs this relation where God as the giver is at the top and man as the receiver is at the bottom. Thus, the relation between man and God is not one of equality but an instance of hierarchy. In this new configuration though man loses previously gained equal status, however, earns provisions to have *dominium.*

So, from the use relationship between man and nature that is evident in Aquinas and Franciscans provisions for man having right over property had been established. It is true that the presence of God is still important. This cannot yet be considered the full rights theory because human being is still circumscribed and not independent of God.

Stage 6: It is in this context that Gerson's intervention is significant. Gerson almost made God's grace nominal. He too agreed with the idea that man derived *dominium* from God through grace. But grace is not personal, as God doesn't have his discretion to either extend his grace to some or withhold his grace from some others. Grace included all, that is, both the believers and the non-believers. It is merely ministerial because even the ungodly priests still possessed grace as God can administer the sacraments. With this the place of God regarding granting *dominium* to man has been reduced to be mere a formal and nominal one. Man is gradually ceasing to be dependent on God.

Stage 7: While Gersonian theory made it easier for man to have rights and to possess private property; this however, carried along with it an important implication which has been highly controversial. That is, man not only has the right to have property; he also has the right over his life. And having *dominium* over property meant his right to own and to sell property. If he can do this with his property, it is but natural that the same applies to his own life. That is, like property he also can sell his own life. This implication came to justify the institution of slavery. Further, restrospectively the present slaves can be seen as those who have voluntarily traded their lives to other in lieu of some returns. The renaissance humanist lawyers have particularly highlighted this implication.

Humanist lawyers rejected two points in the Gersonian rights theory: (i) In the state of nature men could use anything they needed and this provision is very close to what is available in *dominium*. For, nature didn't give us *dominium* in anything, but rather possession for the sake of use. So it is not nature that gives us rights but the society. Thus all rights are civil rights, and more importantly, they argued that, for Gersonian, and (ii) liberty was property and could therefore be exchanged in the same way under the same terms and conditions as any other property. For instance, Gersonians such as Mazzolini had argued that free men were free to enslave themselves unconditionally.

Stage 8: These two opposing views, the natural theorists and the humanist lawyers were present before Grotius, another important contributor to the rights theory. Grotius sought to synthesise both these two schools of thought. He agreed with the humanists that there was no private property in the state of nature. At the same time he rejected the natural theorists partially for making natural *dominium* identical in character to the civil *dominium*. However, for Grotius, the humanists were wrong in denying man any right what-so-ever under the natural order. He pointed out that there could indeed exist a unique kind of right, which might be termed *dominium* by similitude or analogy. Natural man can have rights but rights he enjoys are so only analogously. They defined the rights of the natural man as not strictly property rights. They, nevertheless, are not dissimilar to rights. They belong to the category of right. In saying this, he, in fact, made it possible to see continuity from the natural to the social. He argued that natural man along with having *dominium* also has additional natural right of punishment. Like the state, individuals in the natural state also have a right to punish the wrong doer. John Locke later incorporated this in his description of the state of nature. Thus the rights enjoyed by the atomic individuals in the Grotian state of nature constituted the full moral world, and the civil society becomes an extension of the natural state, since accordingly to him the state cannot possess any rights which are not possessed by the individuals in the state of nature. Thus, in Grotius account, human society has its origin in the nature. Though there is continuity between nature and society, he accepts the view that civil society is the product of deliberate design.

Grotius is also an important thinker in the rights theory because he argued that though men are naturally free to contract and bargain in all kinds of ways over all their property, he, however, maintained that civil laws intervene to prevent certain kinds of bad bargains. That is, though personal liberty was a part of man's property, Grotius distinguishes two types of belonging to individuals: those that can be alienable and those that are inalienable. Inalienable things are those which belong essentially to one man and they do not belong to any other, for instance, man's life, body, freedom, honor and alienable things are those which can be sold in the market. Nevertheless, for Grotius man cannot trade his liberty. In this, Grotius took care of the vulnerability of slavery within rights theory. This meant, taking away from natural man unconditional *dominium*, but through this he could circumvent the possibility of slavery. In his theory, society comes to be portrayed as a watch to guard against the misuse of liberty by man. This has toned down the gap between nature and society. This account of the relation between man's natural state and the role of society, thereby incorporating a realistic picture, renders an important place for man's sociability. Because of this sociable character, man in the law of nature is under an obligation to preserve social peace. This obligation fulfills the most important requirement for the establishment of a peaceful community, and protection of property. In saying this Grotius rejects both Aristotelian position which sees justice as the part of social discourse and the theological position. The latter is evident when he says:

> 'tho' the Power of God be infinite, yet we may say, that there are some Things to which this infinite Power doesn't extend, because they cannot be expressed by Propositions that contain any Sense, but manifestly imply a Contradiction. For instance then, as God himself cannot effect, that twice two should not be four; so neither can be, that what is intrinsically Evil should not be Evil. (in Tuck, 1979:76)

Thus while conceding the importance and the infinite power of God, they nevertheless made his position static, freezing as it were his movements, taking away from him all the provisions to bring about change and reorder the natural status. In his account, God eventually comes to occupy only a nominal role, formally consenting to what is already there. In a way the acknowledgment of God's power has become a mere ritual, and the process of making man more and more powerful with new assignments have lead to this new concept of man.

These remarks of Grotius had angered many theologians as he made God's position nominal, contingent and weak. And he was setting new agenda for man, shaping the autonomous human being by shielding him from God, sometimes by taking him away from God. Simultaneously, he clarified to the angry theologians by stating that he did not reject God. About this he later clarified by situating the relation between God and man on temporality that is sequential. That is, the prevailing view earlier was that both God and man simultaneously enjoyed power. Grotius turned this temporal order into sequential relation by saying that:

> God was at full Liberty not to create Man. The Moment he is determined to create Man, that is, a Nature endowed with Reason, and formed for a Society of an excellent Kind, he necessarily approves of such actions as are suitable to that Nature, and as necessary disapproves of those which are contrary to it. But there are several other things he commands or prohibits, because he thought fit to do so, and not because he could not act otherwise. (in Tuck, 1979: 76)

This places God to be a creator who knows what he has created. Once created, everything will go as preset by him. This rules out the possibility of his interference, in fact interference becomes redundant. The other feature of the work, which was completely new, was Grotius's discussion of the State. The picture of a political society or state, which Grotius presented, was of a group of individuals with a 'Community of Rights and Sovereignty'; a group who had in some way defined themselves as separate from the rest of human society by particular transfer of rights. One such transfer, which he now took to be possible, was the total alienation of all their original liberty by the members of a society of one ruler. This superior authority is necessary as this ensures peace.

In particular, men no longer have a right to defend themselves against the person of the sovereign. Thus, we have a picture where man is slowly becoming free, he comes to have rights and to safeguard these rights he creates society. This is the ground — with minimum entanglement between man and God along with the idea of society not as a creation of God but as man's creation to preserve the natural rights — which has been prepared. Though man has almost acquired freedom, and God is reduced to a mere formality all these, however, are not sufficient for the birth of an autonomous individual. Every thing is ready, still the individual is not yet born. And he cannot be born and his rights not justified unless God is removed from the vicinities. Thus, from the above account it is evident that except a few explicit moves, most of the raw material for the full rights theory, in a non-assembled form is already available. This is what is handed over to the Social Contract philosophers.

Let us note two important features that mark these developments: (i) These developments slowly made man independent of God, and at the same time, and (ii) these developments also maintained some continuities between man and God. The Social Contract philosophers while inheriting the first feature severed the link between God and man. This move was bold and radical. This they could accomplish by introducing three novel and inter-dependent ideas, namely, the state-of-nature, contract, and civil society. These three ideas have been very clearly formalised by the Contract philosophers, particularly, Hobbes, Rousseau, and Locke. It is through the idea of the-man-in-the-state-of-nature, the Contract philosophers could take man away from both God and society and situate him afresh in an imaginary state-of-nature. Through this though they could severe link with God, they nevertheless inherited other two important ideas from the medieval period, namely, the ideas of natural state/law and the idea of individual.

This is briefly the account of some stages in the history of the development of an autonomous human being to whom rights are attributed. Here let me draw your attention to the logic of these developments. This is the history where a part (individual) in the whole (within the traditional theories) has slowly but surreptitiously, grown into a whole. It, in turn made the erstwhile whole (cosmology, society) a mere part. It is also the development where individual has fought against the alleged authority of God, dislodged him, and at the same time occupied God's throne with all its paraphernalia. In doing this individual has become like God, often looking ugly in some others' garments.

In occupying this central position he has been blown out of proportion to fit into God's casket.

The individual has become the creator, creating everything, of course, including his own annihilation. This notion of individual comes to have two features: (i) Insofar as he rejected all history, tradition, anything that has not been made by him, he has become very small, and (ii) however, as he is postulated like God, he has to become all-powerful. This idea of individual had the name of the human being but the power of God. This ambiguity, this deception, captivated the Western thought where the idea of the abstract man is not distinguished from the empirical man. It continues to have love-hate relation with this concept of man, often not knowing the reason for this uneasy feeling. In fact, this idea is often in conflict with the empirical man. The relation between this enlightenment concept of man, whom I termed elsewhere as 'hypothetical concept of man' and the ordinary concept of man, is antagonistic. For example, we do come across in the ecological debates' instances, where the reality of the man-centred universe is antagonistic to man. (Raghuramaraju, 1995)

This ahistorical concept of man has been formulated in the Social Contract philosophers. The three contract philosophers Hobbes, Rousseau and Locke accepted the idea of an abstract man-in-the-state-of-nature. Though the three contract philosophers differed about the attributes of the man-in-the-state-of-nature, they did accept the notion of the individual without social ties. They associated individual with this state. It is this individual who founded the collectivity. This is at the cost of his own annihilation. Thus, this man is both the creator of collectivity and at the same time the annihilator of his individualism. The Social Contract philosophers provide us the thematic for both individual rights and social justice.

Thus, we have in this article recalled the contributions of the medieval theories to the development of rights and articulated an active relation between the medieval and the modern theories. So the concept of human being and his/her rights that we speak today and talk so much about them is the result of a tedious and logically worked out analysis of the medieval period. The richness and the significance of the concepts like individual and his rights is not possible, perhaps, without getting into the genesis of these ideas in some detail. These fundamental developments and more importantly, the very language of individual and rights belong to the medieval period. This contribution cannot be forgotten or discounted. The source of our inquiry need not confine only to the illuminated areas but also should cover the dark areas.

References

Berry, Christopher, 1986, *Human Nature*, Macmillian Education Ltd., London.

Habermas, J., 1977, "The Classical Doctrine of Politics in Relation to Social Philosophy," in *Theory and Practice*, Heinemann, London.

Kymlicka, W., 1989, *Liberalism, Community, and Culture,* Oxford University Press, Oxford.

Kymlicka, W., 1995, *Multicultural Citizenship: A Liberal Theory of Minority Rights,* Clarendon Press, Oxford.

Meldon, A. I., 1977, "Human Rights" in *Rights and Persons,* Basil and Blackwel, Oxford.

Passmore, John, 1975, "Attitudes to Nature," in R.S. Peters (ed.), *Nature and Conduct,* Macmillian Press Ltd., London.

Raghuramaraju, A., 1995, "Of Thinking Machines and the Centred Self," *AI and Society,* pp. 184-92.

Stevenson, Leslie, 1987, *Seven Theories of Human Nature,* Oxford University Press, New York.

Strauss, Leo, 1966, *The Political Philosophy of Hobbes: Its Basis and Genesis*, The University of Chicago Press, Chicago.

Tuck, Richard, 1979, *Natural Rights Theories: Their Origin and Development*, Cambridge University Press, Cambridge.

Tuck, Richard, 1985, *Hobbes*, Oxford University Press, Oxford.

6

Identity, Subject and the Ontology of Self

Ahmed Nizar

In common sense representation self is an interiority.[1] Such an interiority is inconceivable without something exterior with which it is conceptually coupled. Interiority is a formal notion, i.e., a metaphor brought to life by its association with spatial features which if extended capture only formal characteristics of the described. Interiority at once invokes its polar opposite, exteriority, by virtue of which it possesses qualities like

1. This representation is meant, in this context, to suggest not only *self-as-object* ('me') but also *self-as-subject* ('I'). Even when *self-as-object* figures in such representations in a psychologically and sociologically significant sense, it orients toward locating it internally. This diverges from James' view (1950) which tends to explain away the 'I' in favour of an 'empirical self','me'; the 'I' is merely 'a passing, judging thought', and methodologically less significant than 'me'. The common sense representation, in fact conforms to the observations, made in developmental psychology, that evidence or strong inference of reflective awareness is presupposed by any functional concept of self (Johnson,1985: 94). However, Johnson adds, while, contrasting western concepts to other modes, that the self-as-subject, or actor, is experienced primarily in internal states and self-as-object is experienced primarily in external reciprocal social relatedness. But it is not unreasonable to extend the commonsense notion and hold that reflective awareness either is or presupposes a space within, an interiority or forms one. External reciprocal relatedness also presupposes this interiority.

containability which also imply emptiness and boundedness. This spatial metaphor forms a version of the idea of self by rendering it mysterious; mysterious because what this interiority is interior to is enshrouded in mystery. One suggested solution, an opposition of self and not-self, already presupposes self as an entity and therefore hardly explains it. The idealist position it assumes is too transparent to go unnoticed: self is given primacy over other forms of being (?) or rather made ontologically prior to other entities. Just as in the case of mind-body dualism, self and not-self dualism requires something material for the not-self to instance. Here the exteriority with which interiority (i.e., of self) is contrasted is the world, known more confusingly as outer world. This re-enacts the dualism, this time by implying an inner world. However, if the 'world' in 'inner world' is used metaphorically the concept has a materialistic overtone, otherwise it is neutral. In other words, the metaphoric force of the term derives from its use in denoting the physical world and only by extension will it signify a world devoid of whatever that is physical. Such a derived notion of inner world does not involve any ontological commitment. The question of ontological commitment is crucial. Because an indulgence in the use of concepts like inner, outer, etc., is less innocent than it looks. From what may be called just a manner of speaking it needs only a carefree further step to arrive at a real world. These concepts may be rather symptomatic and not simply a consequence of attempts to order the experience. Giving a theoretical status to such concepts might comfortably ignore this. Inner-outer and the like are divisions whose point of origin may be more symptomatic than pragmatic, and which continue to exist for reasons more pragmatic than cognitive. When symptomatic these divisions are co-eval with the identification of the human.[2]

---

2. Thus the Cartesian *res cogitans* might be symptomatic of a changing social world,which later became increasingly individualised, and in which the individual-society dualism found a categoreal status.

Defining self in terms of its difference from the *Other* only avoids a reference to the positivity of this entity but does so by relating it to other *selves*.[3] Such a definition presupposes *selves* without, however, clarifying what they are in themselves if they are to be treated as entities. To add that they are nothing in themselves is barely satisfactory if our question concerns *what they are*. This is because the question what some thing is is ontologically pregnant in the sense that in a *certain way* that thing *is*. To say that it is nothing in itself, therefore, smacks of contradiction. In another respect this definition of self can be said to be compatible with the definition of it as the interiority. For, the *Other* can also be conceived of as an interiority and different too. This, however, renders it as problematic as the definition of self as interiority. Though it is illuminating to posit Self as being situated in the differences among a variety of interiorities, the latter cannot be brought, going by this definition, to bear on the in-being of the self itself. To do this the notion of interiority should be related to that of the self in a substantive manner.

If any entity has the power of directing attention such that it can direct attention at its own boundedness, then such power, by itself, constitutes an interiority in the relevant sense in which one argues for the interiority of the self. That is, interiority is in some way connected to the boundedness of an entity when this boundedness is apprehended by the same entity. This act of apprehension creates, so to say, an amplitude of reflexivity of that entity. In fact reflexivity itself can be understood in terms of a set consisting of an entity, its power of directing attention and boundedness of that entity. In this sense, the reflexive space of an entity is the same as an interiority. But, this interiority is not of any thing other than itself. It is *sui generis*, unreal compared to the entity, but *is* like the entity in the latter's environment. To define self as an interiority, therefore, is to define it in terms of

3. This refers broadly to the structuralist or deconstructionist thesis. The differences among these views are not consequential in this context.

the boundedness of an entity, say, a body, living for that matter and with a power to direct attention; and this directedness of attention may be reflexive, i.e., when the attention is directed at the boundedness itself. The self as an interiority, therefore, *is*, with the entity, body, as its ecosystem but without being the interiority of the entity. The body or the physical is only *causa efficiens* of interiority. That is to say, an interiority, in the sense that it is a self, cannot be confused, at the level of being, with a body. Each has a distinct being, although, with a history mutually influencing. Interiority is not real in the sense in which a body is real, but remains a being so long as the interiority endures. In this sense, the interiority, now the self, is anti-real.This is the ontological status of self if one defines it as an interiority: Self exists and at the same time is not real.

This leads us to some considerations of the principles of ontology, particularly that of identity. The principle that every thing is identical with itself along with two other principles, that every thing is or it is not, there is no third (i.e., of Excluded Middle), and that some thing cannot be and not be at the same time, in the same respect (i.e., of Contradiction), provides, so to say, the determination of the being. Thus, for every thing to be, it is to be identical with itself, i.e., that thing is not itself and something else at the same time. Incidentally, a problem with this determination is that it is only external. The principles together provide an object-oriented criterion, where by object-oriented we mean, the externality of the act of referring, with respect to the being or the entity. An entity is an *ob*-ject if its being could be determined externally. As it is, the principles permit only an external determination. If an entity reveals only or primarily itself in an act of referring which is internal, then that entity is not an object. Referring internally is self-referring. Under the circumstance, we have a *sub*-ject (throwing under) not merely an *ob*-ject. Self-reference, obviously, presupposes the boundedness of an entity besides other things. Ontological principles imply the boundedness of a being in its determination. But this determination yields boundedness only of an object. This is because as shown above the act of referring that picks out an entity is external to that entity. If being bounded is a sufficient condition that something is, it does not also imply that that something is an object. Thus, although self-referring implies boundedness it is not also objectifying. If there is any determination of being here, it could be of a *sub*-ject, understood as something active, i.e., in *sub*-jecting activity. This, however, leaves many things unclear. For, there could be no *sub*-ject understood as an end product of the activity of *sub*-jecting without an interiority in the sense of a reflexive space. The act of subjecting itself constitutes this space. But this is what is minimally required of a self. Therefore, the self is to *be* in order that a *sub-ject* as an end product, *becomes. Sub-ject* is the *manner* or *genre* of self-reference, and not the *act* of self-referring itself. Here, we have a formal definition of self. Such a definition is essential for an understanding of the ontological status of self. It raises doubts about the universal application of the principles of ontology including the one that of identity. The doubt can be formulated thus: how can the principles pick out a being when it is a *duree* of reflexive acts and nothing more?

The same problem can be presented in the language of commonsense. When we identify an entity as one and the same through out an act of reference we are often carried away by an image of that entity as a spaciotemporal continuum. Our model, then, is materialistic as well as objective in the sense that sense-perception is the mode of identification. Therefore, it is quite natural for us to capture its being in an exclusive disjunction: Either this entity is or it is not. More so, when we assert that this entity cannot be and not be at the same time in the same respect. The principles together have an eliminative function also: No entity is a being if it fails to satisfy the principles, which now serve as criteria. Such failure may be due to the model we carry within us about what is an entity. If there is an entity which is not a continuum in space-time, and for which a self-cognition is prior to or at least simultaneous with a recognition or an external determination, then it doesn't fit the model. If this smacks of psycho-physical parallelism it is only accidental. For, in the latter the distinction between reality and *be-ing* is blurred. 'To be is to be real' is an ontological trap, which both rationalists and materialists use liberally. The point of dispute between them is whether the real is rational or empirical (material). On the other hand, if the very experiencing of the *be-ing* is a sufficient condition that some thing *is*, then whatever be necessary for that thing to *be* need not enter in to its ontological determination. Such a *queer* situation obtains in the case of human beings. The sense of being, here, already, by itself, is being. Even when this sense is absent the possibility of being is present. This is because the *duree* of reflexive acts, the interiority, is always a space *in posse* for experiencing the be-ing. Similarly, in this case, the figure stays, while the background shifts. This is because, a reflexive act, despite its changing content, is sufficient unto itself.

Identity as an ontological principle applies in a certain sense to self as an entity. A self in the sense discussed above is bounded. That is to say, reflexive space within an entity (and thus bounded to it) is itself bounded such that the self-referring act forming the space within is identical with itself. In the sense that there is a sameness of self-referring acts, principle of identity is applicable. But such an ontological determination does not pick out simultaneously a self and a body. A body is externally determined, and a self internally, so to say. The ontological concepts, now, therefore have to be made broader and formal. This vouchsafed, at the ontological level, we have two beings: one the self and the other the body. But this analysis will not take us anywhere, because most discussions of identity in Humanities and Social Science contexts do not use the concept of being in this sense.[4] In recent over-theoretical discussions the

4. In such discussions notions of personal identity or social identity are used from psychological or sociological points of view. While aiming to account for the experience of unity or sameness over a time, they slide into normative or descriptive models of identity. Erikson's (1956) ego-identity theory, for instance, focuses on the process of achieving ego-identity. Cases of non-achievement would then have to be equated with non-identity. A similar problem we come across in social identity model, where identity seems to be →

notion of subject assumes the central role. Identity, which often figures in such discussions alongside subjectivity, is an extrapolated idea.[5]

Since the *sub-ject* is not identical with the self the question of identity cannot be raised about it in the same sense it could be raised about the self. As pointed out elsewhere in this paper, *sub-ject* is a *genre* of self-referring and identity may be a mislaid concept with respect to it. Because, it is confusing, if not absurd, to think of the latter as identical with itself. Why should the *genre* of self-referring be the *same* in all its instances? Is it because we think the *genre* is always authored therefore should be the same always? Here again, the possibility of a *genre* remaining the same at every instance of authoring it is arbitrarily envisaged, by confusing authoring and *be-ing*. Can there be some other sense of *sub-ject* that avoids defining it in the manner above ? If there is any, it would soon appear that it presupposes a self-referring act. Unlike self, therefore, *sub-ject* must be a complex notion. Would that mean ontological questions cannot be asked about it? Obviously ontological questions will be relevant if the notion of *sub-ject* is seen as involving self as interiority in

---

→ exhausted by the description of roles and relations of a person in society. Whether at the personal level or at the social existence level this approach reduces identity to a continuity of same properties and relations. This Humean or empiricistic account of identity is a theoretical predecessor of social constructionist thesis.

5. Speaking of Benveniste's analysis of intra-linguistically constructed 'positional field' (of the subject), Shotter (1989: 139) says, "instances of the use of 'I' do not constitute a class of reference, since, like James, he claims that there is no 'object' definable as I to which these instances can refer in identical fashion." Benveniste himself remarks, "what then is the reality to which I and you refer? It is solely a 'reality of discourse. . . .' (Benveniste, 1971: 218, quoted in Shotter,1989: 140). The pre-occupation with 'object' and 'reality' we witness in these statements evidences the rigid views their authors have about identity. Without specifying the authors and contexts one might say that all varieties of social constructionism suffer from this extrapolation.

the fashion defined. *Sub-ject*, if treated as an entity, can thus be defined as an identity in difference.

Even this definition may not satisfy a certain requirement of the recent discussions on subject and identity. For, the identity in question is different from the one in focus in such discussions. The identity in the former, at most can only mean the sameness of *being* in the passage of a *sub-ject*. This, however, is not the sameness of the *sub-ject*. The former refers to a precondition for anything to be called a *sub-ject*. At the same time it is not a determination of the *sub-ject*. It imparts life to a *sub-ject* and facilitates it as a *sub-ject*. In the latter, probably, identity refers to the *becoming* of a subject, capturing mainly the configurations in time. The question of identity could be asked meaningfully only about the *being*, thus intimating an idea of *being-in-itself*. A *being-thus*, in contrast, could be conceived of, in connection with the latter, as *becoming*, i.e., as involving a duration in space and time. The present, in this sense, is only the *re*-presented and this is being-thus, and not being-in-itself. The question of Identity raised in recent discussions is about being-thus, i.e., about representations and not about *be-ing-in-itself*. This notion of identity is not strictly ontological. When strictly ontological the question of identity with respect to the subject will search for the sameness that renders representations, different and diffusing, a semblance of connectedness, only to the extent it provides the subject a ground in the being. The recent discussions on identity, on the other hand, treat the subject as an identity itself while focusing on nothing but representations. It is a well known thesis that representations are significatory and therefore vulnerable to ambiguities and contradictions, thereby allowing analysis and deconstruction to thrive. Such discussions sometimes show a tendency to treat the represented as without depth and as being fully determined. If one proceeds an analysis with this assumption, i.e., the subject is an identity, one might either end up in *discovering* the surprising truth that the subject is a mere nothing, or one would be led to imagine a mysterious depth, *sui generis*, so that identity can still be talked about. In either case the subject is determined even when in one case it is only self-determination. In both, identities are constructed though in one they are only self-affirmations. *Subject-as-an-identity* is an idea which looks for unity exactly where it would be problematic, i.e., in representations. Representations are constructions. This is because, as is well known since Saussure, anything that involves a combination of signs is constructed. Therefore, when *subject-as-an-identity* thesis looks for the same in constructions, i.e., if it also assumes *subject-as-construction*, it falls either into an essentialist or a nominalist position. It is essentialist, when the construction is seen as analysable into a set of necessary components or a certain essence. This essence remains the same in all transformations i.e., in all changes a particular construction undergoes. This is another way of saying that the construction, the subject, is identical with itself. If one argues for the identity of the subject, along these lines, therefore, one tends to show that the subject is the same through out a certain series of constructions. The subject, therefore, must be self-constructing. The assumption that the subject is a construction is nominalist, if, after an analysis, guided by the construction itself, one expects to find no necessary connection among the components of that construction. This would naturally cut a theoretical lane to the thesis that subjectivity is a historically (socially) contingent construction. In this view the subject is both without depth and fully determined externally. Incidentally, recent developments in the history of ideas and study of institutions are greatly facilitated, as well as misled, by this view.

There is a sense in which theoretical notion of subject models after self as a first person experience. It is not in this sense that the self is defined in the foregoing discussions as interiority. If we ordinarily mean by self a source of what is *re*-presented in behaviour it would refer only to a rule-system or a process which is a product, in an equal degree, as the behavior it governs. If this is so we would have no answer to Hume. The question, however, is with regard to theoretically represent the experiencing subject without falling into essentialism or nominalism. Seeing subject as self, manifest or not, is an easy way to a Humean dissolution of the problem.[6] If we resort to the earlier distinction between self and *sub-ject*, as the act and manner, respectively, of self-referring, the problem is still unresolved. For, it is intuitively clear that the words, 'I', 'me', 'my', 'myself', etc., used in first person accounts, imply much more than a mere reference to the act of self-referring. Understanding in everyday life, involves a reference to the content of such acts. For instance, 'I' implies, in inter-personal contexts, a set of descriptions intelligible to the hearer, and experiences representable by the speaker. I is not a mere speaking *sub*-ject, but a *sub-jectivity* proper with a sense of content both for the speaker and the hearer. On occasions such as requiring objectivity, of course, this reference to content is partly held in check. But ordinarily it provides ground for communication. For this reason, for most practical purposes, acknowledging an individual as a self and that individual's awareness of her-*self* greatly overlap. *Sub-jectivity* as representation or construction, thus, seems to traverse the whole of self. If self in this sense is *sub-ject*, i.e., identical with it, then it is both the same as and different from itself. It is different from itself because representations do not obey identity principle. They are perpetually being re-constructed and deconstructed both from within and from without. It is the same as what it is, since at any one instance it is one single projection i.e., *sub*-jecting, (an act). But any such single act is also identical with any other such act. For, in all such projections, i.e., *sub-jections*, the self-referring, or for that matter, *sub*-jecting survives as the same. In other words, what survives is the sameness. The sense of the sameness grounded in the *be*-ing, therefore, is never forefeited. The projections, *sub-jections* (contents) are, thus, projected, *sub*-jected (act), as the same. Though the projections are different or transformed, they do so against a sameness, i.e., of projections or *sub*-jecting (acts). Therefore, if self is subject, it is an identity in difference. Self, in this sense, is

6. Hume says, "when I turn my reflection on *myself*, I never can perceive this *self* without some one or more perceptions; nor can I ever perceive anything but the perceptions. It is the composition of these; therefore, which forms the self."(1739)

projection both as an act and as content. Verily, the self is constructed and then deconstructed, while remaining the same. Rather one might say the self construct and deconstruct itself and survives, open-ended.

For 'identity' to be used in a sense subtly different from one that often figures in the themes connected with the determination of being, a new conceptual ordering is required. Projections as contents are projected. *Projectivity* is, thus, a perennial part of *be*-ing, where *be*-ing is projecting. This very *be*-ing (by projecting) is an identity, where by identity one means a distinctive sense of *be*-ing. This sense is unifying when it is reflected so in projections (contents) which bear the needed distinctive marks. One apprehends oneself as the same, by projecting this sameness. When this project is successful, one has an identity, that too, apprehensible by others. Thus, identity can be attributed to a *be*-ing, by emphasising the *active* in that *be*-ing, but also by sensing it to *be* in a *certain manner. Be*-ing and identity discussed in this sense could, now, be seen as ontologically relevant; but 'relevant' in a highly qualified way. That is to say the implications of the determination of *be*-ing is at variance with the paradigm case of ontological determination. (Before drawing a difference between the two senses, one may stipulate a different use of the terms be-ing, identity, subject and ontology, where, while writing we use the first letter of these words in capital.) The context of determination of *be*-ing, here, is partly or wholly inter-active, in other words, social. This characteristically changes the meanings of determination and *be*-ing, thereby, also ontological inquiries. The new ordering of terms now look as follows:

Where/is inextricably linked with *you* or a name, the power that defines the contours of interaction also defines the identity of the *sub*-ject. This is when other *Be*-ings clearly enter into the determination of the *Be*-ing. Windows of the *Be*-ings are ideas or signs. Therefore, determination of *Be*-ing comes up to be ideological. This is the difference: the interlacing of the ideological and the ontological. The ontological, in the case of *Be*-ing could be partly or wholly ideological. *Sub*-jects are, beyond doubt, projections; but they could be *Subjections*, by which we mean falling under the influence of other *Be*-ings, i.e., by being subjected to the ideas or windows of other *Be*-ings. The *sub*-jection which is self-forming is, and could be the same as, *Subjection*, with 'S' in capital, which is other-forming. This ambiguity in the use of the term sub-ject or sub-jection reflects only the ontological ambiguity of the *Be*-ing, that is human. The question of power featuring in inter-*be*-ing determination, assumes complexity when the ideology or semiology forms a complex system under which every *sub*-jecting turns out to be *Subjecting*. Under such circumstances the identities can be seen as functions of *Subjection*. But the latter *subjects*, not in the absence of *sub-jecting* but despite *sub*-jecting, and through it. Hence, the intertwining of the political and the ontological. Naming or inter-*be*-ing marks already set limits to self-determintion of a *Be*-ing. But this is also the occasion for the identity of that *Be*-ing. Where identity is sensitive to the inter-*be*-ing contexts, it is not just subjected to push and pull, but is also active in this business.

References

Benveniste, 1971, *Problems in General Linguistics*, University of Miami Press, Miami.

Berger, P., 1963, *Invitation to Sociology*, Penguin Books, Harmondsworth.

Derrida, J., 1974, *Of Grammatology*, John Hopkins University Press, Baltimore.

de Saussure, F., 1959, *Course in General Linguistics*, McGraw-Hill, New York.

Descartes, R., 1911, *Philosophical Works of Descartes*, Cambridge University Press, Cambridge.

Erickson, E.H., 1956, "The Problem of Ego Identity", *Journal of the American Psychoanalytic Association*, 4, pp. 56-121.

Foucault, M., 1988, "Technologies of the Self", in Martin, L.H *et.al* (eds.) *Technologies of the Self: A Seminar with Michel Foucault,* Tavistock Publications, London.

Foucault, M., 1988, "The Political Technology of Individuals", in Martin, L.H. *et.al* (eds.), *ibid.*

Hume, David, 1739, *A Treatise of Human Nature*, ed. by L.A.Selly-Bigge, Clarendon Press, Oxford,1978.

James, W., 1950, *The Principles of Psychology*, Dover Publications, NewYork.

Johnson, F.A., 1985, "The Western Concept of Self", in Marsella, *et.al* (eds.), *Culture and Self: Asian and Western Perspectives,* Tavistock Publications, NewYork, pp. 94-7.

Kant, I., 1781, *The Critique of Pure Reason*, tr. by N.Kemp Smith, Macmillan, London,1929.

Shotter, J., 1989 ''Social Accountability and the Social Construction of 'You' '', in: Shotter and Gergen, (eds.) *Texts of Identity*, Sage, New Delhi, pp. 133-51.

Strawson, P.F., 1959, *Individuals: An Essay in Descriptive Metaphysics*, Methuen, London.

7

Emmanuel Levinas' Concept of 'Other'

A Critical Reading Through the Lens of Transcendence

Prasenjit Biswas

As opposed to unifying consciousness of cogito in Husserl and the transcendental Being in Heidegger conditioning the lived experience of the human being, Levinas proposes an ethical Subject whose consciousness is structured as responsibility for Other prior to the realisation of its own self. For Levinas, the consciousness of Other is not a self-enclosed absolute consciousness, but the only mode of existence that acquires the *freedom from possibilities of negation of being*. Further, consciousness is nothingness in all cases when it 'represents' the being and it is substantial only when it overcomes the limitations of being in the form of an unconditional response to the call of the 'Infinite'.

For Levinas, unconditional response to the call of the Infinite is not an ontological activity of the human consciousness, as the In-finite surpasses the self-consciousness and its intentionality. Hence, Infinite remains incomprehensible within finitude of human consciousness and yet, it can be brought or it can come within human consciousness in a state of wakefulness that places human consciousness within the infinity of exteriority. This exteriority makes the human being responsible to other human beings, makes him a subject un-conditioned without any prior commitment. It is in this state of remaining without any condition, the Infinite comes as immanent within human consciousness. This immanence acts as an unconditional condition for the transcendence of the self to the other and beyond. Levinas says,[1]

> The Infinite in its absolute difference withholds itself from presence in me: the Infinite does not come to meet me in a contemporaneousness like that in which neither noesis and noema meet together, nor in the way in which the interlocutors responding to one another may meet. The Infinite is not indifferent to me. It is in calling me to other men that transcendence concerns me. In this unique intrigue of transcendence, the non-absence of the Infinite is neither presence, nor re-presentation. Instead the idea of the Infinite is to be found in any responsibility for the Other.

What Levinas posits here is the *transcendence of presence* of self and being not only in the finite space of consciousness but also in the grounding of this experience of transcendence to an attentiveness and responsiveness to the call of the Other that summons the being. This call of the Other cannot be represented, thematised and expressed within the closed space of consciousness of the being, it is beyond the Ontology of the being and hence also beyond the scope of assimilation of experiences to such an Ontology. Rather, it challenges the being, it's right to be by posing the question of its mode of existence, whether it exists as a participant to what *there is*, or is it an existence stripped off the existent? Levinas opens up such Existential questions in order to develop a positive Ethics of responsibility. The article makes an attempt to first project how

---

1. 'Beyond Intentionality' in *Philosophy in France Today,* ed. by Alam Montefiere, Cambridge University Press, 1983, pp. 112-13 *inter alia, The Levinas Reader*, ed. by Sean Hand, Basil Blackwell, Oxford, 1989, cf. n. 5. Henceforth L.R.

the human subject is constituted by responsibility for the Other and then charts out the existential problem of transcendence that surpasses the imperative of such a 'responsibility for Other' by discussing that neither self-transcendence nor transcendence of Other resolves the existential paradox of acquiring self-identity. Part three of the article presents an outline of a critique of Levinas' notion of transcendence and hints at a revision of the Levinasian concept of 'Responsibility' in terms of a moral struggle for recognition in a modern social space.

I

To begin with, let us ask the question, what is this 'transcendence' and from where/whom to what ? This question is relevant in the context of weighing Levinas' claim of transcendence of the finite being revealed in human consciousness by an allusion to 'Other'. The claim can be weighed only against the limits of human consciousness that cannot conceive the Infinite and therefore Consciousness needs to be extended beyond the limits of being to respond to the call of the Infinite. The question of transcendence, therefore, bring in the question of the possibility that either the Infinite remaining beyond human consciousness remains in-conceivable forever or the Infinite becomes immanent to the limits of otherwise finite human consciousness. The latter becomes inevitable as the human Subject operating with and within the limits of consciousness has to respond to the Infinite which is the surplus or excess beyond the finite with and within the limits of consciousness. Therefore, the response to the Infinite brings down the absolute difference of the Infinite from the self to some kind of revelation of the Infinite at the level of finite human consciousness ('non-absence of the Infinite') and only this is how human consciousness can get a touch of the Infinite. This touch of the Infinite in the finite human consciousness is the concrete and live experience of transcendence that can only be presented by saying, 'Here I am' in which 'I' is just the mark of the subject without any attributable characteristics.[2] But this when 'said' by a concrete person assumes an identification between the Infinite and the finite in the form of owning the referential mark of the subject and thereby obliterates the difference between the Infinite lying beyond subjectivity and the finite subjectivity only to refer to the person who has effaced the difference.[3]

Therefore experience of transcendence comes as an offering of oneself to the beyond and through such an offering the human consciousness thematises a person as a Subject and such a Subject appears to itself as a subject only in response to the Infinite. This is how transcendence structures the Subject: it offers itself in order to attain its identity, but again the affirmation of this identity negates its own subjectivity. Transcendence saves the Subject from such negation of subjectivity situated at the level of an intentional affirmation, when the Subject attains its subjectivity at the level of its response to the Infinite. So, it is a transcendence from the level of self identity, which is represented in the affirmation of itself to carry it to the level at which the being of the subject appears as the respondent to the call of the

---

2. Levinas distinguishes his notion of 'I' from phenomenological-transcendental notion of 'I' in which self-consciousness not only affirms itself as an absolute being but also confirms itself as an 'I' in whose intentionality the world is created as noema. Contrastingly Levinas' 'I' is just the signified mark of something that responds to the infinite, in itself it is empty. The signified merely recognises that 'I' is just there beside its 'Other'. For Levinas, the signified marks the movement of experience within live human consciousness.

3. A concrete person is a singularity, which in being responsible stands out in the difference between 'self' and 'Other'. The 'self' is convicted by the 'Other' to give an answer for the 'Other' and this convicted self appears to itself in its person, this appearance effaces the difference between one's unlimited responsibility and one's singularity. It is the person in singular, to whom the difference is effaced in an appearance of itself. This is how one is thrown back upon itself and called upon to answer for everyone else.

Infinite. This being does not appear before itself, but appears before the Infinite, which is prior to the consciousness of self-identification. The response transcends the finite space of being's consciousness, while it places the being in the continuation of such responses from other beings such that the response opens up the finite space of consciousness of a being to the spaces of consciousness of other beings.[4] Such an opening up of consciousness as a response to the Infinite sets in the being both a relatedness with its counter-parts, a plurality of Others, all of whom are engaged during responses to the call of the Infinite.[5] Such a response does not merge the responses from individual beings into a totality but makes them responsible to remain ever ready to offer themselves to the call of the Infinite.[6] This responsibility of the beings founds a structure of subjectivity which makes being a Subject only as a respondent to something beyond, while this very response produces an ever ready commitment in it and this is what takes Man beyond essence to attain subjectivity in relation to others and in relation to the 'Infinite'. Levinas says,[7]

> The Infinite transcends itself in the finite, it passes the finite, in that it directs the neighbour to me without exposing itself to me. This order steals into me like thief, despite the outstretched nets of consciousness, a trauma

---

4. It is something like standing like a tomb, the debt (responsibility) remains, the way in which I is pledged to the 'Other' without an escape. It is such a proximity to the other in which the self stands with its name being effaced. *God and Philosophy* in *LR*, p. 181.

5. Simon Critchley, *Ethics of Deconstruction : Derrida and Levinas*, Blackwell, Oxford, 1992, p. 131.

6. 'Here I am' is the passivity of offering oneself to God. For Levinas Infinite neither commands nor acts and hence it is beyond the limits of consciousness. It produces only a sense of obeying and offering. *Otherwise Than Being or Beyond Essence* by E. Levinas translated A. Lingis, Martinus Nijhoff, Hague, 1981, pp. 12-13. Henceforth *OBBE*.

7. *LR*, p. 184.

> which surprises me absolutely always already passed in a past which was never present and remain un-representable.

The subject cannot but be affected in the way the being is transcended to a sense of responsibility to the beyond to understand that the non-intentional consciousness in the form of responsibility affirms an 'I' which is without any 'reflection', without any 'ego'. In Levinas' language, 'the subjectivity of subject is responsibility of being-in-question[8] and the subjectivity of this non-intentional mode of 'I' amounts to a cogitation not comprehending the cogitatum which affects it utterly. The experience of transcendence breaks off the repression of responsibility built into the un-conscious 'I' that is engendered by silencing the call of the Infinite. Instead, transcendence turns the 'I' responsible for the very persecution that it suffers in the process of affirming its Ego-self.[9] For Levinas neither philosophy nor phenomenology can reduce this non-intentional consciousness operating unknowingly as knowledge to an identity of being and knowledge[10] and 'Consequently one is forced, no doubt too quickly, to consider in philosophy all this immediate consciousness merely as a still confused representation to be duly brought to light'.[11] Further in Phenomenology, what happens is an 'inversion', the non-reflective non-intentional consciousness that precedes the subject is supposedly placed under the gaze of reflected consciousness[12] to construe a description of the duration freed of all intentions, as being intentionally structured by a play of retentions and protentions.[13] This inversion is what gives priority to an Ontology

8. *LR*, p. 101.
9. *Ibid.*, p. 85.
10. *Ibid.*, pp. 78-80.
11. *Ibid.*
12. *LP*, p. 80.
13. *Totality and Infinity* by E. Levinas, trns. A Lingis, Martinus Nijhoff, Pittsburgh, 1979, pp. 289-90. Henceforth *TI*. *LR*, pp. 45, 103.

more than the desire of the being to express itself.[14]

Phenomenologically speaking, the 'sub-jectum' of the self is conditioned by the unity of the 'being' of the 'essence', but such a conditioned self produces the appearance of an Ego, which merely constitutes the hither side of consciousness, which remains unconditioned because the affirmation of ego not only counterposes the responsibility to the Infinite but also makes it withdraw into one's self, which further negates the possibility of self identity.

The desire of the being to express itself leads to a transcendence of the finitude of the being, while the expression fences the being to the bounds of consciousness of the Subject. Therefore, it is a situation of conflict between the desire to express itself and the desire expressed in finititude that presents a gap, an aporia in human subject.[15] One does not cancel out the other, rather both follows from the experience of transcendence.[16] One can say that being is split between these two moments of its being, one the moment of the desire to express and another the moment of expression of that desire. The former is the moment of transcendence of the finite and the latter is the moment of representation of this experience in the finite.[17] Neither moments retain the 'present' of itself, it slips onto the play of consciousness in being away from itself and therefore, the moment of transcendence becomes the past and the future of the moment of representation, while the moment of representation calls back the moment of

---

14. For Levinas, Western Philosophy has been an ontology that reduced the other to the same in the comprehension of the being. The desire of the being to express itself in its relationship with exteriority, is neutralised in something thematised and objectified that represented the being by suppressing its desire.

15. *LR*, pp. 155-6.

16. 'Experience of transcendence is the experience of the Infinite', *OBBE*, p. 12.

17. *LR*, pp. 176, 178.

transcendence as a step ahead and so on and so forth. Such a suspension of both the moments makes the being neither transcendent nor that which has already become and separates these moments by a play of difference that produces an unbridgeable chasm at the heart of the being.[18] Therefore to be being is overcome by an enigmatic movement of something beyond being and *vice versa* and this presents a subjectivity open to differenciated relation that transforms it onto its complementary state of being.[19]

So far as Levinas' project of overcoming the Eleatic notion of Being is concerned, this double moment of 'transcendence' and 'representation' describes how subjectivity is structured by these two moments in the form of an inbuilt dynamism of reciprocation between complementaries/alternatives, the being oblivious of its horizon of the Infinite and the being awakened to the Infinite.[20] In both these moments the being bears a certain state of subjectivity accompanied with 'being' that remains hostage to the subjectivity which the being tries to overcome by responding to the call of the Infinite. The being hostage to the subjectivity, is the 'Other' of the being that responds to the call of the Infinite and *vice versa* because both these states are two moments of alternation set in a dynamic. One can see how one state causes the other and creates the condition that makes being responsible for the other. There is a perpetual non-coincidence within the consciousness of the being of these two states, through which the being is a Subject so far as it desires discrete representation in the consciousness.[21] Levinas denies

18. In Levinas' inimitable words,

> The responsibility for the 'Other' is the locus in which i.e., situated the null-site of subjectivity, where the privilege of the question "where?" no longer holds (*OBBE*, p. 10).

19. This is the nature of consciousness, which is explained by Levinas in terms of transcendental subjectivity. *LR*, p. 171.

20. *LR*, pp. 79, 169.

21. Non-intentional consciousness offers itself as an internal object of →

any envelopment of the representation of an identity of the Subject by the Subject laid in response to the Infinite, 'the in of the Infinite were to signify both the non and the within[22] and both are anachronistic to each other[23] and hence the human stands outside the subject'.

But the question arises whether this being responding to the Infinite can know the Other beings responding similarly to the call of the Infinite? Even though there is a relation of resemblance in so far as both the 'self' and 'Other' respond to the Infinite, to what extent such an *a priori* responsibility brings the beings into a face to face relation? Levinas' answer to such questions deepens the enigma involved in such questions. His answer is '(. . .) through the non-comprehension of the Infinite by thought, thought is posited as thought, as a posited subjectivity, that is, is posited as self-positing'.[24]

Now this act of 'self-positing' does not satisfy the desire of grasping the Infinite, the 'in' of Infinite produces a negativity of an end that consciousness holds back[25] to return to an end and therefore turns passive. This is beings move to the Infinite that makes it an endless desire for what is beyond being, the dis-

---

→ intentional knowledge and therefore intentional knowledge thematises non-intentional consciousness. Such a thematisation of non-intentional affirms a subject which gets represented in the intentional consciousness. This is how 'subject' in its non-intentional mode is appropriated in the acts of knowledge. Representation makes possible a return to the subject.

22. 'Non' means negation of finite while 'in or within' means idea of the Infinite within consciousness. *LR*, p. 174.

23. The difference between Infinite and finite is such that both do not synchronise within consciousness. The idea of the infinite overcomes the negation of subjectivity, while infinite signifies such a negation.

24. *LR*, p. 176, n. 8.

25. Infinite puts thought back in its place, *LR*, p. 176.

interested and passive Good.[26] Referring back to the question of the divided being that posits itself in 'not-being-able-to-comprehend-the-Infinite-by-thought', doesn't the 'being' recoil into an unhappy state of consciousness? Such situation introduces what Levinas called by the notion of 'there is' to describe the recoil of being into an existential void, 'a presence of absence, . . . it embraces and dominates its contradictory'.[27] But Levinas pointed out that such situations of nothingness are located within human consciousness in such a way that it merely awakens the self from within and distances it as 'an experience of the Subject'[28] and thereby separates the being as a respondent to such a situation. Consciousness acquires the character of incessance[29] to remain independent of there is,[30] the presence of absence is the very possibility of return to presence by a response to what is desired within the horizon. The 'incessance' brings back what is an ontological[31] event that signifies a moment of recovery of meaning in the experience of non-comprehension of the Infinite.

Therefore, the experience of non-comprehension of the meaning of the infinite within the consciousness of being reconstitutes the presence and being in its desire. Transcendence breaks through such desire contained in human consciousness. Even though transcendence breaks through, the desire of the being to return to itself does not alienate it from others,[32] rather it effects transcendence in making him responsible for the Other. Ontologically the absence of others in the irreplaceable response

---

26. *LR*, p. 177.
27. *Ibid.*, p. 35.
28. *Ibid.*, pp. 171-2.
29. *Ibid.*, p. 171.
30. *Ibid.*, p. 35.
31. *Ibid.*, pp. 164-73.
32. The difference that transcendence produces is beyond the difference between self and 'Other'.

of the being to the infinite brings in the absolute law[33] of the 'Other' within the being, to which it responds anonymously. The anonymity of the being in consciousness is overcome in the moment of immanence of a consciousness that ground the transcendental response to being's other. The moment of return of being-to-himself is a moment of immanence that turns being responsible to its own other, which originates in the desire of transcendence. So, desire of transcendence strangely situates being as responsible for the other, even though the act of transcendence remains grounded within the finititude of being. In Levinas' language,[34]

> For dis-interestedness to be possible in the desire for the Infinite (. . .) it is necessary that the desirable (. . .) remain separated in the desire (. . .). This can only be if the desirable orders me to what is the non-desirable, the undesirable *par excellence* the other. The reference to the other is an awakening, an awakening to proximity, and this is responsibility for neighbour, to the point of substituting for him.

II

If transcendence leads the human beings into subjection by the non-desirable 'Other', how does Levinas affirm 'Transcendence is ethics'? Doesn't this conceive ethics to be an exterior responsibility that stands in contrast to transcendence beyond being? If transcendence remains to be the responsibility of each singular being, does not it imply a transcendence from the matrix of relationship in which the being is individuated and imbricated? These are some inherent problems involved in the notion of 'transcendence' primarily because the sovereignty or the will of the being always remains an inequality with the consciousness

---

33. Drucilla Cornell, *The Philosophy of the Limit,* Routledge, London, 1992, p. 54.

34. *LR*, p. 178.

that marks the experience of transcendence.[35] The problem can be posed pointedly, even though self-transcendence is possible, how is the relationship with other beings made possible through the act of self-transcendence?

Some possible answers of this question can be drawn from various levels of Levinas' approach to the notions of being. For Levinas, being arises not as an entity, but as a mode of existence that appears within consciousness as *there is,* which is paradoxical as 'a presence of absence, the *there is* beyond contradiction; it embraces and dominates its contradictory'.[36]

This characterisation of being as 'presence of absence' characterises the existential dimension of being, the abstract field of events such as negation, annihilation and nothingness with its alternate/contrary events like affirmation, creation and subsistence.[37] This existential dimension of being arises out of its encounter with various modes of existence: being not only exists for itself but also exists as *there is* amidst others. This can be observed in the pain, enjoyment and suffering of the being, all of which arise out of an exterior relationship with others that ensue all these various states of being from the response for the other. Such an all encompassing notion of *there is* keeps being grounded in a set of relationship to which the response of the being is expressed in both positive and negative states of mind. Levinas states[38]:

> The mind is a multiplicity of individuals. It is in me and not in another, in me and not in an individuation of the concept Ego — that communication opens.

Levinas' notion of 'me' is a mark of identification of the self by the Ego that substitutes itself for everybody else and this

---

35. *LR,* p. 97.
36. *Ibid.*, p. 35.
37. *Ibid.*, p. 35.
38. *Ibid.*, p. 115.

substitution is freedom prior to all act, commitment and relationship with others. In other words, existence in absolute freedom prior to all commitments is the capacity to substitute oneself for the other. This capacity of substitution remains as the source of being. This freedom assigns being with the character which is 'not itself', but 'for all'. Levinas describes it as[39]:

> It is the setting up of a being that is not for itself, but is for all, is both being and disinterestedness. The for itself signifies self-consciousness; the for all, responsibility for the others, support of the universe.

One can characterise the freedom prior to all commitment as 'responsibility' in which an individual being rises up resolutely to place itself in every situation for bearing any responsibility, even by putting itself in the place of others and the possibility of being turns it inside out, opens it to the other. Levinas characterises it as[40]:

> It is a being divesting itself, emptying itself of its being turning itself inside out, and if it can be put thus, the fact of 'Otherwise than being'.

This fact of 'otherwise than being' is situated by Levinas within the very consciousness of the being as a non-intentional state in which the being 'dare not speak its name, being that dare not be',[41] which has 'no name, no situation, no status'.[42]

This is the state of being in which it remains 'hostage' to the haunting sense of persecution and accusation to which it gives an answer in the form of substituting itself for Others, by accepting a responsibility prior to any commitment for the other.

---

39. *LR*, p. 106.
40. *Ibid.*, p.106.
41. *Ibid.*, p. 81.
42. *Ibid.*

The sense of being accused and persecuted by the other interrogates being's right to be and such a being-in-question experiences the 'face' of the other. Levinas employs negative metaphors to describe this experience of the 'face' of the other which shows up as a naked and defenceless face vulnerable to violence. Levinas gives here a phenomenological description of beginning of consciousness of the Subject, which appears as fixing oneself to a place under the Sun, an extreme exposure of the subject to itself that does not know the reason, a massive consciousness prior to consciousness, a state of passivity in which the subject experiences a solicitude. In this state of passivity and solitude, the subject experiences the fear of being alienated from others and therefore sees itself as the other of itself in its self-enclosed intentionality such that the non-intentional consciousness of 'Other' is already subjected to a perplexing sense of Otherness haunting the being. This experience of otherness within the 'self' recalls the repressed responsibility for the other buried in the unconscious, as if the current state of passivity makes the self invisible to both the self and the other, while the other remains visible to the self in its complete defencelessness.

This situation in the existential dimension is akin to remaining 'hostage' to an absolute other that does not even grant an identity, a state of anonymity of the being facing the 'Other' as the hostage of the 'Other'. Levinas says:[43]

> This subjectivity it denudes under the ego in a passivity of persecution, repression and expulsion outside the essence, into oneself. In this self, outside of essence, one is in a death-like passivity!

In this death-like passivity, the subject not only sees itself as an 'Other', but also realises the passivity of usurping someone else's place, the place of the 'Other'. This is a non-intentional state of consciousness of the 'Self', in which the 'Self' is suspended to the pure duration of responsibility.

43. *LR*, p. 113.

It is in this pure duration of responsibility, the 'Other' remains in non-intentional mode because it is not an object known to the self but the subject of consciousness of being that identify itself with the other in such a way that whatever way the other appears before the being, the being attains that consciousness of other in an experience of encounter.

On the intentional side of consciousness, self sees itself as an other. The self assumes the position of the other to see itself as an other. This 'double intentionality' in identifying itself first with the other in the non-intentional mode and then recovering itself as an intentional 'other' of that 'other' is what makes 'self' responsible before freedom. At first self becomes 'other', the being-for-death through suffering within the finitude of 'freedom' and then it ceases the state of being-in the-sight-of-that-being, the 'other'. Later, the substitution of the 'self' for the 'other' takes place and the being at that state responds to the 'other'. The responsibility that it assumes for the death of the 'Other' at the level of identifying itself as an other turns into a commitment to the other by substituting itself for the other. Commitment to the other is 'positive' in character as the 'self' perceives the face of the other in a face-to-face relationship in 'proximity'.[44] It is positive in terms of the privilege of choosing oneself as a 'me' in relation to the other. But the responsibility prior to the commitment to the 'other' arising in the state of identifying oneself as the other involves a sense of being persecuted and accused as the other is by the 'self'. It is an absolute attention and solitude as well as a 'witness to the inordinateness that commands',[45] it clears the place for subjectivity positing itself in abnegations, in sacrifice[46] and therefore a negativity, 'a persecution that paralyses without annulling responsibility'.[47] Levinas describes this 'negativity' in

44. 'Proximity is fraternity before essence and before death', *OBBE*, p. 139.

45. *OBBE*, p. 138.

46. *LR*, p. 114.

47. *Ibid.*, p. 125, n-29.

various ways: an anarchic liberation from the ego in the 'sensibility'[48] of 'remorse',[49] 'the subject posited as deposed in me', 'I universalise myself'.[50] This mode of assumption of selfhood is 'forced to dispossess itself to the point of losing itself'[51] and such a selfhood is 'traumatic' because it is a passivity of being persecuted. The self can undergo such a trauma of its origination only if there is an inversion of the persecuted in answering to the persecutor, an inversion from 'self' to the 'other'. 'Self' is the persecutor here, while the persecuted is the 'other'. The moment self sees this it assumes the responsibility for the death of the 'other'. Self assumes this responsibility **without fail**, because without this sense of being the persecutor, self is not situated in occupying someone else's place. The answer of the 'self' to the persecuted would be to posit itself as 'persecuted'. This movement from the position of the 'persecutor' to the 'persecuted' happens in a strange sense of responsibility. Levinas argues out that this sense of responsibility is prior to being, rather it is what makes being possible. In other words, the actuality of being is a demonstration of this responsibility which makes being an other, not being otherwise, but otherwise than being, something beyond being. Further, what Levinas posits here has a great bearing on human life and that is the fundamental sense of responsibility for other that gives meaning to every human action. The way a particular act is presented in one's consciousness has to 'face' its consequences that can be understood only in terms of what it does to some other. A mere knowledge of such consequence is not enough to human being; what is needed more is that the human being experiences the consequences of his action by being at the position of someone else who suffers it and this extension to the other makes possible an Ethics of responsibility. Ethics is to place oneself at the position

48. *LR*, p. 114.

49. *Ibid.*

50. *Ibid.*, p. 115.

51. Loss of self is a running theme in Levinas, but the point is that he shows how the self looses itself. *Ibid.*, p. 115.

of the 'other' to realise the consequences of one's action on oneself.

Therefore, Ethics calls for a transcendence from 'Self' to 'Other'. All this happens because of Man's inseparable engagement with responsibility for Other that flows out of the very nature of subjectivity. The structure of subjectivity is such that without an exterior 'Other' it merely represents itself which is not a Subject, a non-being; and in its engagement with the 'Other' it gets empowered to assume a sense of relationship with the 'Other'. This inseparable relationship is what makes subjectivity to assume selfhood 'beyond being'.

Further, what Levinas aims at here is to describe how the labour of the being involves an inseparable relationship with 'Other' that gives deliverance to a persecuted 'self'. The 'selfhood beyond being' is the 'self' that simultaneously bears the brunt of being 'persecuted' (as it occupies the position of other) and relieves itself from bearing the sense of being a persecutor of the other. But then persecution of the self remains a never ending phenomenon for the deliverance of the persecutor 'self'.

Levinas considers this question of attaining deliverance of the persecuted 'self' in the mode of an ethical relationship with the 'Other'. In Levinas's inimitable language:[52]

> A responsibility stemming from a time before my freedom (. . .) before any present. A fraternity existing in extreme separation (. . .).
>
> It is this responsibility of a hostage which can be carried out to the point of being substituted for the other person and demands an infinite subjection of subjectivity. Unless this anarchic responsibility, which summons me from nowhere into a present time is perhaps the measure, or the system of immemorial freedom that is even prior than being, or decisions, or deeds.

52. *LR*, p. 84.

This Levinasian approach to the notion of being as a subject who substitutes itself for the other sharpens the focus of transcendence.

If one takes the very notion of the self as a subject as obsession in passivity for the other, the question comes back, how does an approach towards the other signifies a transcendence from the self? In other words, does the possibility of transcendence from the self also imply a transcendence from the other ?

Levinas's answer to the question can be possibly approached from 'two' notions like 'transference' and 'transcendence'. Levinas' notion of 'transference' is one in which the active sense of undergoing or passion does not occur in the consciousness of the being but lies in the exterior. So the anguish of the being produces an exterior in the form of bearing it against an other and there is a transference of this anguish to the other in the form of seeing it as an anguish for the other.

This anguish can be born by the 'for-the-other' on the condition that 'form-the-other' is already 'for-the-other'. This 'transfer' marks how the subjectivity is constituted by an effacement of the 'anguish' of the self. Therefore, Levinas says,[53]

> One approaches the other perhaps in contingency, but henceforth one is not free to move away from him.
>
> (. . .) This condition or unconditionality of being a hostage will then at least be an essential modality of freedom (. . .)'.

It means that the self in responding to the call of the Infinite responds to its other, as the other also inevitably responds to the call of the Infinite. Both the self and the other attain subjectivity in responding to the call of the Infinite and only in transference of the response as an other, the self presents itself to itself as well as to the other. Hence the 'self' is not a 'seer', before it can 'see' it becomes 'visible' by way of responding to

53. *LR*, pp. 117:54.

the call of the Infinite. It hears the resonance of the voice commanding from beyond.[54] Levinas introduces here the notion of 'God' as absolute 'Other', other than the other. This gives 'God' an alterity prior to the alterity of the other and such a continual transference to the other is what Levinas called, 'transcendence to the point of absence'.[55] Does it mean that transcendence of the self also leads to the transcendence of the other?

If it is so, then within the limits of human relationship, being returns to itself as an other of the 'other'. 'Being' can never come back to itself, it can only return to itself as a hostage to an inalienable Other. Such a play of being in consciousness unburdens itself from the mark of an identity to emerge into an alterity. In•his words:[56]

> The subject as a hostage has been neither the experience nor the proof of the Infinite, but a witness borne of the Infinite, a modality of this glory, a testimony that no disclosure has preceded.

But this Subject witness to the Infinite has its significance only in responding to the summons coming from the face of a neighbour and such a response is always an excess or surplus over the self. In the act of substitution of the self for the other, the self gives itself in a 'hyperbolic passivity' only to recover itself with a surplus, the responsibility for the other.

In this the subject expresses itself by giving over an extra for the other and such a subject appears before the 'Other' and the 'God' through its response, 'here I am !'

Therefore, one can say that responsibility-for-the-other is a way of transcendence of the self and of the other to 'God' and 'Infinite'. This plot of Infinite advances through a process of 'transference' in an endless responsibility by a sign that gives

54. *LR*, pp. 184-5.

55. *Ibid.*, p. 179.

56. *Ibid.*, p. 182.

signals to express the experience of transcendence that goes beyond the being and turns onto language as a 'Voice' that echoes its own sound to be listened to by the being responsible for the other.

III

Thus, Levinasian notion of 'transcendence' assumes an emptiness of the 'ego' in a non-intentional realisation of its otherness, an otherness that alienates being from itself. In Levinasian schemes of things, the non-intentional realisation of responsibility-for-the-other is the transcendence that reveals 'God' to 'Man'. This sounds to be a recuperation of the subject from the already imbricated obligation and commitment to certain beliefs and acts under Modernity[57] to an utopic 'Other' who appears prior to the attainment of the attributes of the Subject. This particular approach of Levinas assumes too much of an autonomy in the Subject to see itself in the position of the other, who is either persecuted or is going to persecute its own other. The subject with an unlimited autonomy assumes to give answer to its persecutor by assuming responsibility for all, by substituting itself singularly for all. Construction of such an euphoric subject in Levinas already proclaims a transcendence from narrowed down constraints of human relationship and ascend to the level of Infinite.

This kind of a subject transfigures the stakes involved in actual moral life and begs the question of remaining responsible to an Other without grounding the other as an existent, but taking it as an alterity for the mode of existence which is responsibility-for-the-other. The other figures in the discourse of responsibility as the unconditioned other to which the self is responsible, but if it is truly an other which is transcendent and which escapes the 'self', how can one presume a responsibility-for-other? The normative assumption of a community with definite moral codes does not allow an unlimited responsibility-

57. *Critique of Power: Reflective Stages in a Critical Social Theory* by Axel Honneth, tr. by Kenneth Baynes, MIT, Cambridge, Mass.,1992.

for-other, except in terms of reciprocation. But the Levinasian 'Other' is a sublime entity beyond reciprocation and prior to all commitment.

Question arises how the self located within a community can return to such a pre-ontological state of transcendence?

The other given in a community does not transfigure as an absolute alterity to the subject in a discourse prevalent within the community. The situation in Modernity does not allow to substitute the 'self' for the 'Other' rather it creates an inalienable double of the 'self' to which the self remains committed to the extent that both of them are 'subjects' to a commonly shared normative order. Does Levinas allow this kind of constraints put on subjects in his notion of transcendence, does he give this notion such a latitude that it images a transcendence of the self at the cost of its limits under Modernity? Perhaps Levinas does not see Modernity as a process of otherisation of the subject to which the subject is compelled to owe allegiance in order to ground itself as a concrete person. Subject as an 'other' is situated as a 'self' under Modernity in which the 'self' cannot become the 'other', rather the 'other' remains responsible to the 'self' as the 'self' seeks solace in the 'Other'. The result is an alienation of the 'Self' as an 'Other' and there is no possible transcendence from such selfhood. This is evident under Modernity when the 'Self' remains as an entity within institutionalised and communitarian networks of society. It no longer assumes as autonomy beyond the defined preccincts of community. Rather it makes itself within the community in its relationship of sub-jection to the 'Other' within community, which is neither the Infinite nor the God.

Further, the process of otherisation as social individuation within modernity cannot be glossed over to arrive at an assessment of Levians' claim of transcendence.

The process of otherisation not only liquidates the otherness of the other by subjecting itself to a dominant genus, but also it produces Other at the margin, which remains alienated from the circulation of dominant symbolic/ideology.

Levinas' responsibility-for-the-other merely makes it possible that the excluded 'other' be drawn near the inside of subjectivity by emptying itself out, without a halt to the process of otherisation. The sheer helplessness of modern man to confront its 'otherness' remains to be a source of 'repression of the social',[58] which in a counter-productive manner cuts short the space of individual autonomy.

Perhaps this can act as a motivational factor in reading Levinas through his lens of transcendence that regenerates an ethical hope in an increasingly hopeless and agonising modernity stricken with the fear of being 'Otherised'. Levinasian revolt against a hypostatised self by its opening to the other disengages the other as an 'other' laid in the process of otherisation without any force to draw it together in a discourse of responsibility. In such a situation where most remain irresponsive to the other, Levinas' attempts to redefine 'self' and 'other' cannot ground the other as the other remains as an other even if the self responds to its maximum. The inevitable exteriority of the process of otherisation keeps on alienating the self and generates a fierce struggle of survival between the 'self' and the 'other'. As Honneth has described[59] this struggle as a moral struggle for recognition dependent upon the mode in which subjects recognise someone. This mode of recognition shapes human relationship between 'self' and 'other'. Levinas' notion of 'other' can be re-worked upon from this notion of 'moral struggle for recognition'.[60]

---

58. *CT*, pp. 57-96.

59. Axel Honneth, *The Struggle for Recognition: The Moral Grammer of Social Conflicts*, tr. by Joel Anderson, Cambridge, Polity Press,1995.

60. In situating oneself in an ethical relationship with 'other', the 'other' has to be recognised. But this recognition is not a one-way traffic, rather it is a struggle for recognition of both the 'Self' and 'Other'. Again the recognition of the 'Self' by the 'Other' under Modernity remains as an 'Other', a distance that cannot be covered. Levinas' notion of 'Other' is re-interpreted keeping in view the conflicting nature of recognition in my forthcoming book, *The Other and the Community : Towards A Revisionary Ethics.*

Part II
EXPERIENCE

8

Life as Literature, Literature as Philosophy*

Bijoy H. Boruah

Life as Literature

WHETHER the relation between life and literature is a relation of difference or of homogeneity is a question that demands a careful discussion within the ambit of aesthetic theory. Any construal of this relation would strike as counterintuitive if it amounted to saying that life in literature is either wholly different from, or intrinsically alike, life outside literature. For either the dichotomy or the assimilation would seem to vitiate the *raison d'etre* of literature as a work of art. Perhaps the mimetic virtue of art in the scheme of human life is such that neither pure aestheticism that insulates an art-work against life outside art, nor documentary didacticism that draws out the message or content of the work by transgressing the aesthetically posited boundary, truly determines the connection between art-life and real-life.

It is true that actual life constitutes the inexhaustible repertoire for the mimetic construction of life in literary fiction.

---

* An earlier version of this article was read in a symposium on "Literature, Philosophy, and the Character of Society", held in the Department of Humanities and Social Sciences, Indian Institute of Technology, Kanpur, in appreciation of Professor S. A. Shaida, on the eve of his retirement. That, unrevised, version was published in *Dialogue: North East Indian Forum for English Studies*, Vol. 1, 1996, pp.1-9.

But mimetic construction being what it is, the writer has the legitimate freedom to improvise life by dint of her sensitive understanding of what actually happens in life. This freedom — for which creativity is another name — is expressible because of the imagination of the writer. The imagination is the creative vehicle through which the authorial freedom finds its accomplishment. The *telos* of freedom is attained in the unitary life magically born within the narrative space-time of the work.

But what is the *telos* of literary or artistic freedom? And how is the life born in the world of fictional narrative comparable to the life we live in the actual, existential space-time? These two questions are of major importance to literary aesthetic. On the latter question, the remarks of Henry James appear to be both perceptive and persuasive. In *The Art of Fiction* James writes:

> As people feel life, so they will feel the art that is most closely related to it. This closeness of relation is what we should never forget in talking of the effort of the novel. Many people speak of it as factitious, artificial form, a product of ingenuity, the business of which is to alter and arrange the things that surround us, to translate them into conventional, traditional moulds. This, however, is a view of the matter which carries us but a very short way, condemns the art to an eternal repetition of a few familiar *clichés,* cuts short its development, and leads us straight up to a dead wall. (1987: 199-200)

The literary artist, for the sake of the *telos* and the execution of her work, draws upon the scattered mosaic of actual life with an attitude of selective arrangement. But this does not mean that the literary product of selective arrangement depicts a fictive life which is a rearranged kind of life, if rearrangement means artificiality.

James adds:

> In proportion as what [fiction] offers us we see life *without* rearrangement do we feel that we are touching the truth; in proportion as we see it *with* rearrangement do we feel that we are being put off with a substitute, a compromise and convention. . . . Art is essentially selection, but it is a selection whose main care is to be typical, to be inclusive. (*Emphasis original*) (1987: 200)

By 'inclusive' James does not mean that the artist must include each and every detail or aspect of life, but encapsulate those features of life that characterize the *universality* and *depth* of human experience. And it is this concern to be inclusive, or to project the universal with depth, that constitutes the *telos* of artistic freedom alluded to earlier.

Take for an example Shakespeare's *Macbeth*. The life of Macbeth is so portrayed as to facilitate us, readers or spectators, to participate with him in his horrendous journey into evil. We are able to share the doubts, fears, desires, ambitions and the sense of guilt that are expressed by the man caught up in an intense turn of events. *Macbeth* is not just a drama narrating the true horrors of murder. It is the living embodiment of certain human possibilities, and it acquaints us with a particular set of circumstances through which we experience horror *for ourselves*. We are brought to face the uncomfortable truth of which we are dimly aware. Indeed, our ability so spontaneously to get inside the mind of Macbeth seems to be a grim indication of the fact that our gaining knowledge of evil through the fictional character is partly a kind of self-knowledge. Macbeth's being revealed to us is, to some extent at least, us being revealed to ourselves. *Macbeth* is, in James's sense, a paradigm case of being "inclusive" of the universal, or the typical, in us.

It may, however, be less obvious how certain literary fictions of a quite different genre than that of Shakespeare's dramas, such as *Alice in the Wonderland* or *Gulliver's Travel* or even *One Hundred Years of Solitude*, can be illustrative of "life *without* rearrangement", and how such a work "is a selection whose main care is to be typical, to be inclusive". For there is a great deal of fantasy in these works, where the fantasy selects and arranges a seemingly very unfamiliar "form of life", to use a phrase of Wittgenstein's. Nevertheless, the point of portraying a fabulous "form of life" is still to transfigure something universal about human experience, whether it is through Alice's adventurous inquisitiveness, or through the *ex nihilo* beginning of the village Macondo that eventually disappears in total extinction. The absurdity or unnaturalism of the life and world portrayed in such works is a literary device deployed to attain the or condition of inclusiveness just because what it is meant to be inclusive of requires the unusual mode of presentation. The same thing can be said of Kafka's *Metamorphosis*, Gunter Grass's *The Tin Drum*, and even the nonsense poems *Abol Tabol* of Sukumar Ray.

It can now be said that life in art-world is, in some sense, continuous with life in real world in so far as there is a universality of human experience that is transfigured in art-life. Yet it must also be said that the selective arrangement that necessarily characterises the controlling imagination of the artist lends an order and meaning to the life-world of the work which is absent from actual life. And we readers and spectators are able to find that meaning in the work because of the way our attention to it is organised and directed. To be able to acquire this special mode of attending to literary art is the first step to being able to view life *as* literature — that is, life as a *possibility* for literary representation.

Literature as Philosophy

What precisely is it about life, or the human condition, which makes itself the subject-matter of literature? What general feature of human experience lends itself to its mimetic transfiguration in novels, drama or poetry? It would only be a partial answer to this question to say that the events of life demand literary narration because life is a story, or consists of stories, and that these stories deserve narrative articulation so as to crystallize the meanings these stories have for ourselves. This of course is true, but a more fundamental point about ourselves as subjects of experience and agents of actions remains to be brought to light.

This fundamental point is philosophical. For it concerns the primary question of being a human individual defined by experience and agency, let alone by personal identity. The primacy of this question consists in the fact that being a human organism implies, minimally, that *there is something which it is like*, for the organism, to *be* such a being. This is true both for the feature of experience and for that of agency. To be in an experiential state means there is something that it is like, for the experiencer, to be in that state – whether the state is of perception or of bodily sensation. And likewise, but in a more general way, to be an agent performing an act, whether physical or mental, means there is something that it is like, for the agent, to do what she does. So we ask, quite naturally and pertinently, what it is like for you to be in pain or pleasure, in happiness or anger, or in a perceptual state like seeing red or hearing a sound. We also ask what it is like for you to write a paper for a symposium, or to clean the toilet that has been messed up by somebody else.

It is because a human being undergoes experiences and acts in the world, where the experiences and actions bear a certain kind of meaning that confers special significance to her existence, that we can meaningfully entertain the general proposition that *there is something which it is like to live a life* – something it is like *for* the person who lives the life. This proposition expresses what we mean by human subjectivity, and it is human subjectivity, understood in the sense elaborated above, that constitutes the subject-matter of literature in particular and art in general.

Literature is a relentless effort to delineate a human world which would acquaint us with what it is like to be a human being or to live a human life. But the delineation is guided by selective arrangement because its *telos* is that of articulating the otherwise unrealised, unfathomed meanings and values which remain there in the depth of human experience. The literary artist is therefore the best depth-psychologist. And it is no wonder that Nietzsche refers to Dostoyevsky as the only psychologist from whom he has anything to learn about the psychology of the criminal, the slave mentality, and the nature of resentment. (See Wellek 1962: 3)

Literary fictions are an exploration of the human psyche, the soul, in the sense in which a sculpture or a drawing may be a study of the human form, the human body in its visible aspect. Dostoyevsky's *Crime and Punishment*, for instance, is a study of good and evil. It is an exploration of the evil that enters into the soul of a man who consents to kill another man, and of the way he finds his way back to the good through the acceptance of punishment. It depicts the contours of motivational complexity, the various incidents and judgements about them that led the motives for the murder up to the committing of it, the different aspects under which the protagonist sees the murder and hence the different sides of his personality that come into play in planning and executing it. In short, the novel shows us what it is like to be persecuted by bad conscience and led by passivity, followed by excessive guilt, to feel weighed down by debt and give in to passive destructiveness, and finally, through a feeling of inner destitution and desperation, to be driven to a violent act.

It would be wrong to take Dostoyevsky as treating the question of Raskolnikov's motive for the murder as a task of furnishing an explanation of that motive. For an art-work is never meant to be an explanatory enterprise. All that Dostoyevsky does as a literary artist is to exhibit the protagonist's complex psychology as a problem, turning the character round and round before our gaze so that we may see every side of it, and then in the end leaving it to us to come to grasp what it is like to live a life enfettered in the web of such a motive.

Human subjectivity is not just what we actually experience and attach meaning to. That may be merely the surface, and there is much more to it beneath the surface. In other words, subjectivity is more than what figures in the phenomenology of ordinary day to day existence. There are various possibilities of experience, nuances of meaning and intimations of timeless values in the texture of life which would remain forever unappreciated but for the depth-psychological vision of the literary artist.

It is in order to enable us to recognise our life-world as non-contingently conditioned by these possibilities, meanings and intimations of timeless values that certain literary works deliberately depict unfamiliar, exaggerated and absorbingly unnatural and even absurd life-worlds. For example, the ability to deny even the deterministic laws of nature as a mode of asserting human freedom — a denial that would apparently be most irrational outside the context of art — gains legitimacy in the life-world of Dostoyevsky's *Notes From the Underground*. For the consciousness of freedom has a phenomenological depth which warrants its expression in a manner as radical as the staunch refusal to subdue oneself to the reign of the laws of nature.

When the reality of human experience is visualised through the lens of literature, what is then perceived is not to be conceptualised as matter-of-fact realism. For the mundane reality transfigured in literature may be recast in the juxtaposition of events with most unusual features, including chimerical scenarios, as found in Marquez's *One Hundred Years of Solitude*. (1970: 422) And the point of recasting and transmogrifying reality is to engender a dramatic effect upon our mode of attention, so that the growing inertia in our sense of day-to-day real life is shaken up, and we are thereby taken in by a sense of heightened awareness of the kaleidoscopic array of happenings. We find ourselves engrossed in the midst of a sequence of events unfolding magically, as if in a dream, even though we are awake and moving about in this actual world. Hence it is not matter-of-fact realism about life, but "magic realism" that becomes the pertinent characterisation of Marquez's mimesis of life.

One Hundred Years of Solitude, is a magnificent illustration of a philosophic artistry of literature. It is a unique mimetic construction of the human world in the sense that Marquez creates a microcosm in the imaginary village of Macondo, and endows it with a microhistory of mankind. The microcosmic world of Macondo with its microhistory of one hundred years is intended to be a synoptic representation, or a total picture, of human existence. The human situation is so poignantly reconstituted that the transience of human life and other things, and the apocalyptic nature of antiquity and decay, both acquire a certain vividness in a radically different, fictive temporal setting. It is a fictional narrative *per excellence,* in which the narrator's standpoint is the point of view of *all* time as *simultaneous* (or, perhaps, the view *sub specie aeternitatis*), whereby one would see the beginning of mankind and its end all at the same time. Compressing the history of mankind into a century is a metaphor for the simultaneity of all time. (See Robert L. Stevens and G. Rolland Vela 1980: 262-266)

But why this fictive experiment with time-frame and this fictive enframing of the life-world of humanity? What is its legitimising rational? I think the rational is philosophic. By this fictive experiment Marquez has enabled himself to view the human world — and to appreciate what it is like for us to live in this world — from a vantage point *outside* this world. It is a fictive making, somewhat akin to the philosophical "ways of worldmaking" (to use Nelson Goodman's famous phrase), by dint of which our lived reality is transfigured from a view point much more encompassing than any view available to the fiction-maker *within* the reality to be transfigured. Not just more encompassing, it is also a viewpoint which lends the creative imagination a deeper kind of freedom to accomplish a poignant articulation of hidden dimensions of the entire existential story of what it is like to live a human life.

We might call this a *transcendental* standpoint, something that any deep literary artist would presumably love to occupy, and assess afresh the real drama of our actual experience and agency in ways that enable us to recognise the sharpness and varying magnitudes of lived reality.

References

James, Henry, 1987, *The Critical Muse: Selected Literary Criticism,* ed. by Roger Gard, Hammondsworth, Penguin Books.

Marquez, Gabriel Garcia, 1970, *One Hundred Years of Solitude,* tr. by Gregory Rabbassa, New York, Harper and Row.

Stevens, Robert L. and G. Rolland Vela, 1980, "Jungle Gothic: Science, Myth and Reality in *One Hundred Years of Solitude", Modern Fiction Studies*, Vol. 26, No. 2.

Wellek, Rene, 1962, "Introduction", in Dostoyevsky, *Notes from the underground*, Englewood Cliffs, New Jersey, Prentice-Hall.

9

Art and Life

Aesthetic Purism Revisited

Rekha Jhanji

THIS article takes up the question of relationship between art and life. Two opposite camps have existed on this issue in the history of aesthetics. One vehemently opposing any attempt to relate art to life and the other equally assiduously supporting the claim that art is valuable primarily as a source of enrichment of life. Hereafter, I designate these as camps of purists and integrationists. While the two sides have put forward significant arguments in support of their respective positions, my difficulty with them is that their positions seem equally incomplete without one another. If we subscribe to the position of the former, we end up reducing art to an empty form; by committing ourselves, on the other hand, to the position of the latter we inevitably reduce art to didactics.

Of the two positions, the purist has been the dominant one for the larger part of this century. This might be so primarily because the principal human concern in our times has been the affirmation of freedom, whether this freedom is political or moral, or is to be exercised in different realms of human creativity. Naturally, then, the pursuit of art too has been viewed as an end in itself, and the demands made on it to perform representational or moral functions are seen as degrading, for they tarnish aesthetic concerns with extra-aesthetic considerations.

I myself started as a purist but have gradually moved much closer to the position of integrationists (Jhanji, 1980, 1981). This article is an attempt to spell out the reasons for this shift. It may be stated at the out set that the integrationist position is not monolithic. There are several shades of integrationist theories. They vary between die hard integrationism where art is subsumed under morality or religion to more softer integrationists who see an intimate relationship between art and morality or art and spirituality. While Plato amongst the classical thinkers could be cited as a die hard integrationist Bharata could be cited as a representative of a softer version of integrationist. Amongst the more modern theorists social realists like Plakhanov could be cited as appropriate representatives of the die hard view. Sartre and Tolstoy could be taken as representing the softer approach of integrating art to morality, and spirituality, respectively. Needless to say that I feel closely inclined towards the softer version of integrationism.

It should help our purpose in hand if we first spell out the purist position in some detail. I believe that Clive Bell summarises some of its basic tenets quite admirably when he writes:

> . . . to appreciate a work of art we need bring with us nothing from life, no knowledge of its ideas and affairs, no familiarity with its emotions. Art, transports us from the world of man's activity to a world of aesthetic exaltation. For a moment we are shut off from human interests: our anticipations and memories are arrested: we are lifted above the stream of life. The pure mathematician rapt in his studies knows a state of mind which I take to be similar, if not identical. He feels an emotion for his speculations which arises from no perceived relation between them and the lives of man, but springs, in-human or super-human, from the heart of an abstract science. (Bell, 1914: 25)

Bell's essay on the 'Aesthetic Hypothesis' makes particularly clear why he takes the position that he does on the relationship between art and life. This is so because he believes (a) that aesthetic enjoyment is intrinsically valuable; (b) that art appreciated for its representational value is not genuine art because it is, then, a means to an end; and (c) that aesthetic appreciation is accompanied by a pure joy untainted by any interest.

Bell is certainly not the first thinker to take such a purist view. Kant's *Critique of Judgment* contains a more systematic exposition of this position. Kant's primary objective was to establish a universal and *a priori* basis of aesthetic experience. He sought to achieve this by emphasising the uniqueness of aesthetic experience, and thereby providing for it an autonomous status. He maintained at the same time, however, that this autonomy does not have its source in caprice; rather, it is founded on those universal and a priori principles which emerge from the transcendental condition of one's humanity. By underlining the autonomy of the aesthetic, Kant wished to assert that aesthetic enjoyment must not be seen as a stepping stone to either morality or knowledge. In aesthetic experience imagination reigns supreme, and is valuable for its own sake. Even though the aesthetic object demands a subjective response from the beholder associated with the evocation and expression of her feelings, that does not make it either relative or contingent. It is both universal and necessary. The aesthetic experience is marked by a disinterested pleasure born of a pure contemplation of form. The beholder is indifferent to the existential status of the object contemplated.

Another argument in support of the purist position is formulated by Susanne Langer. She holds that our response to works of art is different from our response to life-situations because of the 'unreality' of art works. She writes:

> Herein lies the 'unreality' of art that tinges even perfectly real objects like pots, textiles and temples. Whether we deal with actual illusions or with such quasi illusions made by artistic emphasis, what is presented is, in either

> case, just what Schiller called "Schein" and a pure balance, or "Schein" among the husky substantial realities of natural world, is a strange guest. Strangeness, separateness, otherness — call it what you will — is its obvious lot. (Langer, 1953: 50)

For Langer, this otherness of art emanates from its medium, the use of which abstracts it from the world of concrete objects. The colours and lines of a painting, the gestures of dance and the volume of sculpture mark them out from the natural objects as well as objects of mundane utility. A painting is only for seeing, a musical work only for hearing. Langer calls art works "virtual objects". She writes:

> Where we know that an 'object' consists entirely in its semblance. That apart from its appearance it has no cohesion and unity — like a rainbow, or a shadow — we call it a merely virtual object, or an illusion. In this literal sense a picture is an illusion; we see a face, a flower, a vista of sea or land, etc. And know that if we stretched our hand to it we would touch a surface smeared with paint. (Langer, 1950: 49)

Let us now recapitulate the main arguments of the purist thesis. They are as follows:

1. Art is defined as the creation of a coherent form.
2. Its appreciation is valuable for its own sake and in isolation from other pursuits.
3. The pursuit of other values like goodness or truth interferes with the pursuit of aesthetic values. While appreciating art, they should therefore be bracketed out.

It is the last tenet which I have the greatest difficulty in accepting. Let us consider the implications of this position and see if they are acceptable to us.

Is art discontinuous with our experiential world of day to

day existence? The medium of art does bring a break between art works and the world around them. For they are either purely for hearing, seeing or touching. The space, time and events rendered in them are discontinuous with ordinary space and time of mundane life. That is why the purists brand art works as virtual objects. They are primarily valuable for the sensuous experience they provide to the beholder. They neither directly impel one to act, nor add to one's fund of knowledge in the ordinary sense of the term. Kant's distinction between the cognitive, conative and affective realms of human experience was a step in the direction of highlighting the *sui generis* character of the aesthetic experience.

Let us first take up the purist definition of art as the creation of a coherent form, produced presumably by the free play of imagination. But how free is really this free play? To answer this question, we need to consider the nature of imagination. Now, it is true that imagination visualises entities which are either non-existent or are absent in a particular space-time matrix. But this should not distract us from a more significant aspect of imagination, namely, that an absence too can be visualised only if we have a conception of what it would be if it were present. In other words, I wish to submit that despite its otherness from the reality of the ordinary world of our day to day experience, an image is formed in the last analysis by the combinations and permutations of our perceptual experiences. In this sense, both the creation and appreciation of art is ultimately parasitic upon lived life. The objects and events which fill our ordinary lived space and time give us insight into aesthetic objects. To take just one instance, foreshortening as a norm of pictorial representation can be appreciated only because we ordinarily see objects from a certain vantage point that marks out the gradation of their importance in our visual field. Even the rejection of this norm in visual compositions can be appreciated only with reference to our ordinary perception. Without referring to ordinary perception, we cannot grasp the import of aesthetic perception. Thus, one could say that just as ordinary perception, if imposed on aesthetic perception, may interfere with it, it is also nourished by this very perception. Aesthetic experience is sustained by life-experiences to which it constantly turns for its nourishment.

We need not judge art on the basis of its verisimilitude with nature, for that would limit the creative freedom of the artist, yet we need not deny that art is valuable because it is a part of the total human experience. Despite its origin in specific historic-cultural setting to which it addresses itself, art goes beyond its immediate context and reaches out to humanity at large. This is what Sartre meant when he talked of concrete universals in literature. Sartre writes:

> . . . if the public were identified with the concrete universal, the writer would really have to write about the human totality. Not about the abstract man of all the ages and for a timeless reader, but about the whole man of his age for his contemporaries. . . .
>
> As no aristocratic pride would any longer seek to soar above his times and bear witness to it before eternity but as his situation would be universal, he would express the hopes and anger of all men, and would thereby express himself completely, that is, not as a metaphysical creature like the medieval clerk, nor as a psychological animal like our classical writers, nor even as a social entity, but as a totality emerging into the world from the void and containing within it all those structures in the indissoluble unity of the human condition; literature would really be anthropological, in the full sense of the term. (Sartre, 1967: 116-17.)

Unlike philosophy which dabbles in concepts, art projects images which are unique and concrete, yet all these images transcend their concrete setting and deal with the universals of human condition. Art forms which are incapable of this transcendence quickly fade out of the collective memory of humanity or, at best, are remembered as passing fads.

Even when works of art are not of the representational kind, they still encapsulate lived life, encompassing the tensions, the contrasts, the harmony and the unity of life situations as they are experienced by us. The purists draw a mandatory line between art and life because they tend to regard all arts in the light of painting. They seem to discount both narrative and representational arts from their conception of art. As Clive Bell puts it:

> We are all familiar with pictures that interest us and excite our admiration, but do not move us as works of art. . . . Portraits of psychological and historical value, topographical works, pictures that tell stories and suggest situations, illustrations of all sorts, belong to this class. . . . According to my hypothesis they are not works of art. They leave untouched our aesthetic emotions because it is not their forms but the ideas or information suggested or conveyed by their forms that affect us. (Bell, 1914: 16-17)

To take this position is to reduce all works of art merely to formal structures, wherein their content is an inalienable part of their form. Even though we cannot dichotomise the form and the content, yet for analytical purpose we do distinguish between them and aesthetic communication is special because the form and content are an organic whole. An entry into this organic unity of form and content presupposes a familiarity with its cultural context, for that provides us with our first acquaintance with the art work. Since a work of art is not locked in its cultural setting, in order to savour it the spectator moves step by step to a universalised experience. Thus, a true *rasika* has to play between the unique and the universal, the immediate and the perennial. This play can be possible only if one is sensitive to different forms of life as well as the universal dimensions of the human condition. To cultivate this sensitivity the ideal beholder has to practice both identification and detachment.

To be sure, the beholder's identification with the characters in a drama is different from her identification with real persons. In real life situations we alternate between being agents, patients and onlookers. In aesthetic situations, we are constantly aware of the unreality of the events that unfold in them. We can neither be agents nor patients of these situations. We participate in them like children participate in play. It is this playfulness which must have motivated Bullough to contend that aesthetic enjoyment is possible only by putting the aesthetic object out of gear with everyday life situations. But purists like Bullough forget that even aesthetic joy is parasitical on life experiences. Does it not happen that the kind of art works that attract us in our youth do not evoke the same response in us in our old age? Often our aesthetic enjoyment is intimately related to our moral feelings. Does it not happen that when our moral sensibility is outraged our aesthetic sensibility also gets affected? If that did not happen, we would not be concerned about obscenity in works of art. Undoubtedly, the dividing line between realism and obscenity is very thin and no recipes can be given for aesthetic honesty but the problem does keep haunting us in all ages. Obscenity worries us because there is a give and take between life and art — art draws its form and content from life and in turn enriches life. Our imaginative participation in the world of art gives us a vantage point to live life. Right from the time of Bharata'a *Nāṭyaśāstra* to our present times, thinkers have held that the appreciation of art acts as a surrogate for actual life experiences.

Referring to drama Bharata says:

> (In it) Sometimes there is (reference to) duty, sometimes to games, sometimes to money, sometimes to peace, and sometimes laughter is found in it, sometimes fight, sometimes love-making and sometimes killing (of people).
>
> This teaches duty to those bent on doing their duty, love to those who are eager for its fulfilment, and it chastises those who are ill-bred or unruly, promotes self-restraint in those who are disciplined, gives courage to

> cowards, energy to heroic persons, enlightens men of poor intellect and gives wisdom to the learned.
>
> This gives diversion to kings, and firmness (of mind) to persons affected with sorrow, and (hints of acquiring) money to those who are earning it, and it brings composure to persons agitated in mind.
>
> The drama as I have devised, is a mimicry of actions and conduct of people — which is rich in various emotions, and which depicts different situations. This will relate to actions of men good, bad and indifferent and will give courage, amusement and happiness as well as council to them all.
>
> — (*Nāṭyaśāstram,* ch. 1, *śloka*s 108-12)

Aristotle sees drama as a mode of purification of the spectator by generating a catharsis of his pent up emotions. Catharsis occurs by the spectator's internalisation of the imaginary situations. Thus, with the help of the plot, characters and the spectacle of drama, the spectator lives them vicariously by making alive in her psyche an unreal situation and working out her emotions through it. Living vicariously literally means substituting for someone else, therefore it presumes an identification with the other. Usually our identification with another person is due to our emotional involvement with her over a period of a time. For instance, being anxious about a friend or a sibling may originate from the desire to protect her. We could also identify ourselves with the persons or institutions in search of a loftier self-image. Our identification with a religious or political leader may be born of a search for self-aggrandisement. Identification with fictional characters, despite certain similarities with these two kinds of involvements with the other, is quite different. For we know that the fictional personages are unreal, we establish an identification with them through the playfulness of our imagination. We wilfully enter the world of Sītā or Draupadī and shed tears for their plight. We lend our own sorrows to bring to life the sorrow of these characters. Participating in different levels of this grief in turn helps us come to terms with our own personal sorrow that lies embedded in the different layers of our unconscious. Thus, we turn a full circle: as artists we draw our sustenance from our experience of life situations, and by creating works of art we help others around us to understand life and come to terms with its manifold dimensions.

References

Aristotle, 1920, *On the Art of Poetry*, tr. by Ingram Byurater, Oxford, The Claredon Press.

Bell Clive, 1949, *Art*, London, Chatoo & Windus.

Bharata Muni, 1951, *The Nāṭyaśāstra* ascribed to Bharata Muni, English tr. by Manomohan Ghosh, Calcutta, Asiatic Society of Bengal.

Bharata Muni, *The Nāṭyaśāstram*, ed. and comm. by Babutala Sukla Sashri, Varanasi, Chaukamba Publications.

Jhanji, Rekha, 1980, *Aesthetic Meaning: Some Recent Theories*, New Delhi, Ajanta Publications.

———, 1985, *Aesthetic Communication: The Indian Perspective*, New Delhi, Munshiram Manoharlal Pvt. Ltd.

Langer S.K., 1963, *Feeling and Form*, London: Routledge and Kegan Paul.

Sartre, J.P., 1967, *What is Literature?*, tr. by Bernard Frechtma, London, Methuen and Co. Ltd.

10

On Miscommunication

A Study of Two Stories by Milan Kundera

B.N. Patnaik

THIS article is about miscommunication. It aims to explicate some of the essential aspects of the concept and analyses two stories of Milan Kundera, "The Hitchhiking Game" and "Edward and God", for the purpose of illustration. Repeated miscommunication in each story gives rise to the collapse of the relationship between the protagonists and brings pain to them, although the intensity of it is not the same for both.

Miscommunication is a concept that describes a familiar experience in everyday life. One way of stating the essential content of this notion is as follows: it can be said to take place when the participants assign dissimilar interpretations to the utterances, actions, states, etc., they encounter during an interaction. Ordinarily the interaction itself and the relationship between the participants remain unaffected if the degree of divergence between the interpretations is not very significant. Even when it is not so, it need not necessarily happen that the interaction comes to an abrupt end, although the relationship between the interactants may get affected (which may not be transparent to them at that moment), depending on the seriousness of the matter under conversation or the nature of the relationship between the them, among others. It is obviously a different matter when between the participants miscommunication occurs very frequently.

It may be worthwhile to mention here that the available literature on communication hardly deals with miscommunication directly. It does not seem to have been viewed as an interesting concept. It is seen merely as the reverse of communication, when communication is generally viewed as what takes place when the hearer decodes from an utterance the meaning that the speaker had encoded in it. From this point of view, miscommunication takes place when the hearer reads off a meaning from the utterance that is different from the one the speaker had encoded in it. This article, as is clear from the above, does not share this view. It makes no reference to encoding in explicating the notion of communication. The reason is that there is no way to be confident about what indeed is encoded.

Consider in this context, the following example from ancient Indian stylistics. When the husband tells the wife that the sun has set, the wife goes to light the kitchen fire, thinking that by saying what he has said, her husband would not have wanted her to take note of the obvious. Rather he must have tried to remind her that it was time for her to light the kitchenfire. Now from the point of view of the encoding-decoding approach to communication, is this an example of communication having taken place? Perhaps, but one can never be certain that this analysis of the event is correct.

The husband might have made just a casual observation. There is nothing to rule that out. This simple example shows that it is not possible to be sure about what is encoded. Therefore, an explication of the notion of communication must not make any use of encoding of meaning and micommunication is not the lack of communication or the converse of communication, but only an assignment of dissimilar meanings to utterances, etc. by the participants in a communicative situation.

The hearer assigns an interpretation to an utterance in a comprehensive manner; including making sense of the context of the utterance and also making reasonable speculations about the intention of the speaker under the belief that he is sincere and honest in his intentions and is not trying to mislead.

Miscommunication often takes place when the interactants have different understandings of the context, which may in part, be due to their having non-identical information about it, and when they misread each other's intentions. These are surely rather sweeping observations, but have sufficient content for the purpose of the present paper and details need not detain one here.

How does one know that miscommunication has taken place? Only when there is an explicit statement from a participant, such as, "what did you mean?", "I didn't quite get you", etc. Without such an explicit statement (or an action that clearly amounts to the same), it may not be possible for an interactant to know that there has been a miscommunication and a clarification might be in order. For a host of reasons an interactant may not give an indication that he is in need of a clarification (he may simply be shy, or may not like to give the impression that he is not quick in grasping meaning etc.), or even if he does, he may do so in a rather inexplicit manner. The other interactant absorbed as he may be in the conversation, may not even notice or even sense the problem, failing thereby to volunteer helpful clarifications.

To the stories now. The first story, "The Hitchhiking Game", is about two lovers, who distance themselves from themselves, and consequently from each other, so that they can play the game of hitchhiking. Each of them shuttles between two states of awareness: reality and created reality, and each action of the participating character during hitchhiking follows from a governing state of awareness in which he is in at that particular point in time. Communication becomes a problem because they are both not in the same governing state at any time during the game; when one is in the state of reality, the other is in the state of contrived reality. For example, when the young man "softly spoke the name with which he usually addressed her and with which he now wanted to stop the game, the girl said, "you're going a bit too fast!," chiding him for putting his arm around her shoulders and for addressing her that way (pp. 8-9).

The young man's action followed from an awareness of the state of reality but the girl viewed the same from an awareness of state of created reality, where she finds herself as a young and attractive hitchhiker and her young man as a motorist driving along the highway,who had given her a ride in his car.

The lovers were going to Low Tatras for a long-awaited two-week long vacation from the dull routine of their lives. The girl decided to play the hitchhiker and the young man joined the game, and having started the game, they could not extricate themselves from it. Both wanted the game to end, but at different times during the game. When one wanted it to end, the other did not. Therefore, the game went on till it was over owing to its own internal logic and when it did, they found themselves completely alienated from each other with no hope of a bridge and with thirteen more days of their vacation, not to look forward to, but to endure.

The girl was the hitchhiker: the initiator of the game; the man simply joined it. This corresponded to their roles in real-life hitchhiking when during a drive they would find the petrol exhausted: the man would hide, and the girl would thumb rides to a petrol station and back to the car and her man. The game of hitchhiking is constricting, as all games are, since once the game starts, a player does not have the freedom to withdraw from it at will. Besides, it is an unusual game that the players played; "unusual" because they, the real-life lovers had to pretend to themselves and to each other that they were strangers. Besides, what is the notion of an ending of a real-life hitchhiking? The destination reached, the hitchhiker leaves. But the game the young man and his girl were playing, could have no comparable notion of an ending with the girl leaving, since the players, who were lovers, were to spend the vacation together, once the game was over.

The story opens with a reference to the several earlier instances of actual hitchhiking by the girl to get petrol. The young man and the girl talked flirtatiously about it. The girl had always felt jealous imagining the possible encounters with women thumbing for a ride that her man would have had while driving alone. This apart, despite her intentions to give herself fully to him, she always had the feeling that she had not been able to do so, that she had only inadequately reached out to him, which she knew, was due to her shyness about her body, which in turn was due to her old-fashioned upbringing. She always suspected that other girls, as hitchhikers, who must have had a ride with him, didn't have this inhibition and that for this reason he must have been more at ease with them. For the girl, playing hitchhiking was a means of experiencing an escape from her own inhibitions, thereby transforming herself to one who would be more desirable to her man, and perhaps at a less conscious level, a means of finding out her young man's responses to the imagined girls' overtures to him and his own overtures to them during such encounters. So she initiated the game and he joined:

> She stopped and began to wave at it like a hitchhiker waving at a stranger's car.The sports car slowed down and stopped close to the girl. The young man leaned toward the window, rolled it down, smiled and asked "where are you headed, miss?" "Are you going to Bytritsa?" asked the girl, similing flirtatiously at him."Yes, please get in", said the young man, opening the door. The girl got in and the car took off. (p. 6)

The hitchhiking game — the entire event — is structured out of a series of sequential actions starting with the girl's waving to the approaching car for a ride and ending with sexual intercourse in a dingy room of an ordinary hotel in an unfamiliar town. Conceptualisation of an entire hitchhiking event by the young girl and her man had emerged largely from their reading of trashy literature. The man had never visited a whore house, and the girl had no experience of anyone trying to take advantage of her during her rides to the nearest petrol station with strangers, when the petrol in their car would get exhausted. The game comprised a series of actions and pieces of conversation that complement each other. Speech in the story can, in fact, be viewed as not just invitation to action, but also as action, at least in some instances, such as the following one:

> After her third vodka and soda, the girl got up and said flirtatiously, "Excuse me". The young man said, "May I ask you where you are going,miss?" "To piss, if you'll permit me," said the girl and walked off between the tables back toward the plush screen (p.17).

Uttering "piss" constitutes part of the girl's attempt to seek release from herself. The story mentions how earlier, her shyness about her body did'nt allow her to utter the word, and how during their drives together, the man's question as to why she wanted him to stop the car for a moment near a cluster of trees had always irritated her. Uttering the word was like casting off of a layer of her dress; when she did finally strip, she merely completed an act that had really started here.

Thus, she was trying to free herself from herself so that she could become a stranger, a real hitchhiker, the kind of woman who, she had always believed, her young man would have found more attractive. This was a paradoxical act in a sense: she was trying to be closer to her man by becoming a stranger. One meaning of the girl's flirtatious utterance of the word "piss" was that she was now liberated which was in consonance with her role as a hitchhiker, but the meaning that the young man assigned to it was that her present lack of modesty was indeed real and not a put-on act, and this single action of hers reduced her stature in his eye to that of those other women whom he had known and had rejected. (p.15)

Consider the following drinking ritual. It starts with the man raising his glass and saying "To you" and the girl responding, "Cann't you think of a wittier toast?" (p.15) and ending with the young man's crude toast "To your belly, into which your sould descends,"to which the girl responds "To my belly" (p.16). Subsequently they drink to her breasts. The girl's action could mean that she was trying to give her young man something that she had not been able to give him so far, namely, the pleasure that "flirtation gives to a person" (p.16). But the young man did not assign the same interpretation to her action; instead, he saw in it a kind of vulgarity that he found disgusting. He was downright rude when at one point he proposed the following toast: "To your soul which lights up when it descends from your head into your belly, and which goes out when it rises back to your head" (p.15). Totally absorbed in her role as a hitchhiker, the girl didn't see the disgust behind these words and didn't realise that her man was already confused and that he had started seeing the game as the real thing.

From the toast onwards it is all a story of physicality, of bodies. For the girl this physicality is not just part of her play acting at one level of conciousness, but of an assertion of her release from her own inhibitions about her body. Thus, on her way to the toilet when a drunken man spoke to her, she "thrust out her breasts, and fully experienced every movement of her hips, then disappeared behind the screen" (p.18). But this play acting was for the young man a real life act of seduction of a stranger, by not a hitchhiker, but his own girl. Thus what was play acting for one was nothing but abject treachery for the other, and what for one was an act of being able to give onself totally to her man was a grossly crude act for the other. The hitchhiking game ended with two bodies, two sensual bodies, alien to each other, "engaged in love making without love". The players were united physically, but the lovers were alienated mentally. As a result both knew that the game had ended, but whereas the girl was pitifully pleading for a return to the pre-game state, the young man was striving unsuccessfully to at least be compassionate to calm the girl, if nothing more.

Before turning to the next story, one is tempted to invite attention to the following:

Consider the action of the girl's thrusting out her breasts and moving her hips in response to an intoxicated customer's address, "Combien, mademoiselle?" (1992, p.18). It lends itself to at least two interpretations. One, the girl was innocently proclaiming a release, however temporary, from her inhibitions, in the intoxicated mood of a player absorbed in a game. Two, she gave a seductive response to the customer. The youngman read the second meaning. He didn't see that the girl was only playing the game. Then, the youngman's "Do you prefer them one after the other or at the same time?" in response to her saying that she didn't mind having several men in one night if they're good looking, again can be read in at least the following ways: (a) the hurt lover's anguished cry for understanding and help from his beloved, and (b) the suggestive, seductive and leading remark of the man who has given the lift to the hitchhiker. The girl assigned the (b) meaning to the question. She failed to see that her youngman was not playing the game.

Turning to the second story, "Edward and God" is the story ot Alice and Edward and of miscommunication between them resulting in failure of their relationship. Post-revolution Czechoslovakia provides the backdrop to the story of the lovers. Young Edward found a teaching job in a small town, thanks to the ugly, ageing directress-comrade, who was always after young men. Soon he fell for Alice whom he purused with "a seriousness that was almost genuine" (p. 207). Alice, a religious girl, was virtuous and regarded extramarital sex as sin. Thus in the beginning "during their evening walks he had tried to put his arm around her so that he could touch the region of her right breast from behind, and each time she had siezed his hand and pushed it away" (p. 207). Later when he suggested that they visit his brother in the country during that weekend, she rejected his suggestion outright. Although she allowed him to kiss her, it was much later that she "became reconciled to letting him stroke her breasts" (p. 212). But "at her navel, she drew a strict and uncompromising line below which lay the area of sacred prohibitions, the area of Mose's denial and of the anger of the Lord" (pp. 212-13). No argument, theological or emotional, of Edward's would succeed: when citing St. Augustine, Edward said, "Do you understand, Alice? Love God and do what it pleases you to do!", she replied, "Only what pleases you will never please me." To Edward's response that she didn't like him, she said, "I do, . . . And that's why I don't want us to do anything that we shouldn't do!". (p. 214)

As Alice persisted in denying him her body, Edward embarked on an effort to win her by going to Church with her and by conducting himself there in a manner that was conspicuously over-religious. When Alice would not kneel because that would spoil her dress, he chided her for not being adequately religious. Once as he picked up a rusty cross from the street and crossed himself, a petty school official saw him doing so and reported the matter to the directress, who, incidentally had earlier seen him once outside the church herself and had expressed her disapproval of his church going.

He was summoned to a meeting with four officials of the administration including the directress and there, not at all out of any truthfulness or seriousness, but on account of other considerations that one might ignore here, he took the stand that although he did'nt want to believe in God, he somehow did. The committee was annoyed, but at the same time noted his frankness and honesty and at the instance of the directress, directed her to "take charge of him" and re-educate him. This was to the liking of both; as for Edward, his job was secure, since he knew that the directress was after young men and in fact, after him himself, and as for the directress, it gave her an opportunity to reach the youngman.

The re-education essentially meant spending evenings at the lady's house. In the first meeting, he called her "pretty" which pleased her immensely and she encouraged him to visit him from time to time, and "just before he left she lightly stroked his hand, so that this foolish fellow went off with the sprightly feelings of a winner" (p. 225). So each had his or her own secret agenda, and each felt that he or she, in pursuing a well-defined, specific agenda, was making a fool of the other.

On the Sunday, following this first meeting, Edward saw Alice a changed person, and two days later the matter became clear to him. The news of the meeting at school had gone out in the mean time and it had become a rumour in which Edward's status had been elevated. He had emerged as a man of courage and a defender of God, who had stood up for Him during his "interrogation". Alice had heard of it all and was immensely proud of him. He was now her hero and for him she was willing to do anything. For Edward,

> . . . they were an unexpected gift. Of course, Edward knew that they were an undeserved gift, but he said to himself that if fate withheld from him deserved gifts, he had a complete right to accept these undeserved ones (p. 228).

Edward exploited the situation to his advantage and when he suggested to Alice that they spend that weekend together at his brother's cottage in the country, she agreed.

Two days after this, on that Thursday, when Edward went to see the directress, he noticed that she had got for him his favourite drink. He had to get himself drunk, so that he could respond to the sexual advances of the ageing, ugly woman. He was still dressed when she returned from the bath-room with nothing on but a transparent nightgown, and invited her reproach: "why are you still dressed?" But from now on it was he who took the upper hand that evening. From uttering an uncertain instruction — "Undress completely" — to her which she readily carried out, he graduated to issuing the firm order "Kneel!" and as she carried that out,

> "Take those hands off," he called her to order.
> "Clasp them!" Once again she looked at him uncomprehendingly.
> "Clasp them! Did you hear?" She clasped her hands.
> "Pray", he commanded.
> She had her hands clasped and she glanced at him devotedly.
> "Pray, so that God may forgive us", he hissed. (p.234).

And at the end of it when she said "Amen", he "violently lifted her off the floor and dragged her onto the couch" (p. 235). Her craving for sex had reduced her to "a naked revolutionary . . . being humiliated by prayer" under orders of a subordinate and it is not his love of God (there was none), or his hatred of her that made him humiliate her this way, it was merely a wild attempt to make his body get over its revulsions at the ugliness of the woman to whom he knew he was doomed to make love that evening.

On the appointed day Alice and Edward went to the country to spend the weekend in his brother's cottage. As Alice was quite relaxed, Edward was trying to define for himself his attitude towards the change in her. He concluded that it was derived from an illogical attitude on her part which in turn was based on a mistaken perception of what he had done:

> Why should Edward's sufferings for his fidelity to his beliefs have as a result Alice's infidelity to God's law? If Edward has not betrayed God before the fact-finding commission,why should she now betray Him before Edward? (pp. 235-6)

Edward didn't articulate such thoughts and try to draw her attention to the illogicality of her attitude exactly as he had earlier not tried to correct her on the facts about his "martyrdom", lest she denied him what he had all these days been after. But he was quiet, although in her cheerfulness Alice didn't notice it. Later in the evening when they went to bed, Alice insisted that even the shutters be closed, so that the light of the stars do not enter the room.

But for him the meaning of her offering herself to him had changed and her behaviour only gave him "a certain vindictiveness and anger" (p. 236). "It irritated him how she experienced everything without inner conflict - self-confidently and easily" (p. 236). He had been looking forward to making love to her but when he did it, it gave him no joy. The girl had happily fallen asleep, leaving Edward irritated, thoughtful and confused. She was completely at ease with herself the following morning as she moved about in the house naked, as Edward wanted her to be. It intrigued him that she didn't mind remaining naked in the light of the morning, whereas only a few hours earlier she had insisted on shutting off even the light of the stars from the room.

It is only then that she noticed that he was thoughtful and asked him about it. He said he was to see his brother after breakfast, an answer that satisfied her, so unsceptical she was about the situation. In the afternoon as they were travelling back in a compartment where they were all alone, Edward was thinking about the meaninglessness and the futility of his relation with Alice. A series of misconstructions had determined its course. He brought up the matter of their sexual act the previous night and said that he was "miserable" that they had done it and in reply to her protest that it was he, who had wanted to do it, he condemned her exclaiming," . . . a person who is able to betray God is able to betray man a hundred times more easily" (p. 241). When they reached the station he said "Good bye" to the shocked and tearful girl and left, ending their relationship. The rest of the story is of no interest to us for our present purpose, except the following: he reproached himself for having lost the girl, felt the loss for a while and then forgot about it all.

Consider Edward's relationship with the directress. The directress wanted him and created a situation which helped her to achieve her goal. She never let him know about her intentions about him but she never knew that he was aware of the same all along and that he too was manipulating to be in control of the situation with regard to her. There was this assymetry about them, although both were manipulators with respect to each other. But there was no miscommunication between them. They didn't assign different interpretations to the utterances they encountered. The directress's undressing had the same interpretation for them both, namely that she was offering herself to him. A little earlier when she had told him ". . . I am not a boring woman! That I'm not!", and he had responded saying "No", there was dishonesty in the reply, but it was not given two different interpretations by them.

To turn to Edward's relationship with Alice. It was again assymetrical in that whereas Edward manipulated things with respect to Alice so as to be able to achieve his end, Alice had trust in him and never suspected that he could be manipulating. There was miscommunication between them. When she undressed and came to his bed, this action was assigned different interpretations by them both: as far as she was concerned, she was offering herself to him, but as far as he was concerned, it was an act of betrayal on her part.

Miscommunication in both the stories is due to the interactants' understanding of the situation in which they were placed, in different ways. In the first, at a certain stage the youngman was no more playing the game whereas the girl thought both of them were. In the second, Alice thought that Edward was sincere and honest with respect to her, as she was to him, but indeed he was not. To complicate matters, Alice drew a valid and positive conclusion about Edward from the inaccurate information that she had gathered about his conduct in the so-called "interrogation", whereas he drew a valid although a negative and unfair conclusion about her from her willingness to give herself to him.

What can redeem a situation created by miscommunication is the participants' recognition of the reality of such a situation and their willingness to seek clarification. This did not happen in the stories under discussion. The girl in "The Hitchhiking Game" got increasingly absorbed in the game and failed to notice that her youngman was not playing the game and was revaluating her instead. Every action of hers, verbal and non-verbal, looked so natural to him that he was beginning to think that deep inside she was a very different person from the one he had all along presumed she was:

> If she was able to do it so well, he thought, it really meant that she really was like that. After-all, no alien soul had entered into her from some-where in space. What she was acting now was she herself; perhaps it was that part of her being which had formerly been locked up and which the pretext of the game had let out of its cage. (p.16).

The girl's problem was not that she was insensitive; she was too trustful and too secure about the youngman. On the other hand, he didn't insist on her getting out of his game frame at later stages when he hadn't really started revaluating her, because by then he had felt deeply hurt. He was hoping for her to realise his situation on her own. In the other story, Alice had absolute trust on Edward and never felt that there was reason for scepticism on her part. As for Edward, he was a clever manipulator, and as such was in no need of any clarifications from the girl.

Now to a final question in order to conclude the paper. Why is it that in the stories relationships collapse, owing, to a significant extent, to miscommunication and virtual lack of any serious attempt to redeem the situation? The protagonists seem doomed to miscommunicate in the world of Kundera's stories under discussion. It must be borne in mind that the participants in an interactive situation need not be destined to miscommunicate; there is as much possibility of their assigning the same or nearly the same meaning to utterances as there is of their not doing so. Then what explains miscommunication in the stories?

The answer may lie in Kundera's understanding of the predicament of man in the world. The following from "Edward and God" is a succint statement of the same:

> . . . a man imagines that he is playing a role in a particular play and does not suspect that in the meantime they have changed the scenery without his noticing, and he unknowingly finds himself in the middle of a rather different performance (p. 229).

Under the circumstances what sense can he make of the world where he finds himself? What meaning can he assign to actions, words and relationships with confidence? Unsure of himself, he is unclear about everything. Miscommunication is the more likely prospect. One need not ask "under what conditions does communication take place?" It's not Kundera's problem — at least in these stories.

References

Fiske, J., 1990, *Introduction to Communication Studies,* Routledge, London.

Kundera, M., 1992, *Laughable Loves*, Rupa and Co., Delhi

Mortensen, C.D., 1997, *Miscommunication*, Sage Publications, New Delhi.

Windahl, S. and Signitzer B.H. (with J.T. Olson) (1992), *Using Communication Theory,* Sage Publications, New Delhi.

11

Marxism and Aesthetics

S.S. Barlingay

I

In this article I discuss whether aesthetic problems would appear differently if Marxist philosophy is accepted. *Prima facie,* I do not think that aesthetics would appear differently if Marxism is accepted. In fact, the fundamental principles of aesthetics should not undergo any change even under Marxism. Aesthetics cannot be classified as capitalistic aesthetics and Marxist aesthetics. "Beauty", which is the main subject-matter of aesthetics, does not differ from a capitalist to a common man, nor from a worker to a peasant. Marxists may emphasise certain aesthetic problems on account of their understanding of social reality. Further, Marxists may regard what can be rationally and scientifically thought about aesthetics as Marxist aesthetics.

Here, I am neither interested in showing that aesthetics follows a certain law of dialetics; nor in showing that if one tries to deduce certain theorems of aesthetics from the law of dialectics, one is committing a great mistake. Of course, both the laws of dialectics and the theorems of aesthetics arise in the same social reality. Therefore, one is likely to be consistent with the other or at least, one would not be inconsistent with the other. Just as one cannot distinguish between capitalist science and socialist science, and just as a socialist does not reject the science formulated in the capitalist world, similarly, he need not reject everything that has been accepted as beautiful in a non-socialist society. Whenever we discuss problems concerning social reality — and I do think that the problems of aesthetics concern social reality primarily — social philosophy is always in the background, like a light-house. From this point of view, I shall be forced to discuss some concepts of dialectics, particularly because dialectics not only gives us a certain picture of social reality, but it also supplies us with methodological tools.

The Hegelian-Marxist dialectics gives us the evolutionary picture of history. If we draw a temporal graph of history in a series represented by *T*1, *T*2, . . . *T*n, then, the successive events are likely to present a more progressive state of society. For the Marxists, like Idealists, truth is determined by the particular context and so, is never false or incorrect. They do not believe in the true-false dichotomy.

It is certainly true that our world is not created by man, but it is the man who gives meaning to the world, and that it is constantly evolving. When we talk of history, we talk of this human world. We can only talk of concrete events from which abstract principles cannot be separated. The human world is primarily social. Individualism should be discarded; for Marxists, Idealism and Realism are forms of individualism alone. An individual is, of course, a part and parcel of the social reality; but social reality also comes into existence on account of his self-consciousness.

Self-consciousness, however, represents a split from consciousness. To be aware of myself is to treat myself as separate from the reality. Just as consciousness comes into existence as an evolute, so self-consciousness is also an evolute and consciousness of others is also another evolute. Splitting of this kind marks alienation and is of the form 'I am different from the remaining.' Alienation principle, which plays a big role in the social history of man, works in many different ways and at different levels. A worker in the past may for example, regard his work of art as a part and parcel of himself; but due to alienation, he might today think that it had different stages. Some Marxists distinguish between objectifying and alienation.

But even so distinguished, they would only be the same process, perhaps, represented by two points removed temporally.

Of course it is possible to conceal the more remote point representing alienation as the negation of negation, and the less remote point (i.e., objectification) as mere negation. Li Che Hou making such a distinction, says that beauty is the negation of the sense of beauty and art is the negation of negation of the sense of beauty. But theoretically the temporal process is infinite, and one can, therefore, say that there are several negations. So writers such as Plekhanov see alienation even in the impressionist and cubist movements. The impressionists in their paintings do not depict the objects, but only colour their impressions, alienating colour from form. In these movements, both representing a kind of Subjective idealism, the object is left aside and it is the subjective which is given importance to.

For the Marxists, alienation in any natural or social process is due to a dialectical logic, represented by thesis, antithesis and synthesis. The stage of synthesis represents the unity of opposites. I may be allowed to say that "unity of opposites" is the positive depiction of the "negation of negation". The negation of negation may enable us to propose the compatibility and co-existence of these different elements because, in the negation of negation, every element appears to be the contradiction of the first in any temporal process, including the social process. However, they are not contradictories; they are only different. Every successive element is different from the previous element, but both can successfully exist together. So if we take one cross-section of this process we can have a perception of several differences together, e.g., in musical *laya*. If we leave our prejudice that the differences are incompatible, in any picture of such a cross-section, one may find a variety of events based on a variety of principles, going together. I think it is this fact which proves that whether it is a capitalist state of society or a socialist one; there would be several things in common. It is this commonness which is responsible for our common aspects of beauty. Marxists such as Caudwel, Plekhanov, Fischer, Lucas,

Li Che Hou and Hung-I-Yang emphasise the common elements between capitalist or feudal aesthetics and socialist aesthetics for this reason.

For the communists, it is in the society that man attains a fuller measure of freedom than the beasts, because society is his creation. This is in a way a queer doctrine, for, we do sometimes feel that it is in the society that man's freedom is curtailed. For the Marxists, what we regard as freedom apart from the society is not freedom at all, as there can never exist a state where an individual exists but the state does not. What is regarded as freedom in the capitalist and feudalistic states is merely a licence to exploit others and such exploitation always gives a picture where there would be (i) right to exploit others and (ii) inability to erase the exploitation. The inability to erase the exploitation is evidently not freedom, and by freedom, cannot be meant the freedom of a particular section of the society. So, in a sense, freedom must be compatible with everything that makes the society.

Plekhanov describes art as a means of intellectual communication. The word "intellectual" deserves attention. Often, we equate intellectual activity with logical or mathematical activity, but perhaps one has to distinguish the two. In logical activity, there is no freedom, whereas in intelligent activity, there is choice. What Plekhanov would like to say perhaps is that the creation of an art requires such freedom. Although such freedom may also be ultimately be determined by the state of society, feelings and emotion are unimportant. The intellectual has a larger scope than the logical, and determines the world of human activity.

Since a sociology or dialectical logic is presupposed in human thinking, for the Marxists, (i) our concept of beauty is relative to man and exists only in the human world, (ii) it presupposes certain laws of society which are dialectical in nature and (iii) like language, this concept of beauty is evolved and realised in the evolution of society. Marxists do recognise the element of form as different from the elements of matter or content; but they do not think that with every change in the matter or content the form of the society also invariably changes. Let us see the implications of such thinking on the problems of aesthetics.

II

The foremost problems of aesthetics are what is beauty; where are we to find it; and how it is created. In English, the primary word is 'beauty' (*saundarya*) and the adjective 'beautiful' (*sundara*) is formed by adding the suffix, 'ful' to it. On the other hand, in Sanskrit or in other Indian languages the primary word is *sundara* and the abstract noun *saundarya* is formed out of it. This Sanskrit construction seems to be nearer to experience.

Let us see how the words 'beauty' and 'beautiful' are used. First, we use the word in the context of natural phenomena and facts, of which man is not the author. For example, we describe the sunset, the morning and the evening colours of the sky, humming of bees and the shape and colours of flowers, the sound of springs, the light of the moon, the green colour of the lawns, the waves and the tides of the sea and the sea beaches, etc., as beautiful. Secondly, in the same way we also describe the picture of Monalisa, paintings of Vermeer, the Taj Mahal, as beautiful. We also make statements such as, "The statue of Venus is beautiful", "Ellora and Ajanta caves and cave paintings are beautiful", "The poetry of Mardhekar who is a contemporary Marathi poet and critic or Eliot is beautiful", "Pandit Ravi Shankar plays beautifully on sitar." The context in the two kinds of statements is different. The first, relates to the natural environment, where man is spectator; in the second, man not only knows objects as beautiful, but he also creates them. In the first context, there appears to be a binary relation between man and the thing; In the second, there appears to be a relation more complex, involving the relation between man, man and thing. Regarding the classification used here, it may be pointed out that there are borderline cases which are difficult to be classified, for instance, the voice of Lata Mangeshkar, M.S. Subha Lashmi, or Nurjahan. It may be difficult to classify these instances strictly in the first or in the second. If voice is taken as a natural gift, then they will go in the first set, however, if voice is taken as some thing more than the natural gift accounting for the artists manipulation of voice, then it may be classified in the second.

It may be admitted that in our ordinary language, when we say that the sunset is beautiful, we regard the predicate beautiful as belonging to the sunset. In the impersonal and realistic aesthetics of Mardhekar, it is clearly accepted that if a shell is said to be beautiful, this is so whether or not man perceived it. Beauty, for Mardhekar, is a quality possessed by a thing. Marxists regard this as capitalist aesthetics, and I do not debate whether this view is because of capitalism or naive realism.

To regard beauty as a characteristic of a thing is to put it on par with length, breadth and thickness. But there appears to be a difference between the statement, 'the sun is round', and 'the sun is beautiful'. When saying 'the sun is beautiful', we mean that the sun *looks* beautiful. When saying 'the sun is round', we mean that the sun *is* round. Of course, people may say that the statement 'the sun is round' also is to be understood as 'the sun looks beautiful', and then there is no further answer. However, in our ordinary language when I say 'my radio-set is big, heavy and of brown colour', I am not saying the same kind of thing as my radio-set is beautiful. If at all the first three qualities become significant in my second judgement, it is only in the manner that my second judgement is passed on the first three qualities. That by which I pass my judgement and that on which I pass my judgement are not identical and cannot be measured by the same yardstick.

For Marxists, this valuational aspect of the relation between the creator and the object is lost sight of due to alienation. But it may be realised that even traditionally, when we evaluate a thing, we do it for somebody. If we eliminate this, it would not be possible to value or even exchange two things; even barter is based on the utility that the two things have for men. So, although we do say 'this is valuable' or 'that is beautiful', the syntax of such expressions is incomplete. It should be reasonable to ask, 'for whom?'.

It is one thing to say that man is necessary for evaluation and another to ask whether his evaluation would be private. The reply to the second question is, whatever is expressible in this way must necessarily be public. An evaluation is not a pattern of unmeaningful sound, or a kind of whistle, which can be treated as mechanical. When man reduces something to something else, there is a motive or purpose behind it. So when we attribute beauty, we have already accepted that the context is no more private than our expressions are for communicating to others.

It will be interesting here to resort to an analogy. It may be granted to the realists that things exist in the world in their own right, although they may be dependent on human beings for their being known, they are not dependent on human beings for their existence. So, in such cases, it may be possible to distinguish what is and what is known. But in other cases, such as pain, the pain in my body cannot be separated from the knowledge of my pain. It is not possible to think that there is pain in my body and I don't feel it. The pain does not exist unless I feel it. It would be desirable to distinguish three words, to be, to see, and to appear. In the act of seeing and appearing, the seer is certainly presumed. In the act of seeing, the subject is active, whereas in the act of appearing, the subject is merely a recipient. On the other hand, in order for a thing to be, it is not necessary that the seer is necessary. When an agent exists, then distinctions between 'seeing' and 'appearing' are made. In the process of 'appearing', the process part is so very feeble that gradually the difference between them vanishes. It is on this account that we say that 'something *is* beautiful,' and not 'something *looks* beautiful.' We accept that what *looks* is what *is.* We are continuously drifting from existence to appearance and are giving the appearance the status of reality, which is possible only in the human world.

Man is also aware that he is imperfect and he tries to make good this imperfection by certain illusions. At least, the Marxists hold that, in creating art, man is continuously going from reality to illusion, in the creation of which man feels elated and enjoys his own illusions. It is due to alienation that the world becomes different from us. That the world is different, objective and separate from us, generate in us a feeling that we should create our own world and be happy with it. For some Marxists, objectifying the world is the first alientation and the creation of an invented world is the second alienation. Value is not a name of anything which exists. We can create words, even substantives without there being any bearers. The formation of such substantives may distort our understanding of the things. There is 'evaluating' the activity and not indicating, identifying or describing the substantive. But in our thinking, we forget this evaluating part and use the noun 'value'. This transformation is a kind of Platonism, classified by Marxists under alienation. An action is a part of man's behaviour. As soon as we take cross-sections of actions and regard them as separate entities, it is forgotten that the actions belong to man. This is one way of alienating man from his actions. When we say that something is beautiful, we accept the matter and form of that phenomenon. Sometimes this acceptance is due to tradition and social history. Attributions of beauty has at least three constituents, matter, form and acceptance. Matter and form may be cosmocentric, but acceptance can never be, making the whole phenomenon anthropocentric.

Acceptance can also be related to the forms of things as well, and logic and mathematics come out of this relation. It is not necessary that the object of acceptance should only be some object other than the human. When man is concerned with himself, or other members of his own species, it will in fact be a mere anthropocentric world. Man, himself, however belongs to the cosmocentric world. So although, we can talk of this world as anthropocentric, such a world arises in the interaction of man and the rest of the world.

Man's acceptance may also be concerned with his reaction to the experiences of objects in the world. This reaction is not subjective, otherwise he would not have been able to talk about it to other men. That he is able to communicate his reactions to others is a sufficient ground for ascertaining that his reactions are inter-subjective or social. Suppose *A*, *B* and *C* are talking about an object *X*. They may address *X* as *P*, *Q* and *R* respectively. But equally, they may address *X* as '*X*', the latter being called 'an objective attitude'. This attitude does not only signify a relation between *A*, *B*, *C* *vis-a-vis* *X*, but also an inter-subjective relationship between '*A*, *B*, *C*' and *X*. So, whether it is a relation between two or more men, or man and things, the relationship is always inter-subjective. Whether it is Logic or Mathematics, Ethics or the Social Sciences and Art or Aesthetics, you will always find inter-subjectivity there.

The truth of a proposition, such as '*X* is heavy', is decided by what the case is, but not `*X* is good or bad' without their being a person who passes such judgement. But man is not a member of this 'case'. When we evaluate '*A*' as good or bad, then, '*A*' and his behaviour are the constituents of the case. '*X* is heavy' can be the case whether or not man, or other beings with cognitive power exists. But '*A* is good' cannot be the case unless not only *B*, but the other person who passes such a judgement exists. The first is not controlled by us, but in talking about social, moral or aesthetic truths, we control what is the case.

In judgements of beauty about natural objects and about man-made objects, anthropocentricity is common. But the sociality of a human being is more vivid and manifest. Although sociality is anthropocentric, the anthropocentricity where there is sociality and the anthropocentricity where there is absence of such sociality, are different. It would not be possible to measure art objects with the same rod of beauty as in the case of natural objects. Our arts are at least partly determined by the social evolution. This theme is asserted by the Marxists emphatically, following from the idea that it is in an evolving society that man realises his freedom. Art is definitely due to man's freedom, and if it changes form as man evolves, then at least in some sense, the marxist thesis will have to be accepted.

I made a distinction between a beautiful object which is not man's creation and that which is, the second being an object of art. In the first case, the issue is merely about our appreciation, whether the thing has a certain structure and whether it is beautiful. In the second, the question is not about structure alone. Whereas, it is possible for me to think that the structure exists even in my absence, it would not be possible for me to think that there was beauty in the structure in my absence. What we call beauty belongs to the category of meaning and function. Structure belongs to the category of symbols alone. The relation between the structure of an object and beauty should be understood in the same way as we understand the relation between a symbol and the meaning of the symbol.

Unlike the case of natural objects, the artist not only creates beauty but also a structure whose reaction for the observer would be beauty. The problems which, therefore, arise in the case of art objects are: (1) when we evaluate an art object, is beauty the standard by which we evaluate? (2) Does an artist create an art object for creating beauty? My answer, as also the answer of the Marxists, for both, would be in the negative. As Bergson says, primarily, an artist's intention must be to create a structure. He might have a rough idea that his structure is likely to be beautiful and that an observer's reactions, agreeable. But how this will happen, he does not know. This uncertainty is due to the freedom of the artist and the fact that his idea about the painting is continuously evolving. So, although the concept of beauty may lie at the back of the artist's mind, the exact nature of the relation between the structure that is created and its relation to beauty may not be pre-judged.

Can we say that beauty is *common* to all beautiful objects, just as the quality of being a 'man' is common to all men? In such a case, we will have to say that there is something in common between music, poetry, sculpture, etc., but what that something is, will be difficult to decide. We cannot formulate dicta or rules, as in logic or ethics, about beauty, or any criterion by which we can say that such and such an object is beautiful.

If at all, such a criterion will have to be negative, by which, at the most, we would be able to say that some object would not be beautiful. The object and the characteristic which we name as beautiful are inseparable. What we call beauty is not a purely formal quality which can be separated from the object.

In language, of course, like other separable characteristics this also will have to be separated, for we do not have any method by which we can write a sentence where one kind of predicate can be shown as separable from the subject and the other kind can be shown as inseparable. The two propositions, 'He is my friend' and 'This is myself', are described in the same manner. From this, however, it does not follow that the formal aspects are totally absent when we say something is beautiful. The structure always has some formal qualities. But the logic of the structure and the logic of the reaction to the structure should not be identified. Rabindranath Tagore and Susanne Langer tried to identify them. Mardhekar proposes that symmetry, contrast and balance are the formal criteria of the structures that are beautiful. But we cannot say, 'For any *X*, if *X* has symmetry or contrast or balance, or all of them together, *X* will be beautiful'. Indeed, we can see that symmetry and contrast, if not contradictory, are at least opposed to each other and so, the same object cannot have both. Space and time, as Susanne Langer says, certainly play an important role in art structures and if the spatio-temporal elements are absent, then indeed, there would be no beautiful objects. But one could not also say that if these elements are present, then, beauty is also present. I, therefore, draw the conclusion that in beauty, which, according to me, is of the form of a judgement, the formal and non-formal elements have to go together and they cannot be separated.

III

Let us understand 'beauty' further, by first seeing the function of a concept. A concept enables us to communicate. It usually takes a linguistic form, and belongs to the region of the meaning of a word rather than the symbol. Concepts can as well be found in actions. Concepts are not private, but this does not necessarily mean that they are universal. For a concept to be public, it must, like relation, be at work where there are at least two individuals, if not more, constituting an universe. This concept of 'universe' is the operational field of the context and is different from that traditionally held to represent 'all'. The concept 'universe' suggests that man's world may go on increasing or decreasing as the 'tribe' increases or decreases, so such a concept is more of a *tribal* character than of the *universal.* A concept, then, need not be of the nature of something common to different objects. It could be such as Wittgenstein's concept of family resemblance.

When Plato talks of concept he has before him a model of a material object, having a common reference. An universal for him exists like a particular with the only difference that the universal is a heavenly particular. He, therefore, thought that an universal must have three characteristics: (i) it must exist, (ii) it must be common for all and (iii) it must communicate. Of these, the first two are simply special cases of the third. What is really necessary is that the concept must communicate and they get this ability on account of their publicness.

How is the publicness of the universal achieved? The concepts are public, right from the beginning but in the cultural history of man, they get enriched and get public acceptance, setting value standards. The concept of beauty, for example, is determined at least in judging the concrete forms from the cultures in which these forms are evolved. Apart from culture, it would be impossible to judge something as beautiful. 'Beauty', in this manner also, is related to man. As Plekhanov and other communist writers pointed out, what is beautiful for a white man need not necessarily be beautiful for a Negro. Objects like Raffell's Madona are the products of a certain civilisation. Turgenev says, the principles of 1789 are more valuable than the Venus of Melo (*Plekhanov*). The point here is not that the form of value is different in different cultures and history, but that, when we talk of beauty, the form and content get mixed up and such a mixture becomes the object of our judgement. From this it follows that some indeterminate and indefinite forms also gradually get evolved, lending further support to the recognition that beauty does not represent one common form. Beauty is discovered in different forms, in different cultural and historical patterns. All concepts are not formed in the same manner, though they serve the function of communication.

In a sense, the Marxists are right when they say that art flourishes with social progress. Communication is social in character, and art is concerned with a type of communication. But it may be possible to communicate something at one level, but not at another level. To understand these different levels requires training and this understanding comes as society progresses. But this does not mean that there cannot be any decay of art as society progresses. The two propositions are not opposed to each other, and it can very well be imagined that as society makes industrial strides, the poetry may become more and more artificial. Of course, not anything and everything that is communicated is art. Both natural beauty and artistic beauty give rise to communication, but there is one difference. In natural beauty, the communication is just epistemic, is concerned with nothing but appreciating. Man has no control over its creation. This is not so with regard to the work of art. Here the sociality is not only concerned with the knowing of art, it is also concerned with the creating of art. I may, however, say that whether it is a natural object or a work of art, we will have to understand it at three different levels, the *level of content*; *the level of form and the level of acceptance.* In the case of natural beauty, there is communication at the levels of form and acceptance. In the case of an art object, there is communication even at the level of matter/content. Since matter, form and acceptance can be distinguished but not separated, and since they point to the essential limits of appreciation or aesthetic activity, I feel that in the context of object of art in particular, beauty alone would not give us the aesthetic standard. Sociality and communication will also have to be taken into account.

In one sense, it is absurd to say that there are two types of aesthetics — the Capitalist and the Marxist. It may, of course, be true that the Marxist may be more sensitive to some kinds of aesthetic problems and this sensitivity may be due to sociality and communication. The Marxists' presuppositions are the following: (a) the human world is real and constantly developing; (b) its development is according to rules of dialectics; (c) human freedom realises itself in society and whether it is human development or natural artistic development, it is due to alienation.

Alienation has meaning only in the context of a self-conscious, living being. Man is such a being. Alienation takes place when man feels separated or alienated from himself or he is separated from skill or possessions. Take the case of human labour. A man's labour cannot be separated from himself. But if we treat this labour as separate and say that the labour is concretised in the form of his creation, we say there is alienation in this respect. Self-consciousness is also an alienation from consciousness. Similarly, when one talks of conscious and unconscious mind, it gives rise to alienation. If a man begins to think that he is a woman or *vice versa* and intensely tries for sex-change, it would again be a case of alienation. Our experience tells us that the substance part and the quality part cannot be separated. For example, a table and the length of that table cannot be separated, but if we view them as separate for our convenience, we are imposing alienation on the object. But here, the 'we' is important, for it suggests that alienation is always in the context of man. In one sense, objectification is also alienation, but by objectification, an art object is not created. If we want to distinguish between the earlier part of the temporal series and the latter part of the temporal series, then such as Chinese writers one could say that the first is negation and the second is the negation of negation. The fact, however, is that what we call objectification is only an element of the same series which goes by the name of alienation.

This objectification is necessary both for life and art. That we have a tendency to become many (*bahu syam prajayeya)* means that we have a tendency to separate or differentiate. These newly created parts are due to alienation. It is alienation which in fact, acts as a medium of communication, and if alienation is carried beyond a certain extent, its communication with the original object is lost or forgotten; the alienated object becomes independent. Even that which is merely the extension of the self of the artist or the craftsmen, in as much as it is an activity of the artist, becomes, as Marxists pointed out, a commodity. One can see the different methods of alienation. The dance cannot be separated from the dancer, the music from the musician, although it is now possible to record it. But a painting always existed apart from the painter, as also is the case with poetry. The tendency to become many has two opposite effects in the context of art: (1) The object which is, in fact, linked with the artist, is regarded as an absolutely independent entity. This leads to some kind of vulgar Realism where the link between the artist and the object is lost sight of; and it is forgotten that the art object has a role in the communication process as a medium. Or, (2) the art object that is created, is given scant attention, resulting in some form of Subjective idealism.

It is because of such tendencies that the evaluation part, which is also, in some sense, communication, is forgotten. When we say that something is beautiful, that we are evaluating is not forgotten. But when we say that something is a beauty, beauty being a noun, it is thought as if it was an independent entity existing in its own right and is of the nature of colour, fragrance, length or weight. All this happens at least partly because of different kinds of sociality, playing a part in the whole process. The concepts are formed in different ways sometimes emphasising the special characteristics and sometimes the common characteristics. But both of them have a kind of publicness at least in their cultural background.

Although, as discussed earlier, the concept of beauty is an open concept, we should further distinguish varieties of open concept. The aesthetic concepts on account of their communication with cultural history, may be regarded as vaguely developing concepts. When we talk of beauty, the particularities and the generalities can be distinguished but cannot be separated.

How is the art object, which is an idea in the artist's mind, objectified? The process of objectification, or if anyone wants to call it alienation, is due to man's freedom. Of course, this freedom is always limited or manifested by sociality. For in the first place, man's individuality is also so formed and secondly, he is at least partially modified by the environment. Since the objectification of art, as also the emergence of the idea of art, is due to man's freedom, one could also see that art is autonomous. But when the autonomy of art is asserted, we are not denying the social context, or the communication aspect of art.

Where the beautiful object is in nature, the communication is about the object. Where the art objects are created by man, it is not only about the object but is also through the object. The communication, so to say, passes through the object. In the first case, the communication is of the nature of perception, in the second, it is both perception and creation. *A*, *B* and *C* may discuss their responses to a beautiful sunset, but their medium is through ordinary language. This process is roughly comparable to cognition. In the art process, communication is between the artist and the appreciator(s), and the communication need not necessarily be in 'one time'. The artist may create something in the past and the appreciator may appreciate it now. How is this communication carried out? It is *about* the ideas which are objectified. The objectified idea has taken the form of an art object. The communication, so to say, penetrates through the art object and reaches the appreciator(s). If the appreciators and the artist are living in the same period, the former may also communicate something to the latter. It is about the artist's ideas, but it is also about the art object. In such cases, the communication is *through* the art object and also *about* the art object. Between every appreciator and the artist, the communication is of this type. When several appreciators talk of the art object, it is about the art object, and not through the art object. When the artist and the appreciator are not in the same time, communication is through as well as about the art object, but dialogue is absent.

I have stated that communication requires publicness, and that publicness can vary to a great extent: It can be universal or tribal. I may also state a limiting case of this publicness: the dream. In a dream all that we experience is conveyed to us by concepts which are public. There is a possibility of the dream being conveyed to others. But while dreaming, we are not able to convey our experiences to others except in some rare cases where we start talking aloud. Dream is a limiting case of inter-subjectivity, where the publicness of concepts is naturally limited to one individual. The case where ideas are born in an artist's mind is something like a dream. A dream cannot be separated from an individual. The art object, on account of this objectification is separated, and is separable.

IV

What we call art is a compound, consisting of content, form and acceptance of form. There are two kinds of arts, those which are based on structure, and those which are based on the meaning and understanding. In the second type, the structure also enters the whole as content. But of course, there is no rule that the structure should always be of the nature of content so far as the meaningful arts are concerned. Even one structure may become the content for another structure. The acceptance is a judgement. All these three elements which can be discovered in an art-object, cannot be separated from one another. That is why there cannot, for example, be a formal science of art. In such a formal science, the content part would be ignored and there would not be rules about acceptance. Acceptance is a judgement; judgement is a kind of measurement and a judgement is not concerned with the rules of measurement. It is concerned with the measurement of a thing that actually exists. It is possible that the judgement part may be inter-subjective and so also the form part. It is also possible that the formal part may be a hidden judgement. But these will be judgements at two different levels, where one judgement becomes matter for another judgement. Thus, for example, when we say that the judgement of a judge is not correct, we are passing a judgement on the judgement. This is something that happens in the Arts. The significance of Art lies not only in the form but also in the content.

The content of art is certainly due to atoms in reality, but the illusion that is concerned with art, lies in the arrangement of these atoms. When we say that the art is realistic, what we mean is that the atoms are real and although the relations of the atoms are not actual, they are possible. What we call actuality is only one of the several possibilities. It is, therefore, possible to think that actuality is one contingent case and therefore is not a manifestation of reality from every angle. The other possibilities though, in our ordinary language are illusory, are to be taken into consideration in order that we should be able to understand the complete reality. All the possibilities which are of the nature of illusion, give perfection to reality, as the communist writers say. For them, art and literature are illusory but they point to the possible dimensions of reality and give perfection to it. Here again, what the Marxists say is significant without there being anything specially "Marxist" about it.

If all that I have said is correct, then it means that art is not to be judged by beauty alone. It is judged by sociality also. So, there are two kinds of sociality, one concerned with beauty or judgement, and the other concerned with matter and form. They operate simultaneously or in quick succession, but at two different levels. Another conclusion which follows is that, sociality can be of different orders. For example, there is the sociality connected with morality. This sociality too cannot be excluded from the orbit of art. Thus, different arts will manifest different kinds of sociality. The controversy whether art is for the sake of art, or art is for morality, thus becomes meaningless.

How is this social content in art manifested? We must first make a distinction between registering or reporting, and expressing. It is this expressing which manifests the social content in art. Registering can be mechanical. Even a camera may register, but expression requires a human being. It is the thought which takes the form of an art object. It is something which takes the sensible form, the form with which other people are already acquainted, because it is public and therefore provides material for the understanding of thought. One man's thought is conveyed to the other by communication, but it is the expression which carries it from one man to another.

Objectification is another name for expression with which the artist's or man's 'mental' state may be expressed through bodily expressions. It may also be expressed through words or sound symbols or may be expressed through *mudrā*, acting or science. The primary pre-supposition in this respect is that man can express. It is not merely in the sphere of art that the expression becomes significant. The whole behavioural pattern of man is connected with expression. Eliminate the expression part and there will be no difference between a man and a stone. How do I know that a man is angry and that the stone is not? The only reason for our thinking that the stone cannot be angry is that the stone cannot express itself. In the case of two stones, there is no scope for sociality. In the case of two men, the element of sociality becomes primary. Of course, the sociality can be extended beyond human limits, such as the social context between a man and a dog. This sociality is possible on account of the freedom of man and in the case of art, the art object is also created on account of this freedom.

For sociality, the primary thing that is required is to recognise the other person as the other person. If I recognise the other person as only a part of me and my extension, then it is the beginning of slavery. It is also the beginning of treating others as things. So in a way, the society requires recognition of others which means alienation, or transformation of one into many. But alienation also may be responsible for destroying sociality. The social context may ultimately create the feeling of non-recognition or strangeness even between the artist and the art object. Marx has talked of a process of alienation and how with industrialisation that which is produced by craftsmen and which the craftsmen earlier regarded as their own, comes to be regarded as a commodity. Thus, gradually the attachment which one has for one's creation is lost. So alienation requires some kind of detachment, but if one has too much of attachment, then also there is alienation in the sense that the true nature of the thing is kept away from us. If a being is regarded as a thing, it really means that man is alienated from other men and in such cases, the sociality also gets damaged. With the growth of our civilisation, the alienation in both these forms occur. In alienation, the art object would be treated such as a vegetable in the vegetable market. This is how in the industrial civilisation a man with money can buy either an artist or the 'creation' of an artist. This is also the process by which, once an art object is forgotten, and only a relation between an art object and the appreciator (or a purchaser) is formed. Once this happens we forget the distinction between the naturally beautiful object and the art object that is beautiful. The beautiful sunset and the Monalisa are measured by the same standard.

V

Imagination also plays an important role, both in the understanding, and the creation of aesthetic objects. What does this imagination consist in? In fact, even if we talk of wild or free imagination, I may not think that it can be completely free. It is bound to our experience. The process of building concepts or discovering universals is not different from that of imagining. Suppose I see a flower. In my very perception, I start thinking of the size, the smell, the shape or the texture of that flower. If I want to know the smell, I smell it, if I want to know the texture, I touch it, etc. All these processes which combine in my perception get separated in my explanation, or in my expression of the same. Nevertheless, they are bound with the perception. In fact, when I form different concepts including that of the flower, I concentrate on one particular aspect, and try to find out whether this aspect has anything in common with the other flowers. Thus, I try to separate the different images connected with the flower, from the flower or the substance itself. These separated details are the universals, and in language, we again combine them to describe the flower. But just as they could be combined in the reverse order in which they were separated, similarly, they could be combined in whatever way we want them to be combined. The softness of the flower may not be combined with the flower itself. It may, now be combined with the physique of a woman. When we imagine, the imagination is free or wild; we, in fact, are referring to the various possibilities of such combinations. When an artist combines a certain form, an ordinary man is able to appreciate it, but an ordinary man does not know that this is one of the several possibilities. What the artist does is to visualise these different possibilities and select one of them for the combination. It is imagination in selecting the possibilities that makes the artist good or bad.

Conclusion

It is on account of alienation and sociality that the ideas in the man or the artist are expressed. But they are also expressed because the artist has freedom to express them. The artist like every other man collects the atoms of his experience and then selects them. He gives them a form. Giving a form is in a way his power of imagination. But in a way, it is also the limitation of his freedom. So in the process of objectification both imagination, freedom and some kind of controlling the freedom becomes operative simultaneously. What I feel necessary is to note that the form which the artist gives and the content through which is given the form cannot be separated. There is no logic or rule governing the beauty of the content. Of the two equivalent forms one may be beautiful and the other may not be. This is because the content plays an important role in the process of beautification. Similarly, the same elements which make one object beautiful, may make another object ugly. Here the beauty is determined at least partly by form. In a way to give form is to give acceptance to the form. And as we have seen, acceptance is valuation or evaluation.

12

Ethics, Aesthetics and Human Existence in G.E. Moore

Hasna Begum

I

THE famous English philosopher, G.E. Moore's (1873-1958) normative ethical theory has a special focus on an ideal human existence mainly comprising of moral and aesthetic aspects in human life. The fusion of analysis and common sense is a unique characteristic feature found in his philosophical writings, particularly in his writings on ethics. There is a logical connection and sequence in his writings on different philosophical topics. In this respect, in his views on normative ethics a latent logical sequence is found between the ideas of 'ethics', 'aesthetics' and 'human existence'.

Underlying Moore's normative view of ethics there is a belief in a peculiar kind of spiritualism. Of course, his spiritualism does not commit to the belief in the existence of any 'spirit' or super-human being. He believes in the existence of beings which are either empirically known or knowable. The former kind includes all kinds of natural beings and qualities, and the latter includes, goodness, beauty, number and/or all kinds of universals which are and could only be exemplified in natural objects. The existence of any 'spiritual being' or anything other than the above two kinds of things aroused in Moore a kind of disbelief, or to be more precise, agnostic attitude. However, spiritualism in which

Moore seems to have some sympathy is not classical ontological spiritualism, which negatively means the denial of anything which is purely and crudely material. His conception of spiritualism implies: (a) the fulfilment of feelings and the consciousness to be achieved through cordial and warm relationships among fellow beings and (b) the aesthetic enjoyments from the objects which are beautiful and at the same time devoid of any kind of evil or ugly elements in them.

II

When Moore writes on the moral ideal of human beings in the sixth chapter of his famous book, *Principia Ethica* (1903), he emphatically says that 'the Ideal' includes three kinds of values: (i) Unmixed goods, (ii) Mixed goods, and (iii) Positive evils. The human ideal is: to expand the amount of unmixed goods as best as possible; to accept the existence of a minimum amount of mixed goods (which have evils and ugliness causing pain and sufferings) with the objective of minimising the present and possible future positive evils; and, thirdly, to avoid all kinds of positive evils and ugly existents.

Unmixed goods, in Moore's view, comprise of only two kinds of experiences and feelings, personal affections or friendship and aesthetic enjoyments. He asserts without hesitation that these are the two things which ". . . include *all* the greatest, and *by far* the greatest, goods we can imagine, . . ."(1903: 189). Further, he adds that: "By far the most valuable things which we know and can imagine are certain states of consciousness [which are referred to as 'spiritual'] which may be roughly described as the pleasures of human intercourse [meaning 'pleasant' and cordial relation among human beings] and the enjoyment of the beautiful object. . . . This simple truth may, indeed, be said to be universally recognised. What has *not* been recognised is that it is the ultimate and fundamental truth of Moral Philosophy. That is only for the sake of these things ... that any one can be justified in performing any public or private duty; that they are the *raison d'être* of virtue; that it is they —

these complex whole *themselves*, and not any constituent or characteristic of them — that form the rational ultimate end of human action and the sole criterion of social progress: these appear to be truths, which have been generally overlooked" (1903: 188f)

This view of normative ethics discussed in Moore's latter book, *Ethics* (1912), could not gain much popularity, compared to *Principia Ethica*, among the latter philosophers. This is mainly because of the pronounced acceptance of analytic fervour in the attitude in them. Thus, the analytical tool which was originally meant by Moore himself to bring precision in moral literature, unfortunately contributed to overshadow the main purpose in all his ethical writings. The main purpose being, the introduction of a moral ideal that helps in qualitatively upgrading human existence. However, during Moore's own life-time his normative ethics was given much importance by an aesthetically-oriented literary group, called the "Bloomsbury Group" in London (*vide,* Begum, 1982). Further, it is important to note that, the value of his normative views is getting its due importance. Some contemporary philosophers have begun to comprehend the necessity of developing an anti-materialistic and anti-hedonistic (in its crude form) philosophy of life, which has a strong potential force to take over the crude materialism of today. It is generally accepted by such thinkers that human fellow-feeling, friendship, and contemplation of what is beautiful in nature and art objects, are important for human existence. It is the acknowledgment of this kind of existence which can uphold human dignity. In contrast, crude lust for pleasure from material comfort and enjoyment is something which devalues human worth *qua* human beings.

This is what specially concerns us today as the developments in science, importantly as in the fields of medicine, biology, genetic engineering are opening up possibilities of many more new inventions and discoveries, e.g. cloning and space travel (exploring the planet Mars has already become a reality). In this new situation thinkers are seriously compelled to find the ways and the means to control the already acquired knowledge and technologies for the sake of human welfare and society. Moore's normative ethics which emphasises friendship and aesthetic enjoyments can become a good guideline towards the salvation of mankind from greed, physical lust and love for what is evil and ugly.

III

Here let me bring to light Moore's aesthetic theory underlying his normative morality. Though Moore didn't write particularly on aesthetics, in his attempts to clarify the nature of the non-natural quality of goodness the presence of his latent view on aesthetics are subtly felt. For instance, he writes: "It appears probably that the beautiful should be defined as that of which the admiring contemplation is good in itself." (1903: 201) In this the core of Moore's views on beauty, taste and art can be detected quite clearly. The subordination of the conception of `beauty' to that of goodness is a novel approach in aesthetics. This becomes even more pronounced when he writes,". . . the pursuit of beauty for its own sake must always be postponed to the pursuit of greater good, which is equally attainable".(1903: 84)

Moore is not a nominalist. He is more sympathetic to Plato though he rejects Plato's concept of the theory of forms as universals. However, it is interesting to note that, Plato's theory of ideas are closer to Moore's aesthetic theory. Here it may be recalled that Moore in early Cambridge life was influenced by the then broadly accepted ontological idealism (*vide*, Schilpp 1942: 12ff), which was later renounced by him, had some effect on his belief in universals and in the supreme worth of goodness in the context of human existence.

Plato, in his *Republic*, places the idea of 'the good' at the apex in the hierarchy of ideas. In Plato's *Republic*, philosophers are the guardians of the state who are wise and just and they become wise and just by grasping thoroughly the idea of 'the good'. Once these philosophers know this supreme idea, they cannot but become good and just men, and rule accordingly. 'Beauty' and other ideas play a subordinate role to 'good'. This subordination of beauty to good in Plato is also subscribed by Moore. Thus, we conclude that Platonic conception of 'the good' influenced Moore. He, while explaining the nature of intrinsic value as non-natural, extensively discusses the relation between 'goodness' and 'beauty'. However, as already noted, Moore's main thrust was not to give a comprehensive aesthetic theory. He was primarily interested in refusing the claim where good is wrongly defined as natural, committing naturalistic fallacy.

Moore in both *Principia* and 'The Conception of Intrinsic Value'(1922) offers his observations on the relationship between goodness and beauty. In *Principia* Moore argues that there is only one intrinsic value, namely, goodness, and beauty is to be defined only by referring it to goodness. In the essay (1922) both goodness and beauty are intrinsic kind of values. 'Intrinsic value' is a generic concept, and goodness and beauty, more or less on a par with each other, are its species. Moore seems to say in this essay, unlike in *Principia*, that beauty is also an intrinsic value like goodness as it is intrinsically value possessed. Thus, it apparently seems to follow that Moore holds two different theses: one in *Principia* and another in the essay regarding the status of 'beauty' in axiology.

In *Principia* (1903: 201f) there is the double recommendation as it accounts for both the apparent connection between goodness and beauty and the no less apparent difference between the two conceptions: ". . . it [the definition] leaves only one unanalysable predicate of value, namely `good', while `beautiful' though not identical with, is to be defined by reference to this, being thus, at the same time, different from and necessarily connected with it." From this and his statements in *Principia*, 1903: (57, 202) it implies that:

(i) to say that a thing is beautiful is to say that though it is not itself good, it is a necessary element in something which is good;

(ii) "to prove that a thing is truly beautiful is to prove that a whole, to which it bears a particular relation as a part, is truly good"; and,

(iii) there are two different predicates of value: 'goodness' and 'beauty'; but there is only one unanalysable predicate of value, namely 'goodness'. The main contention in *Principia* regarding beauty is that it is to be subordinated to goodness as it is defined only by referring it to goodness.

In the essay (1922) Moore gives the following definition of intrinsic value:

> To say that a kind of value is 'intrinsic' means merely that the question whether a thing possesses it, and in what degree it possesses it, depends solely on the intrinsic nature of the thing in question.(1922: 260)

In this definition it is obvious that by `definition' Moore doesn't mean `analysis of a complex whole into simple parts', as he does in his treatment of the alleged definitions of good in *Principia*, but he only means `explanation of the meaning of the intrinsic nature of value'. Further, by the expression 'a kind of value', Moore means not goodness and evil, since his writings clearly indicate elsewhere that goodness and evilness are the positive and negative aspects of the ethical value which is intrinsic. So, kinds of value which are intrinsic, as stated clearly in the definition are `beauty', on the one hand, and the particular sense of `good' on the other with which Moore has been mainly concerned. (Schlipp, 1932: 582) Thus, understood, `beauty' is the aesthetic value which is intrinsic in the above sense, and `good' is the ethical value which is also intrinsic. However, Moore doesn't say that these two kinds together exhaust the field of intrinsic value. As an ethical pluralist he presumably keeps open the possibility of other kinds of intrinsic value. In *Principia*, he refers to `beauty' and `goodness' as the "two objective predicates of value, `good' and `beautiful', which are so related to one another that whatever is beautiful is also good." (1903: 201f) Here he seems to put forward a short outline of what he explained later about these two objective predicates of value which he later explains in the essay as kinds of intrinsic value.

Moore compares and contrasts these intrinsic kinds of value with right, wrong and duty; the latter, he says, are objective like beauty and goodness and unlike them are not 'intrinsic'. He writes in the essay (1922: 257) that unlike right, wrong and duty, beauty and goodness are themselves intrinsic. He also says that, former are instrumental and always have a fixed relation to an intrinsic value. That is, they have a fixed relation to intrinsic value as goodness or as beauty. It is noticeable here that according to *Principia*, though beauty is an intrinsic kind of value, it has also a fixed relation to goodness (the fixed relation of different kind). If this is so, then the right, wrong, duty, even when they have a direct relation to beauty, they have an indirect fixed relation to goodness since beauty itself has a fixed relation to goodness. The above is consistent with what Moore says in the last chapter of *Principia* that the most important of all valuable things in the world are personal affections and aesthetic enjoyments. (p.188f) These are two kinds of good things which are purely good and hence unmixed with any kind of evilness or ugliness. The last chapter includes many passages which clearly show, on the one hand, the subordination of beauty to goodness and, on the other, the necessary fixed relation of the two concepts. He says,

> . . . we may admit that the appreciation of a person's attitude towards other persons, or, to take one instance, the love of love, is far the most valuable good we know, and far more valuable than the mere love of beauty, yet we can only admit this if the first understood to include the latter, in various degrees of directness. (1903: 204)

From what Moore says here, it is quite interesting to note that not only is his aesthetic imbued with moral value, but his ethics is laden with aesthetic value. For him, whatever is beautiful must also be good, and whatever is good must also be beautiful.

To be good, a thing has to be far removed from evilness as well as from ugliness. Aesthetic enjoyments and personal affections could then only be enhanced in the universe, thus making it a highly intrinsically valuable whole.

It is, thus, plausible that for Moore goodness and beauty are not of equal value. Though both are intrinsic values, unlike other values (e.g., economic value), however, goodness, which is directly concerned with human relationship and human well-being, is much more important and primary. Thus, it should be promoted whenever it can be promoted. Beauty too is of intrinsic value, but the importance of it is secondary to goodness and consequently, the pursuit of beauty for its own sake must always be postponed to the pursuit of some greater good. That is why the contemplation of the beauty of, for example, 'The burning Rome with its wailing people' by Nero for the sake of the contemplation of beauty itself at the cost of human sufferings would never be considered intrinsically valuable by Moore. He wouldn't consider it to be beautiful at all. But the contemplation of ugliness, which we find in Zaindul Abedin's paintings of the Calcutta Famine of 1943 and in Van Gogh's paintings of the miners and the mining village in the Netherlands, would certainly be considered by Moore as beautiful, because here the contemplation of the ugliness and pain though negatively, has a direct relation to what is good. These paintings create in us positive feelings for our fellow human beings, thus enhancing general affections in us and are therefore, valuable both morally and aesthetically.

It seems that by subordinating beauty to goodness Moore means that though beauty is intrinsic like goodness, it must not be desired for itself when it is against moral goodness. This is why Moore categorically says in *Principia* that the beautiful is to be defined with reference to what is good, though he all along seems to maintain that beauty is a kind of value which is both intrinsic and objective. He thus attempts to save aesthetics, particularly aesthetics bereft of morality which can lead itself to sadism as evident in the example of Nero. Moore through his aesthetics, which is under the control of morality, circumvents the possibility of contributing to the increase in misery and cruelty.

IV

The idea of moral good and the concept of beauty for Moore seem to imply that in human existence there is a peculiar and common aspect which comprises of moral and aesthetic awareness, i.e. *consciousness* of the fact that humans have moral and aesthetic feeling in them. Where Moore says that 'personal affections' and 'aesthetic enjoyments' are the kinds of value which are the source of all kinds of private and public activities, he proposes to mean that it is the acquisition of these two kinds of experience in humans which marks them different from other existent beings. Humans are the only beings, so far as our knowledge goes, who have the abilities and also the conscious desire to acquire more and more of such experiences. This driving force or motive in human beings makes them choose a life full of activities which, as a consequence, makes it plausible to acquire such intrinsically valuable things or experiences of the mind. This might lead to enhance bodily pleasure as well, but the main focus *is* and *should be* on the spiritual, as opposed to material or corporeal pleasures.

As already mentioned above, Moore's description of the components of the moral ideal and his view on aesthetics subordinating it to moral goodness, taken together, makes us conclude that he certainly puts emphasis on establishing a world order in which humans are ideally full of friendly and aesthetic feelings without causing any misery and pain to fellow beings. He explicitly mentions about avoidance of human misery as such. Implicitly he seems to suggest that to cause misery to any kind of being is to compromise his/her ideal world order, as pain and sufferings are considered to be the Greatest Evils.

Moore, in *Principia* (p.200) carefully and quite clearly compares the intrinsic worth of 'love of God' and 'human love' and asserts that 'human love' is undoubtedly more valuable than 'love of God', because it may so happen that God does not exist, but we know with certainty that humans do exist. Love for a thing where there is no assurance of its existence devalues its intrinsic worth. Human existence is something which cannot be doubted and hence when we love a fellow human being, — the mere fact that our object of love does exist makes it more valuable. Moreover, Moore goes on further to explain and elaborate this idea in the sixth chapter of *Principia* by saying that love for someone will be intrinsically more valuable when it is reciprocal and not one sided. In the case of human love for God the reciprocity is even more doubtful since God's existence itself is doubtful, and also His reciprocity cannot be experienced through empirical experiences. It could only be an object of belief. Even in the presence of such a belief love of God becomes of little value, because the belief itself is questionable. Again in the absence of such belief, this kind of love loses all its meaning and becomes devoid of any intrinsic worth.

According to Moore, an ideal human existence requires the acquisition of intrinsically valuable things, which consists of '*both* some feelings and *also* some other forms of consciousness', (1912: 153) which must be acquired during his/her life time. Because, in Moore's view ,

> . . .it may be doubted, whether we shall have any future life at all, and that is even more doubtful, what, if we shall, that life will be like. . . .(1912: 13)

So, an ideal human existence implies 'to be existing in this world only'. But, at the same time, though this ideal existence includes concrete positive experiences, these experiences are not merely physical, devoid of feelings and consciousness. Here by 'concrete experiences' Moore seems to mean experiences, either physical or mental, to be felt and enjoyed during one's own lifetime, and not to be postponed for a 'future life', meaning 'a life after the extinction of that person'. From this it does not follow that he neglected the hope of any compensation which the person might get 'in some future life' (i.e., life after death).

Here still one more important point needs to be mentioned regarding Moore's view on an ideal existence. He refuses to agree with any kind of moral egoism, and asserts with confidence that, '. . . every action which most promotes the general good always *also* most promotes the agent's own good; and *vice versa*'. (1912: 141ff) But he also maintains that, even if and when the above mentioned consequence doesn't follow in every case it,

> . . .seems . . . self-evident that it must always be our duty to do what will produce the best effects *upon the whole*, no matter how bad the effects upon ourselves may be and no matter how much good we ourselves may lose by it. (1912: 143)

The supreme end of human existence is not, and should not be, the acquisition of intrinsic goodness only for one's own self at the cost of increasing intrinsic negative value in the whole world. Friendship and cooperation among fellow beings, even in the cases where one's own good lessens, may make the world as a whole a place better than our conception of heaven. In this way humans are able to create a world full of 'beauty' and hence goodness. Moore at the same time holds, in practical life situations it seldom happens that the agent's 'chosen' sacrifice either directly or indirectly, does not cause good for *himself* as well as for others at the same time. The agent's sacrifice with the end of changing the world into a place full of 'personal affections' and 'aesthetic enjoyments' certainly would produce in him a peculiar kind of consciousness, which is good in itself. A human person has the capacity to get satisfaction from merely imagining a world full of worthy feelings and devoid of anything ugly and evil. This capacity enables human kind to choose to sacrifice one's own good for the sake of universal good. To promote this ability is what a human person ideally should do. Moore's ideal utilitarian view tries to solve the unresolved paradox involving ethical egoism and universalism in this way. This is very much evident in his latter book, *Ethics*. Human existence, thus, in him gets a new and unique perspective by subtly refusing to accept the above mentioned presumed paradox.

For Moore, enrichment in positive intrinsic values, in the form of feelings and conscious comprehension of such feelings, make a human person's existence worthy of being human. The place of the moral ideal and the aesthetic model, as offered by him, thus attaches a new element which is peculiar only to human existence. This peculiarity involves combining both spiritual and material into a harmonious and coherent organic whole. This is what could be considered to be any unique contribution by Moore, which opens a new door to comprehend a conceptual frame of normative ethics which in its *form* gives emphasis on realism, but in its *content* includes idealism of its own kind. This is quite different from the ontological or epistemological idealism of earlier philosophers.

V

As this article is meant to be dedicated to Professor S.A. Shaida who also wrote recently on friendship, aesthetics and human existence. (Unpublished 1996-97) Let me paraphrase a few excerpts from Professor Shaida's own writings:

(i) True friendship may make one of the friends feel so happy to know that in some special sense she/he has been able to have some positive effect on the other friend's being. But she/he may also wish to assure the other that what the other feels is also something which has a responsive chord in her/his own self. The friend's relationship which is and would always be reciprocal (cf. Moore 1903, ch. VI) in all possible senses. One advises the other never to allow herself/himself to sink into the abyss of discontent and despondency. Life at every stage has the capacity of unfolding new dimensions and possibilities which all humans must exploit and enjoy to the fullest. Expectations and hopes give flips to our desire and give us strength to face the problems and the difficulties that beset us.

(ii) True and ideal friendship is unrestricted acceptance of the whole being of the friend as she/he is. In a sense, I would call it 'complete surrender' of oneself ('surrender' in a creative and reciprocal sense), because one should not keep any aspect of one's existence concealed from the friend. It is a life of sharing everything and feeling or 'living' the pains and pleasures, hopes and aspirations, with so much understanding that one need not even say everything in verbal 'languages'. Both the friends have complete faiths in each other. (cf. *Ibid.*) It is such a fortunate thing to happen and a wonderful relation which transcends the dichotomy of selfishness and selflessness. In making one happy, the other feels greater happiness and at the same time one knows if she/he is happy and this makes the other happy. The experience of true happiness in friendship brings about the fusion of the two selves/beings.

(iii) About the concept of beauty in human beings I would agree that essentially it is applied to certain features as qualities which we characterise as virtues and values. (cf. *Ibid.*) Form definitely dominates the contents of aesthetic expressions. Except in music, (cf. *Ibid.*) most of the fine arts are embedded in the content. We transform the content to more and more sophisticated patterns and forms and give new meaning to them in our creative imagination. The ability to transcend a certain level of existence doesn't minimise the place of those levels [of consciousness] which are thus transcended.

The above paraphrasing of Professor Shaida's views does help most to conceive and comprehend with a deeper understanding of the theories offered by Moore about the three subjects mentioned in the title of the article. Human existence ideally, as a complex whole, constantly goes on struggling towards transcending the given situation to arrive at a higher state of consciousness, not by ignoring the concrete reality but by transforming it, with a complete (or more or less complete) understanding of the choice one makes. This idea implies a great responsibility on human persons, who generally and ideally are supposed to be capable of bearing the burden with grace and without any regrets.

References

Begum, Hasna, 1982, *Moore's Ethics: Theory and Practice*, Dhaka: Dhaka University Press.

———, 1995, "Moore: Aesthetics Imbued in Morals", *Art: A Quarterly Journal*, Vol. I, No. 2, October 1995, pp. 7-10.

Moore, G.E., 1903, *Principia Ethica,* Cambridge, Cambridge University Press.

———, 1912, *Ethics,* Oxford, Oxford University Press.

———, 1922, "The Conception of Intrinsic Value", *Philosophical Studies,* London, Routledge & Kegan Paul, pp. 253-75.

———, 1942, "An Autobiography", in Schilpp A. (ed), *The Philosophy of G.E. Moore*, Cambridge, Cambridge University Press.

Schilpp, A., 1942, *The Philosophy of G. E. Moore,* Cambridge, Cambridge University Press.

Shaida, S. A., Unpublished correspondence with the author.

Part III
ETHICS

13

Moral Principles

P. R. Bhat

1. The Problem

SEVERAL attempts have been made to build and rebuild moral systems without much success. Great religions have tried to bring some moral order in the society, so is the case with great leaders and philosophers. Some attempts were in the direction of founding universal ethics; some others were in the direction of contextualising them. Some found moral principles in religious scripts, some in social conventions and rituals, some in social contracts, some others in emotions, feelings and still some others found them in human reason.

If a moral theory is found to be elegant, it may not be applicable in several moral contexts. For instance, Kantian categorical imperative[1] has hardly any application in the professional contexts, especially where the moral relationship is between unequals: a client and a trained professional. Contextual theory, such as Act-Utilitarianism, emphasises evaluating each and every action taking the context and consequences of action into consideration, can hardly permit any valid generalisations. If telling lie is permitted in one context, it may not be permitted in another context. Thus, evolving moral principles and organising life in accordance with them is made impossible.

---

1. Kant, I., *Fundamental Principles of the Metaphysic of Ethics*, tr. by T.K. Abbott, Longmans, Tenth edn., 1959, pp. 60ff.

Psychological, emotional or for that matter religicus foundation of ethics would have their limitations, for they appeal to only a limited segment of the society. For instance, the psychological hedonism though is universal in form is simply false. Not all individuals behave as hedonists and seek pleasure all the time. The emotive theory has large appeal, yet it does not influence who has self-control, rational and objective. Any morality that is based on a religion cannot have appeal to all simply because no religion is globally accepted. Thus, the best option we have is that of rational foundation of ethics since all men are rational even if not always.

2. The Social Contract

A rationally inclined individual is attracted naturally to moral philosophy of Hobbes. His theory of social contract[2] appeals to several thinkers. Hobbes discusses the human nature and takes it to be of extremely selfish. He then imagines the lawless state of nature where each individual is totally free to do what he feels right. This situation naturally leads to the state of war because he believes that each individual has adequate intelligence and ability to be a threat to life of any other person on earth. This is unbearable to any individual that his life is on constant threat and agrees to have social contract for mutual advantage. This social contract, thus, is found on the fear of life and safety.

We may react in two ways to this theory. Firstly, such a social contract, perhaps, is the fiction of the philosopher. Apart from this being historically untrue, there is no reason to believe that the social order would not have come into existence for any other reason. Secondly, the social contract makes fear as the foundation of norm, which may be true of animal kingdom, but is not suitable to explain norms of human beings. Further, even if there was a social contract, why should one honour this contract made by our ancestors is not answered adequately.

2. Woodbridge, F. J. E., (ed.), *Hobbes Selections*, Charles Scribner's Sons, 1958, pp. 285 ff.

How the commitment of our ancestors becomes the commitment for us is not clear even if we are to be grateful to the cultural heritage that we inherit from them.

What is required is to explain why the social contract should be honoured by a member of the society. That is to say, social contract makes sense; for that matter "contract" makes sense only within a moral framework where promise must be kept is accepted as a value. Social contract cannot, then, be the foundation of our value system. The fear cannot be the source of morality is evident here. If fear is the source of morality, absence of fear should make us a beast. But that is not expected to happen. It seems obvious to Hobbes, at least, that if we become civilised once, we do not become uncivilised again! Social contract is for the advantage of everyone. True enough, but for an opportunist, it is a disadvantage. If he agrees to the social contract and subsequently does not keep his promise, he would have better advantage than his counter-part. It is possible to think that eventually the opportunist is the loser since no one would believe him. This may be so only if the opportunist does not keep relatively less important promises. But to be an opportunist at times would certainly be advantageous to the individual where the general norm of the society is that one should keep one's promise. Social contract theory can appeal to those who already believe in the institution of promise. It fails to explain why should one keep the promises, at least, in those cases where one does not have the fear of being caught and punished.

What is then, required is an account that can give foundation to the norm of promise keeping. What makes us the moral agent is our freedom. The human freedom is distinctly different from the freedom exercised by animals, call it due to rational ability that we possess or due to our other abilities such as intelligence, imagination and expectation. Consider again the Hobbes' notion of the man in the state of nature. Surely, this state lacks all norms and principles and the drive for action would be either instinct or desire. Acting on instincts and feelings do not require any moral thinking, and hence no moral principles are required either. A free human agent, might act on instinct and feelings; but in either case, he cannot be said to have exercised freedom. Acting without thinking is not an action for which we are either praised or punished. That is to say, no moral responsibility can be attached to actions performed without thinking. We may hold an agent responsible for not thinking, but not for the actions performed without thinking. There is the direct link between the freedom and the moral responsibility.

Since man is a gregarious animal, one person's freedom comes in conflict with the freedom of others. There is no way one can measure whose freedom is important in the state of nature. The principle that prevails in such situation is: might is right. But when it is the matter of human abilities, whether physical ability is superior to the mental ability cannot be so easily decided, and thus the situation would arise where one cannot clearly know who is mightier than the others. Struggle for powers and dominance has remained all through the history of man and the power hungry man does not respect any principle, leave alone moral principles.

Certainly, the state of constant war is Hobbes' fiction. If animals can co-exist with all their instinctive behaviour, there is no reason to believe that human beings could not have survived such a tension of constant threat to life. Yet such a situation of constant war would not have been the best possible alternative. By sacrificing some freedom, individuals could gain multiple advantages. This is the basis of the social contract, where each individual learns to restrain himself from harming others and allow others to exercise their freedom. He sacrifices his freedom and gains security and cooperation. Any breach of this implicit contract attracts punishment that is nothing but curtailment of the freedom of the defaulter. Thus, social contract is founded on human freedom and not on fear.

Another acknowledged social contract is in the form of common language that they spoke. Language cannot exist without the formation of rules and rules are conventionally accepted. That is to say, by exercising our freedom, we have evolved symbols having rules. We have made linguistic rules and by following those rules we are in a situation to gain the advantage of communication. Certainly rule-governed behaviour presupposes much restraint on the part of the users of language. Each and every word has to be used in a systematic manner. Clearly, if man wanted to retain his full freedom, he would not have used language. Without the loss of freedom, i.e., without abiding the rules of language, both syntactic and semantic, one would not have succeeded in evolving such a powerful language that we have today. A principle that is commonly presupposed in both the evolution of language and of morals is that treat similar things similarly. We have learnt to use rules. Rules are presupposed in both social contract and use of language.

If anything has made man rational, it is his ability to use rules. A moral person, then is necessarily a rational person. It is not possible to imagine an irrational person being moral or immoral. We do not call a mad person as moral or immoral. That is to say, there is some basic link between rationality and morality. This basic connection is made explicit in social contract and the use of language. R.M. Hare made it abundantly clear both in *Language of Morals* and *Freedom and Reason*[3] that our language including the language of morals is governed by rules, and as the user of language we are committed to the principle: if *A* is red then anything that is similar to *A* in all relevant respects would also be red. This universalisability principle would be applicable to both descriptive language and moral language. Certainly, Hare is right in indicating that man can be rational if and only if he is systematic and regular in using his terms. If one refuses to universalise the use of words, then he is not either competent user of language or he is necessarily biased, i.e., intentionally uses the words in the deviant manner.

Use theory of meaning believes that meaning lies in the use

---

3. Hare R.M., 1952, *The Language of Morals,* OUP, Oxford, p. 94 ff.; R. M. Hare, 1963, *Freedom and Reason*, OUP, Oxford, p. 30 ff.

of the term. If that is the case, any use must be universalisable. That is to say, "This pen is red" is meaningful, "All pens are red" also should be meaningful. That is to say, meaning and extensions are internally related. If we know the meaning, we know the extension of the word. Given this, what is important to note is that there are certain predicates, they necessarily limit their use. For instance, we cannot say that all needs are basic needs. If we say that then the term "basic need" would lose its meaning if all needs are included as part of its extension. Similarly, we cannot say everyone is "hardworking". If we use this predicate to everyone, then the distinction between "hardworking" and "lazy" would not remain. Ethics uses the terms such as "right" actions as opposed to "wrong" actions, "good" as opposed to "bad", "virtuous" as opposed to "wicked", "kind" as opposed to "cruel" that are necessarily contrasted. What we notice from this is that we do not believe that ethics is universal and each one of us would be virtuous and good though Kant would visualise such a possibility. Use theory of meaning also cannot allow us to universalise these predicates to such an extent that all the extensions of its opposite also are included within the scope of the term. If we universalise them, then a predicate would make its opposite necessarily vacuous having no application. This is not a useful thing to happen.

3. The Categorical Imperative

Another rational attempt to build an ethical theory was that of Kant. Kant spoke of maxims. These maxims are nothing but certain considerations tempting for action. When we universalise with respect to certain desire, it is one like proposing a rule for the use of a word. And this rule for the use of the word could be proposed only in one manner: the rule proposed be the same for everyone. This is because, the law of identity requires that the same rule be applied to similar things. And for this reason, there is no choice but to permit the same rule to everyone. Like, Wittgenstein, Kant believes that if there is a rule for the use of a word, it should be used very consistently and systematically.

This is the same spirit in which R.M. Hare also speaks about the case of descriptive meaning and universalisability of moral judgements. The meaning is use, and the use gives meaning is also implicitly admitted by Kant's theory. Without the consistent application of rules, there cannot be any meaning to the words.

Kant has ensured the subjective desire to enforce the moral principle. It is only the subjective desire that was converted into a maxim. That is, the agent has the desire to act; after having such a desire, he subjects this desire to rational scrutiny and he would act on the maxim if and only if it meets the formal requirement of universalisability. Moreover, the procedure of universalisation adds the rational motive to act in that particular way: it shows the meaninglessness of the contrary behaviour. For instance, on universalisation, a rational being realises that he cannot permit everyone to act in the manner that loans taken are not to be returned. He realises that there would be no institution of lending any loan since loans would be forced gifts if universalised in this manner. Thus, Kant's categorical imperative has two strong motivations: first, the subjective desire for action since each individual's desire for action is the beginning point; and second, it would be irrational to act in the contrary manner since if he were rational, he must admit that every one else similar to him should also be permitted to act in similar manner.

4. Essentially Contested Terms

Contrary to the feeling that a moral agent should universalise his maxim, we may find some difficulty in universalising. There are certain notions that are mutually exclusive. For instance, stealing and the right to private property cannot go together. If we grant the right to possess private property, we need to protect them from stealing. Similarly, non-killing and self-defence cannot go together. Either we should permit killing or should not speak of self-defence as a moral act. The case of trust and cheating are such that they cannot be together. If we need to be dependent on others, we cannot be cheating. Thus, an ethical system can accept one on these pairs of opposites.

Yet we notice that a moral system invariably claims that self-defence is justified and murder cannot be ignored. And it would equally hold that one ought to tell the truth at the same time use the directive to doctors not to reveal the nature of the disease to keep the confidence of the patient high. Cheating is not allowed by the general norms of the ethics, yet a psychiatrist can pretend to be kind and a personal friend of his patients.

5. Justice and Equality

A rational approach to ethics is marked by our use of the notions of justice and equality. Justice has, at least, two criteria and each of the criteria would force a rational being to act in that particular manner. For instance, one of the criterion is treat similar things similarly, and the other criterion is treat dissimilar things differently. But both of these are formal criteria. They give us the formal guidance and we must know how and when to apply them, otherwise we may cause injustice rather than justice. For instance, if we claim that a rich man should have a seat in a crowded bus, whereas, a poor person should stand; this would be a wrong way of discriminating. Instead, if we claim those, senior citizens and children, should have privilege to sit and travel in state owned transport services, that would be the right way of discriminating. Similarly, we should not discriminate between individuals when it is the matter of medical treatment. We should not say that children and senior citizens should be medically treated whereas youths need not be. Suffering, whether it is of young or old is equally bad; every effort should be made to remove suffering without discrimination.

What is important to note is that both the formal criteria are opposed to one another in a certain manner. That is to say, justice seems to follow some **golden mean**; any extreme seems to be necessarily rejected. This golden mean is between the two extreme points of abstraction and contextualisation. In extreme abstraction we tend to say that all objects are similar in one aspect or the other, and in the extreme contextualisation we tend to claim that each thing is unique. Any value system based on either extremes should be rejected since the value seems to be misplaced.

6. The Golden Rule

Following The Golden Rule was considered to be rational and just. The rule "Do unto others as you would have them do unto you" is said to be a formal rule, since it speaks of nothing in concrete as to what one ought to do, and yet it is prescriptive in nature. When the rule is interpreted in a general manner, it has two difficulties as pointed out by Gewirth.[4] The Golden Rule can be considered from two distinct points of view: one that of the recipient and the other that of the agent. In the former case, the agent has to act toward others as he would want them to act towards him if he could have the desires of others. Hence, he must treat them the way they want him to treat them. And in the latter case, the agent has to act towards others according to the principles on which he would want them to act towards him.

Having realised the above difficulties, Gewirth speaks of moral rationality where the rule of moral action requires that the rules must serve to harmonise the interests of all the persons affected. Thus, the notion of rationality that is embedded in the Golden Rule is that of ensuring that you do not hold double standards. Gewirth claims that an agent should limit his rational desire because he has to grant unlimited rights to others. And therefore, he suggests that one should limit to the Principle of Generic Consistency. The principle of generic consistency states: *Act in accord with the generic rights of your recipients as well as yourself*. But this is no good argument. Given the fact that many are not in his situation, i.e., the president of a country, might invoke a principle where he says that all presidents should be above the constitution. This the individual knows does not cost him anything, and moreover, there are very few individuals who

4. Gewirth A., 1982, *Human Rights: Essays on Justification and Application*, University of Chicago Press, Chicago, p. 130.

can avail of such a provision. For this reason the argument is ineffective.

Firstly, it is a misnomer to claim that there are rational desires. To have the desire to be rational is not the same as rational desire. There is no doubt that we would like to be rational and consistent. But this desire is desire to be moral and just, but does not spring from one's rationality. If that were the case, highly rational people must have been necessarily moral. However, it is not difficult to find counter living examples against such a claim.

Secondly, even the principle of generic consistency is also very broad and limited at once. On one interpretation, freedom of others could include anything that the other individual wants to do; and his well-being is not less vague in comparison to the notion of freedom itself. The other individual might think that his having a car is essential part of his well-being, and some others may contest this on the ground that the basic needs are more fundamental and qualitatively different from such an item of luxury. They may not include possession of a car as essential part of one's well-being. Given this generality of freedom and well-being which the generic principle speaks about, any ethical controversy can remain untouched. If we take this principle of generic consistency at the abstract level, then the principle is as useless as Kant's categorical imperative.

Thirdly, the striking drawback of the principle of generic consistency like the Golden Rule and the universalising of the maxims and resultant categorical imperative, is that it is applicable only to individuals among morally equals. We can compare between only those who are morally comparable. For instance, two adult males can be compared with one another; and two children can be compared with one another. It would be difficult to hold both adults and children equally responsible for their actions because they are morally unequal agents. This principle generic consistency or its counterpart in the form of the Golden Rule or that of Kant's universalisability criterion is totally silent on morally unequals, such as between professionals and their clients; teachers and students; parents and children. Needless to say that most of the hotly debated moral issues are often between morally unequals. For instance, paternalism as a moral issue would arise in the context of gardians, doctors and lawyers: whether they have the right to decide what is good for their children and clients respectively. Applying the principle of generic consistency, we cannot expect children and clients to decide what is good for their parents and professionals respectively.

7. Social Foundation

No society can have all members equal. Each and every society has a way of taking care of helpless, if not in a satisfactory manner, to some extent their needs are taken care. Each and every society has a mechanism to transfer the values to its next generation the cultural wisdom it inherits in the form of proverbs, legends and epics. These cannot be useless, since the social existence largely depends on them. There are several proverbs that capture the moral fabric of the society. For instance, "as you sow, so you reap", "self help is the best help", "cleanliness is next to Godliness", "health is wealth, duty is God", "haste is waste", "love is blind", etc., indicate prudential and moral advice to the youth. *Jātaka* stories, *Pañcatantra* are stories meant for children to imbibe the right values of the society. Epics such as *Rāmāyaṇa* and *Mahābhārata*, apart from teaching political philosophies, do give moral messages through examples. *Bible* and *Koran* are no exceptions to this. No moral system would be teaching anything contrary to all these proverbs, legends and epics. The moral values embedded in these literary works themselves may not fit fully within a moral theory; yet moral principles that are to be practised by the members of the society cannot be entirely different from them. There might be difficulty in deciding which proverb is to be applied in which moral context.

Certainly, it would be unreasonable to think that a large number of members in a society are immoral, though possible to imagine that all women and children are ill-treated by dominant men. Yet it is difficult to conclusively say whether majority of the members are immoral. Even in the list of cases where one has identified the ill-treatment given to women and children, the ill-treatment may be the consequence of custom and tradition. For instance, the *burkha* system or that of shaving of the head of widow, etc., could be the result of certain social custom and therefore cannot be counted as clear cases of ill-treatment. No doubt that the society at large is responsible for such practices, and there is much point in engaging oneself in bringing social change, yet these cases cannot be identified as clear cases of immoral acts. Thus, wherever the ill-treatment to some sections of the society is prevalent, it is, in principle possible to appeal to the rational mind and make them realize what they practise is unjust. What we would require, is, perhaps, lengthy discussions with certain influential individuals in the society when they are not emotionally charged.

8. Rational Actions

After rejecting the possibility of universal ethics, can we still speak of rational ethics? Let us begin with the question: What is a rational action? This cannot be answered without knowing the relationship between reason and emotion. This issue is very important because without carefully delineating the relationship between the two, we would not be in a position to solve the moral issues. The concept of the golden mean of Aristotle in a modified form is applicable even in this context of rational action. We need to acknowledge that man has both rational and emotional dimensions. Reason would tell us what are the best ways to achieve the goals if the goals and different methods of achieving them are given. Moreover, what is regularity, consistency, contradiction, etc., is given by our reason. Emotions can be described, perhaps, in terms of their intensity. Children and women are relatively said to be more emotional. Some graduate from getting often emotional to a more stable states of longer duration. With hardly any exception, every one goes through certain emotional states; but some are often emotionally charged and some others are not so frequently. This has something to do with cultural, economical, psychological and biological constitution of an individual. Without undermining the importance of these factors, we might say that every individual has emotional states: extreme and normal. What may be counted as extreme is where the emotion takes over the person and the individual has no control over himself; and what may be called normal is the least emotionally charged state with respect to an individual.

Speaking from the point of view of an individual, what we may identify a decision to be most rational would be the one which is taken when one is in least emotional state. This has something to do with our biology. When we are excited about anything, the blood supply has to be diverted to motor organs rather than to our brain and thus there would normally reduction in our capacity to think and reason. However, if the excitement is about the very idea of something, we may be lost totally in thinking and pursuing the idea. This happens only to the intellectuals who are emotional about their rational thinking. This case of emotional state leading to further rational thinking is only an exception.

Our thinking ability is reduced when we are emotionally charged can be noted with one simple example. When we are angry, for instance, we have the urgency to act. Even if there is no reason to take immediate decision and act instantaneously, the individual feels the compulsion to act immediately when he is in the state of anger. In other words, there is urgency to come back to our normal senses as early as possible after execution of the decision. This is, perhaps, the reason why there is such an urgency to act when we are under emotional states.

What we should not fail to notice is that we know that we are emotional when we are in the state of emotions; we know that we are angry, depressed, sentimental when we are in those states. Thus, the self-knowledge about our emotional states is available to us. But often we do not make use of this information in our moral decisions. We need to utilise self-knowledge of this type very constructively, for what is right and what is wrong can be defined with reference to these emotional states in the following manner. Consider for instance, the relationship between the rational decisions and our emotional states. We may describe our different emotional states from one extreme of being very happy to the other extreme of being very depressed. The normal state would be somewhere between the two extreme points when we feel neither happy nor unhappy. For instance, a decision might be taken when one is extremely happy to give charity and gain moral praise by being altruistic; and a different decision might be taken to commit suicide when one is extremely unhappy. These decisions when reconsidered would seem quite legitimate when we are again in those extreme emotional states. However, both these decisions seem to be extreme decisions and thereby hasty and unreasonable when we are in the normal state of emotion. Giving away large sum of money as charity may not be considered to be the right thing to do and the idea of suicide may be considered to be even foolish from the point of view of least emotional state.

In this context, the pressing issue is this: if a decision taken in a particular emotional state seems legitimate and right when we are in similar states, how does one choose which emotional state is the right one? A pragmatic approach to emotions could be the following: of the 24 hours a day, some hours are spent in sleeping and some are spent in doing other daily routines. Not that we cannot be dreaming dreaded things, not that we are not emotional while eating, bathing, etc., but normally we are not involved in taking decisions when we engage ourselves in these activities. If psychologists are correct in informing us that a restless mind would eventually become mad if enough rest is not given to it, then we need to take a normal man as emotionally stable and has emotionally less charged longer hours in a day or in a week. Thus, a rational individual takes moral decisions when he is least charged by emotions. Moreover, he would be in a position to interact with others on moral issues when others too are rational, i.e., in their least emotional states. And such interactions lead to improved moral decisions on several issues concerning the individuals and the society including the ills of customs and religions.

Acting morally is more difficult than being rational. In any rational exercise, we tend to say that a rule determines its extension. For instance, if we know the rule of addition, we would be able to do the exercise of adding given any numbers almost mechanically. The situation is different in the context of morality. Following moral principles blindly may not result in moral actions. For instance, keep the promise cannot be applied blindly. The gun borrowed should not be returned if its owner needs it for shooting himself or his wife.

There are two difficulties of fundamental nature in implementing our model of rational conduct. First, what should be done if a person is not in a position to come to his normal senses until he decides on a moral issue? This may be viewed as arguing in a circular way. We cannot expect a person to be rational unless he is least emotional and if the issue involves the individual it may be said that the very thought of the moral problem puts him in an emotional state. For example, consider a lady having a child is considering the moral justifiability of giving divorce. But the very idea of the child not having the benefit of both the parents living together makes her emotional about the whole thing. She may attempt several times to rationally consider the issue and become emotional invariably and thus not being sure of her decision. As we mentioned earlier, the agent knows that she is in an emotional state and the best thing she could do is to pose the moral issue to another person who is emotionally stable and is unlikely to be upset by the very issue at hand and get the advice. Second, there can be difficulty in consulting any other individual for a moral advice in addition to the problem mentioned above. For instance, the lady may be further pre-occupied by the idea that informing others in order to seek moral advice itself puts herself in a vulnerable position. What should one do if one does not have any emotionally free mental state even to seek moral advice from other moral agents?

As is obvious in the above account, there is no way of

reaching a rational decision on the moral issue regarding this issue of divorce. But to think that every moral issue might be one like this is to stretch the argument too far. The lady has to make up her mind and consult others if she feels that she becomes too emotionally charged when she considers the issue at hand. The fear that she becomes vulnerable may be unfounded since she is worse off as it is: the undecided state of moral problem makes a person more vulnerable than the possible consequences of consulting someone on such matters. The only way out is to be morally brave under such circumstances. Here too, the solution lies in the agent's realising that obsession too is not good. Thus, moral discourse is possible when individuals are in their least emotional states and seek the moral advice from some other person who shares the social values.

9. Concluding Remarks

How do I ensure that I act morally? Social groupings cannot be avoided. We do groupings on the basis of professions; we also group people according to their age and sex; according to their physical disabilities. Grouping according to economic and social status also is found to be very desirable. In any case, morality recognises groupings and has different ethics meant for different groups. For instance, we have several ethics recognising the social groupings: business ethics, psychiatric ethics, medical ethics, juvenile ethics and so on. The same moral principle, e.g., help the needy, is applied differently to each group. A refugee cannot be helped by giving alms; he needs to be rehabilitated; and a beggar needs alms. Exceptions to moral principles are also made sometimes. For instance, if cheating the patients is allowed by pretending in psychiatric ethics; telling lie to the patients by the doctor is allowed in medical ethics; but neither of them is allowed in business ethics.

The universalisability that we need to use here should be the one that does not deny the social groups their ethical rights. This is possible when we go for linguistic universalisability. That is to say, the universalisation should not be across the groups eliminating the privilege granted to some groups. Tell the truth, must be applicable normally to everyone though the doctors are not covered by this moral principle when they are practising. If universalisation renders a moral term useless, we should not be accepting that maxim as ethical. For instance, if we hold that we have the right to property, then we cannot defend stealing as ethical. We cannot universalise the desire to steal simply because we have granted ethically possessing of private property. Similarly, we cannot universalise the dowry system because when we universalise extraction of money by force, it would not be any more gift by the parents-in-law. Dowry system too goes against the principle of right to property. To be short, we should not act on that maxim that would deny the rights of others if universalised. Thus, our rational approach is inspired by Kant but not Kantian.

We may note that we are different from others who are highly inspired by Kant. For instance, the universalisability criterion is accepted by Singer but he uses this criterion in the context of utilitarianism of his version.[5] He would like to universalise a maxim to compute the consequences to know if contemplated course of action is desirable. He would then decide on utilitarian ground whether a course of action is morally sound or not. There is merit in this, but we do not subscribe to this view for it has demerit too. Though, utilitarianism needs to be respected as the second best alternative, we need to protect the interest of the minority; and we need to respect the contribution from our tradition. Since utilitarian criterion takes into consideration of the totality of happiness gained by a course of action, majority of the moral decisions may go against the minority. Moreover, the traditional values that have been long tested and have been serving the societies cannot be rejected on utilitarian criterion. We need to adopt de-ontological stand when it comes to the matter of rights of distinguishable groups.

---

5. Singer M., 1963, *Generalisation in Ethics: An Essay in the Logic of Ethics, with the Rudiments of a Systematic Philosophy*, Eyre and Spottiswoode, London, pp. 13-60.

The other philosopher who has highly inspired by Kant but is quite different in his approach is R.M. Hare who accepts the universal nature of moral judgements by characterising universalisability as essential feature of his prescriptivism. Prescriptivism is more of a language of morals rather than a moral theory. It offers us a sound explanation as to why have moral judgements their moral force. If Stevenson felt that they have the persuasive power, Hare felt that this persuasive power should be distinguished from the prescriptive element that is there in a moral judgement. Prescriptivism, in an uncommitted manner can describe the prescriptive element in a moral judgement and hence to that extent it is a descriptive account of moral language. But in advancing his account of moral language, Hare has rightly recognised the universal element that is present in moral language as is the case with ordinary language. Hare has drawn our attention to the consistency that is required for any intelligibility of language, thus demonstrating how no talk of ethical system without the universal element would be fully satisfactory.

Since prescriptivism is non-committed to any definite position in philosophy except that it opposes naturalism and intuitionism, we cannot be adopting such a position to seek for a system which is action-guiding. We are in search of moral principles basically to guide us in our moral decisions and actions. Though, we agree with Hare in accepting this moral force that the moral judgements have, this force cannot be so clearly distinguished from the cognitive force. For instance, Socrates believed that virtue lies in the knowledge of what is good. If one knows what is good, he naturally would choose that course of action, he insisted. If there is an unscrupulous person, the prescriptive elements of moral judgements would have no impact on him unless he is already committed to the value system. And if we overlook this aspect and speak of moral language *per se*, then prescriptivism becomes irrelevant to the issues at hand.

Habermas is yet another philosopher who is highly influenced by Kant but he has a different programme for a rational individual.

He tried to incorporate rational element in his discourse ethics where each participant is believed to be ideal and situated ideally.[6] That is to say, leaving aside the practical differences, we are made to believe that such a possibility exists where each one is just and fair to the other participant in the discourse. Again, we find the account unrealistic and unattractive for two obvious reasons. First, if individuals could be just and fair to the others and if individuals could be rational, there would not have been any occasion for us to deliberate on the issues: a good moral system would have prevailed long before all philosophers were born. Second, discourse ethics undermines the fact that different individuals brought up in different cultures will have difficulty to evolve a common platform where rational exchange of ideas could take place.

This difficulty would remain even in our framework. If it is a highly complex society one such as ours, it would be difficult to morally decide which course of action would be appropriate. For instance, should the inheritance law regarding private property be religiously based cannot be easily settled rationally. Since individuals from different community within the society may be brought up in such a manner that they view things in accordance with their religious rights. Morally persuading keeping aside the religious considerations and cultural considerations may be very difficult. Yet, if there is anything worth pursuing towards so that we reach a standard of morals, it would be a rational one as explained in our previous section.

What should be noted here is that we are inspired by Kant in the sense that we speak of limited universalisability, at the same time, we believe that classification is inevitable. We believe that we need to make distinctions within the society, grant different rights to different groups without which it is impossible to defend

---

6. Habermas, J., 1973, *Legitimation Crisis,* tr. by Thomas McCarthy, Heinemann, London, p. 107ff. Also see the reply by Habermas (1982) to his critics in *Habermas: Critical Debates*, ed. by John B. Thomson and David Held, Macmillan Press, London, pp. 227f.

our fine sense of justice. What cannot be permitted is to allow individuals to make distinctions to such an extent that the whole system collapses and becomes a toy in the hands of a relativist.

14

Resituating Duties in their Rightful Place

Satya P. Gautam

THE rise of liberalism can be seen as a response to political tyranny and religious oppression. Historically, liberalism was a movement for freedom from the arbitrary exercise of power by the feudal and religious institutions. Supporting a view of basic civil liberties, what have presently come to be known as human rights, liberalism gradually developed as a modern political ideology which gives primacy to the freedom and rights of the individual against any undue interference from powerful institutions — whether political or religious. The main concern of the liberal thinking was to question any form of absolute and arbitrary rule by proposing rule of law and limited government. The ideal of the "rule of law, not of men" called upon its adherents to strive to ensure that the law itself will rule and not the arbitrary wishes of any powerful individuals. To use Locke's words, government must be by "settled standing laws" and not by "Absolute, Arbitrary Power". The central concern of the liberal tradition was the protection of the individual by recogning the significance of every individual, the equal worth of all individuals irrespective of their religious denomination, class, race, or socio-cultural affiliation. Thus, in its origins, liberalism was a revolutionary doctrine which aimed to provide specific rights to all adult citizens. Though the liberal doctrine was articulated and defended in different ways by various thinkers, it has been rightly pointed out that,

> . . . one point constantly recurs in each and every manifestation of liberal thinking. It is this belief that the liberty and welfare of the individual and the justice and security of society depend upon there being clearly defined and enforced legal relationships between all of its members. No man may rightly be considered outside or above the law. (Manning, 1976: 14)

Thus, setting up of an impartial and efficient juridical system was seen as a possible way of dealing with the problems that can arise due to conflicts among individuals in their pursuit of wealth, power and status. An articulation of a framework of legal rights and rules has been an important part of the growth of liberal political theory.

In the history of liberal thought, we come across arguments for a minimalist government based on the principles of (i) self-protection, (ii) natural rights and (iii) moral autonomy.

Self-Protection

Liberals hold the human individual as a sovereign creature who must enjoy his life in an unhindered freedom. For protecting the individuals from any injury or harm, they have concentrated on setting up regulative barriers between individuals on the one hand, and the individual and the state on the other. The instances of misuse of power by the officials of the state, torture and killing of its own citizens by any government have been regarded as sufficient to demonstate the benefits of liberal institutions. RULE OF LAW and MINIMAL GOVERNMENT are expected to provide protection to relatively powerless citizens against the arbitrariness of an all powerful state.

Natural Rights

People are endowed with natural rights. These rights can be discovered by human reasoning. Right to life, liberty and property were recognised as basic rights. Liberal morality of rights can be characterised, using Mark Johnson's metaphor of traffic,

(1993: 119) in terms of a right-of-way to move unimpeded along an action-path towards some purposive destination, where you have a right-of-way, the others have a duty not to obstuct your metaphorical movement along the action-path. Of course, this exercise of rights presupposes a mechanism which would balance or regulate the exercise of rights among all the individual members by some sort of social accounting. The minimal responsibility of the liberal state is to act as an institution for the protection of these rights whenever any violation comes to its notice.

Moral Autonomy

Individuals are morally autonomous in the sense that they have no obligation that they have not explicitly or implicitly accepted. Individuls are regarded as being capable of determining for themselves, independent of any traditional authority, obligations which are binding on them by making their own choices based on their conceptions of happiness and goals of life. As such, morally autonomous individuals have only such obligations or duties which are solely a result of their own acts of will. All obligations are, therefore, conceived in terms of the generic notions of the social contract, of which consent, explicit or tacit, agreement, promise and convention are different forms. In the liberal view, normal life of individuals is not an integral whole but an aggregate of specific and identifiable obligations. This contractual view of obligations tends to ignore or trivialise all such obligations, however profound they may be, which cannot be brought under contractual terms; e.g., the liberal political and moral theory is generally silent on obligations towards one's family or the community. The liberal believes that he has fulfilled his obligation towards his community if he has not violated its laws.

Classical liberalism viewed human beings as, by nature, solitary and selfish. Human beings are seen as competitive in their struggle for survival and comforts. The view that at bottom all human beings pursue their own individual interests can be found in the writings of Hobbes and Bentham. Hobbes held that the only thing which could move a person to action was thought of his own good. Bentham believed that all human actions were motivated by the desire to aviod pain and gain pleasure. The natural condition of human beings is a state of conflict. The civil society is founded solely on the basis of a social contract among naturally hostile individuals. The political community derives its moral authority solely from the consent of the governed. Thus, liberal politics is a politics of accommodation among natural adversaries who have, through their individual reason, somehow learnt to transform themselves as fellow citizens in their quest for peace, harmony and order. Not all versions of liberalism, however, put forward a doctrine of egoism as found in the writings of Hobbes. Rawls, for example, does not assume that no one is capable of "disinterested" concerns for the welfare of the other. Rawls' theory of justice as fairness assumes the possibility of an impartial consideration of the interests of others as well as oneself. Nevertheless, the individuals, whom Rawls assumes to be planning the hypothetical society as an exemplar of principles of justice, are primarily concerned with maximising their own share of social goods. Thus, they are in competition with each other for such shares as their own individual self-interest, whatever it may mean under the viel of ignorance, is their fundamental concern.

Liberal theorising about justice is based on an atomic picture of individuals and their social relations. In this picture, each person acts according to her own goals, choices and intentions. Quest for well-being or happiness of an individual is characterised in terms of satisfaction of human needs and desires. Satisfaction of desires is not regarded as a means towards an end but as an end-in-itself. Consequently, an unlimited production of goods, both material and cultural, and creation of other services and facilities becomes the prime goal of social life. A legal contractual framework of rights and obligations, granting individuals right to use that they own and to transfer or acquire such rights, is a salient feature of liberal social theory and practice.

The demand for equality comes from or on behalf of the

most disadvantaged sections of society. These include women, oppressed minorities, landless, homeless and the unemployed, slum-dwellers and other marginalised people. They seek equality of opportunity, equality before the law and emancipation from drudgery and subjugation. They struggle for their empowerment by seeking an active participation in restructuring the economic and social relations affecting their lives. This requires redistribution of wealth and incomes, changes in working conditions by assigning a welfare function to the state. Inequalities in wealth are intimately related with inequalities in privilege status, educational opportunities, political influence and power. These disparities in various areas of social life considerably restrict the freedom of the victims of inequalities, undermining their self-respect and making it impossible for them to live a life of satisfaction of their minimal needs. In view of the challenge from these sections to the stability of society, the modern liberal theory faced the issue of reconciling the claims of liberty and equality in their affairs of the liberal political order. Liberalism approaches the issue of social justice out of concern for the equal liberty of citizens. If all citizens are to exercise their rights in practice, governmental interventions may be necessary for a redistribution of social resources and opportunities. In dealing with the conflicting claims of egalitarianism and libertarianism, the issue of redistribution of rights and benefits, privilages and powers has been handled in the liberal tradition at a very abstract level. By defining justice through a process of reasoning which totally abstacts from social particularity, liberal theory does not identify the actual causes of oppression, exploitation, powerlessness which result in the subjugation of different groups or individuals within the same group.

Contrary to the universalistic stand adopted in the liberal political theory, issues concerning justice or injustice cannot be adequately delineated without taking into account the concrete conditions that produce and/or reproduce the relations of privilege and oppression, domination and exploitation, subjugation and victimisation on the basis of gender, class, race, ethnicity or any other systematic social basis. Everyday language usage clearly suggests that 'injustice' is suffered by the victim. A paradigmatic case of injustice arises when something is done to someone which is not his due. Outstanding instances of such injustice will occur either when, in cases of judical murder, an action done with the aim of inflicting harm is directed at a person or persons known to be innocent of any fault, or when, a person known to be guilty of a serious misconduct is allowed to be judicially acquited. Judgement of guilty and innocence cannot be made without taking into account the specific details of the situation in which the actions of a person are being judged. It is important to note that discourse about justice and injustice would lose all its significance if we lose our sensitivity towards the difference between 'guilt' and 'innocence'. We learn to acquire this sensitivity not through context-free abstract principles but by learning to participate in a specific value-recognising and value-preserving practice of our respective communities. In seeking to be universal and independent of actual social structures and situations, rationalist liberal theories of justice create an unbridgeable gulf between the ideal principles and their actual practice. Such theories are the result of the fallacious assumption that it is possible for philosophers to produce the unchanging and universal truth about justice from the nature of reason itself.

Any careful consideration of the subtle and prolonged debates among the various contemporary political philosophers in the Western world would clearly show that whether it is Rawls or Nozick, Sandel or Walzer, MacIntyre or Taylor, they are all trying to reinterpret the shared understanding of the place of principles of distributive justice in the competing ideals of social life already developed within the Western political traditions. Theorising about justice, as they practice it, are attempts to clarify, for the 'democratic' culture to which they belong, political norms and values of thier own institutions and to resolve the apparent contradictions in their beliefs and practices. Their disagreements and resulting contraversies are rooted in the competing ideals of good life and the ways in which these can be pursued or not in contemporary social and political circumstances. Rawls' own recent concession that his theory of justice is relevant only for constitutional democracies would support the context-specific character of such debates. (1993)

The liberal theory has placed an exclusive emphasis on the rights of abstract individuals. In an attempt to carve a clearly marked out space for each individual to exercise his rights without any hindrance, the dominant ethos is that individuals are expected not to meddle with each other. This approach results in negative injunctions such as 'Do not cause suffering' rather than a positive injunction to help others. Such an individual-centric ethos is of an isolationist character and ignores the fact that the human 'self' acquires its identity and has worth solely in and through relationships with others. Human needs and interests, skills and goals do not get formed in a vacuum but in a social context of relationships with other people. Human *need for* relationships cannot be understood as merely instrumental to isolable individual ends. Recognising the essential social character of individual existence, growth and development, communitarian critique of individualism have been offered within the contemporary Western political thinking. The communitarian critique has offered three types of arguments which may called as political, moral and philosophical critiques of individualist liberalism.

Political Critique

In pursuit of private interests, we neglect to cultivate the virtues and responsibilities necessary for becoming citizens of a just society. Far from the liberal imagination of autonomous individuals capable of reasonable self-government, the manipulative information-technologies and impersonal complex bureaucratic procedures turn the members of modern liberal societies into disempowered, indifferent, isolated individuals incapable of struggling against injustice. By absolutising the rights of abstract individuals without paying sufficient attention to the concrete conditions of their real growth and development, liberalism has destroyed responsible and participatory citizenship by undermining civic virtue. It has failed in providing an adequate foundation for a truly democratic community of free and equal citizens. The communitarian critique underlines the need to revive the traditional ideals of citizenship which teach human beings to guide their conduct by the considerations of the common good and not merely their private interests. By extending the domain of justice from the sphere of quantitative distribution of goods, opportunities and services to qualitative aspects of dignified human living, the cultivation of civic virtue may enable human beings to take control of their common life. Instead of living a life of passivity and conformity to the demands of consumerist culture, administered very efficiently by the invisible forces controlling the market, individuals need to come together to rediscover the significance of solidality, care and communion in their lives at an individual and collective level.

Moral Critique

Liberal theory and practice may have helped the Western societies in being liberated from the control of tyrants and priests. But its atomistic view of individuals makes it almost impossible for many people to imagine the genuine bonds of common life with fellow citizens or even with one's family and friends. At an abstract plane, people imagine themselves to be free individuals forgetting that their real lives are embedded in particular communities which constitute, at least in part if not completely, their identities. Individuals have loyalties and duties towards their parents, siblings, children, teachers, students, colleagues, and friends. These duties are not always acquired, as the liberal doctrine of moral autonomy would persuade us to believe, through our free acts as individuals. Only by reviving the practice of adhering to special and general positive duties, restoring the moral authority of the community over the individual, we may be able to restore moral meaning in our lives. Responsibilities linked with various roles would have to be identified and developed context by context because the demands of these roles may not be universal and may be significantly context-dependent. This affirmation of duties and obligations would also contribute towards a check on the erosion of the normative character of social institutions and roles associated with them.

Philosophical Critique

Individualistic liberalism is defective because it rests upon an incoherent view of moral reasoning and the nature of the human self. The quest for a rational polity — founded on universal principles of public good — against which one might measure the practices and principles of any particular community is misguided. Moral ideals are essentially contested because they share, what Pitkin calls, "a tension between purpose and institutionalisation". (Pitkin, 1972) Our value-preserving institutions, and the activities we routinely observe in order to safeguard justice in our society, are oriented towards a goal or ideal standard of what constitutes justice. We may criticise our practices and institutions in terms of this standard or we may try to adopt the standard in conformity with other current institutional practices. The interpaly between these two polarities is the dynamic which produces changes in the rules for correctly describing actions as just or unjust. However, we cannot temper with either the standard or the institutions in a way that would obliterate the distinction between an innocent person and a guilty one. For without that distinction, the word `justice' would cease to have any application. Pursuit of justice, like preservation of other values such as truth, turns on an unspoken bond of trust. This bond is a pre-supposition for articulating any principle or arrangement which aspires to balance the conflicting claims of individuals on goods and services available to them. A just community is not merely a means to the end of distributing and exchanging goods. A just community teaches its members to live and to live as well as possible, learning to respect others so that they may learn to respect themselves. It is through such a learning that we become capable of becoming sensitive to the difference between guilt and innocence, injustice and justice. Recognising the normative character of our social being, we learn to respect our duties without any fear of losing our rights.

References

Johnson, Mark, 1993, *Moral Imagination: Implications of Cognitive Sciences for Ethics*, University of Chicago Press, Chicago.

Manning, D.J., 1976, *Liberalism*, St. Martin Press, New York.

Pitkin, H.F., 1972, *Wittgenstein and Justice: On the Significance of Ludwig Wittgenstein for Social and Political Philosophy*, University of California Press, Berkeley.

Rawls, John., 1993, *Political Liberalism*, The Columbia University Press, New York.

15

Objectivity and Prescriptivism

Jagat Pal

THE purpose of this article is to show that the notion of objectivity has no logical place within the conceptual framework of R.M. Hare's theory of prescriptivism. The criterion of universalisability, advocated by Hare, should not be understood as a criterion of objectivity by which we can judge any value claim whether it is objective or not. According to this view, the criterion of universalisability is a criterion of rationality by which we can judge whether somebody is using a value judgement rationally or not. Hare does not derive the notion of rationality from the notion of objectivity as the objectivists do. He clearly maintains the distinction between them. Instead of deriving the notion of rationality from the notion of objectivity, he in fact derives it from the notion of universalisability with which he does not conceptually connect the notion of objectivity. On his view, neither the notion of objectivity logically rests on the notion of universalisability, nor does the notion of rationality logically rest on the notion of objectivity. For him, value judgements are bereft of objectivity; but they are not bereft of rationality. This, he shows by isolating the notion of rationality from the notion of objectivity and connecting it with the notion of universalisability. To establish all these points, let me first begin with the notion of objectivity that is a crucial notion in deciding of the issue.

When we reflect upon the notion of objectivity, we find that it is used in two different senses: non-derivative and derivative. When we use it in non-derivative sense, we generally use it in the context of physical things, events, and facts. We do not use it in the context of mental things, events and facts. When we characterise physical things, events and facts as objective in contrast to mental things, events and facts, we do it on the basis of their external, independent ontological existence. We do not derive their objectivity from the other sources. The ground of their objectivity lies in their nature and outside of them. But when we use the notion of objectivity in derivative sense, we generally use it in the context of judgements and statements. When we characterise them as objective, we do it on the basis of their corresponding objective facts about which they make assertions. We do not call them that they are objective on their account. We call them that they are objective on the account of their corresponding objective facts different from them. We derive their objectivity from the process by which we test them. The testing process of their objectivity always requires evaluation against some external independent touchstone relevant to them on the basis of observation. The postulate of external independent existence of reality, thus, constitutes the logical touchstone for objectivity against which we test the objectivity of our judgements and statements. And this testing process we conduct on the basis of inter-subjective observation. We derive their objectivity from both the sources. Since the notion of objectivity conceptually involves the notions of externality, independency, and inter-subjectivity, for any claim to be objective; it must not only make an assertion about the existence of some external independent reality, but also must be capable of being tested and re-tested against that reality about which the claim in question makes an assertion on the basis of observation.

What would happen suppose if we define the notion of objectivity in terms of the mere act of assertibility. The result, I think, is quite obvious. We will have to admit that subjective judgements are objective in character because they do make assertions about the facts, that is, mental facts. We cannot say that subjective judgements don't make assertions about any fact because to say so would amount to mean saying that they are not descriptions of subjective facts which they are. So just on the basis of the mere act of assertibility we cannot maintain any distinction between subjective and objective judgements because both these judgements possess the characteristic of assertibility. Not only this, if we define the notion of objectivity in terms of the mere act of assertibility, we will have to admit that a judgement is objective even when what it asserts is not there at all which is absurd to admit. Because the absence of an objective fact abnegates the objectivity of a judgement. The objectivity of judgement always hangs on the objectivity of fact. It is because of this reason I claim that the act of assertibility does not by itself render the objectivity of any judgement even though it is essentially required for any judgement to be objective.

This has been rightly stated by H.I. Brown (1987: vi, 202) This means that if any claim makes no assertion about any objective reality, the claim cannot be said to be objective at all. In fact, in such cases the question of the testability of the objectivity of a claim does not arise at all. It arises only when we logically assume that the claim in question makes an assertion about some objective fact. But here we must not forget to note that the mere act of assertibility does not by itself render the objectivity of any claim although it is essentially required for any claim to be objective. For any claim to be objective, it is also essentially required, besides the act of assertibility, that the asserted fact must have its own external independent ontological existence outside the domain of our mind. Then and then alone we can legitimately talk about the objectivity of that claim, otherwise not. So if any claim makes an assertion about the existence of some mental event, we cannot test that claim on an objective basis. Nonetheless, it is perfectly quite possible that a claim may involve a reference to some objective fact and yet that fact may not be accessible to our mind. Under such situation we cannot logically say that the claim in question possesses the characteristic of objectivity just on the basis of the mere act of referring without knowing of its referent. We can say with the authenticity about any claim that it is objective only when we know that there is a corresponding objective fact against it, otherwise, not. That is the reason why for any claim to be objective, it must not only make an assertion about the existence of some external independent existence of reality, but also must be capable of being tested and retested against that reality about which the claim in question makes an assertion on the basis of observation. It is on the basis of this ground we characterise a claim as subjective when it makes an assertion about the existence of a mental event no matter whether it exists in the mind of the author of the claim or in the mind of other person or persons. Not only this, we also do not characterise a claim as objective when it is coloured by the author's emotions, feelings and preferences, etc. So when we make the distinction between subjective and objective, we do it on the basis of the conditions of externality, independency and inter-subjectivity. When any claim satisfies these logical conditions, we say that it is an objective claim; and when it does not satisfy them, we say that it is a subjective claim. The conditions of externality, independency and inter-subjectivity, thus, constitute the logical grounds for our objectivity on the basis of which we evaluate and test the objectivity of any claim.

The above stated conception of objectivity might give this impression, because of the involvement of the notion of inter-subjectivity, that it leads to the path of relativism. But this is not so for the simple reason that because the notion of objectivity in the derived sense does not include in its meaning only the notion of inter-subjectivity. Besides the notion of inter-subjectivity, it also includes in its meaning the notion of independency and externality which conjointly excludes the notion of relativity from its meaning. In other words, the notion of objectivity in the derived sense leads to the path of relativism only when we identify it with the notion of inter-subjectivity. And to identify it with the notion of inter-subjectivity is to commit a self-contradictory mistake because the notion of objectivity, besides the notion of inter-subjectivity, contains in it the notions of independency and externality. But when we take the notion of objectivity in its full sense, that is, in the sense of independency, externality and inter-subjectivity, it does not lead to any path of relativism. Because the factors of independency and externality always abnegate presence of relativism. It is because of this reason by calling any judgement objective in the derived sense one is not logically committed to any relativistic position.

What I have said can also be seen to stand valid from another angle. The criterion of inter-subjectivity is an epistemic criterion by which we test the objectivity of any judgement. But it does not by itself constitute any ontological ground for objectivity. It is not a touch stone against which we can judge whether a judgement is objective or not. The objectivity of judgement is always derived from its corresponding objective fact which is thought to have its own independent ontological existence of our mind. And this is tested by conducting inter-subjective observations. That is the reason why when we call any judgement objective in the derived sense, we do not logically commit ourselves to any relativistic position because its objectivity always hangs on the peg of objective fact.

R.M. Hare also subscribes to this view. (1989: 33) When we judge Hare's theory of value judgements with the above account of objectivity, we find that they cannot logically be characterised as objective judgements. The reason why we cannot logically characterise them as objective is that because they do not meet the logical requirements of our objectivity. For any judgement, as we have seen, to be objective, it must not only make an assertion about the existence of some objective fact, but also must be capable of being tested and retested against that fact about which it makes an assertion on the basis of observation. All these conditions, since Hare's value judgements do not satisfy, we cannot logically characterise them that they have the logical property of objectivity. This fact is quite evident from Hare's conception of value language itself. (1981: 83-6) For Hare, the language of value judgements is not one sort of descriptive language. We do not use it to describe any fact natural or non-natural that could be said to exist independently of our mind, and can function as a logical ground for the objectivity of a value judgement. Since value judgements, on his view, are not used to make assertions about the existence of objective facts, the question of their being objective simply does not arise at all. It would arise only when we assume that value judgements do make objective claims when we use them and this Hare's theory of value language does not assume. From this point of view, we can say very well that Hare's theory of value language is characteristically different from the theories of objective naturalism and non-naturalism. Because, according to these theories, value judgements, when they are used, they are used to make objective claims. For the objective naturalists and the non-naturalists, value words are on par with descriptive words like 'red' and 'green'. They do not differ in their logical behaviour. They belong to the same class. Like descriptive words, value words too, for them, are used to refer to qualities. For the naturalists, value words are natural qualities referring words. While for the non-naturalist's value words are non-natural quality referring words. Nonetheless, both these theories do agree on the logic of value words that it does not differ from the descriptive words. They do have the same logical status, that is, both are used to refer to some qualities. Hare does not accept this account of value words. He rejects both the theories of naturalism and non-naturalism and advocates the view that the logic of value words is characteristically different from the logic of descriptive words.(1965: 7 ff.) For him, value words are not quality referring words at all. Their logical role does not consist in the act of referring to some qualities. Value language for him is one sort of prescriptive language in the sense that when we use it, we use it to guide choices and actions directly or indirectly either of our own or other person of the society. (1952: 127) But we do not use it to state any fact natural or non-natural which could be said to be existing independently of our mind. In other words, since in his view to guide is not to describe any fact, we cannot say that value judgements are descriptive in character on his account. If it were the case, Hare would not have called himself as non-descriptivist. (1989: 33) Since value judgements, he says, are not descriptive of facts, we cannot logically characterise them to be objective judgements. They fall out of the domain of our objectivity.

Whatever I have said so far also logically follows from Hare's dichotomy of fact and value which we can see in the following way. According to Hare's dichotomy of fact and value, no value judgement can be logically derived from the judgements of facts alone because there always remains a logical gap between factual and value judgements. Since, the notion of objectivity is conceptually connected with the notions of externality and independency of the fact and the notion of fact is conceptually different from the notion of value, we cannot logically derive the objectivity of value from the objectivity of fact for the simple reason, that there always remains a logical gap between them. If it were the case, it would have been possible, Hare argues, to settle value disputes on an objective ground. Because, even if we agree on the fact, we may not agree on the value aspects of that fact. This is logically quite possible. It is because of this reason Hare claims that we cannot logically settle value disputes on an objective ground. But to say this, he says, is not to say that value disputes cannot be settled on a rational ground. On this view, this is possible because value disputes do not fall out side the domain of rationality, but only of objectivity. Hare establishes this by dissociating the notion of rationality from the notion of objectivity, and connecting it with the notion of universalisability. (1989: 34-5; 41-4) The thesis of universalisability is a logical thesis. It rests on the notion of consistence.

However, from the foregoing discussions we should not infer that Hare must be a subjectivist because he is not an objectivist. Hare is neither a subjectivist nor an objectivist; he is a prescriptivist. He does not believe in the view that value judgements are descriptions of subjective facts, that is, they are used to describe the states of mind and dispositions of people. He is not an objectivist because he does not believe in the view that value judgements are descriptions of objective facts, other than the states of mind and dispositions of people. Value judgements, he says, are not fact stating judgements at all. Not only this, he is also not an emotivist either since he does not believe in the view that value language is of the expressions of feeling, emotion and preferences. If it were the case, he would not have advocated the thesis of universalisability which goes against the thesis guiding. They always entail imperatives which descriptive judgements do not. (1952: 178) Hare's view of value language, thus, is not only different from the views of the naturalists and the non-naturalists but also is different from the views of the subjectivists and the emotivists. Hare, no doubt, does agree with both the subjectivists and the emotivists on the point that value judgements are bereft of objectivity. But he does not agree with them that value judgements are also bereft of rationality. From this point of view, we can say that he agrees with both the objective naturalists and non-naturalists. Like them, he too believes that value discourse is rational and hence does not fall out side the domain of rationality. But he does not agree with them that rationality logically rests on the ground of objectivity. For him, the notion of rationality logically rests on the notion of universalisability. He does not entertain the view that value judgements are descriptive of facts. In his view, value judgments are neither descriptive of subjective facts nor objective facts of any kind. That is why he says about himself that:

> I am a rare bird who is neither an objectivist nor a subjectivist, but believes that both these schools of thought are vitiated by the same error, namely descriptivism. (1989: 31-2)

It is obvious that if Hare were a subjectivist or an objectivist, he would not have said that he is neither a subjectivist nor an objectivist. This statement of his goes against Professor Shaida's view (1989: 277), that Hare is an emotivist who believes in the intersubjective truths of moral judgments. Hare doesn't, either fully or partially, take any side with either objectivism or subjectivism.

No doubt, Hare maintains the view that value judgements do contain in them both descriptive and prescriptive elements. But on the basis of this ground we cannot characterise him that he is a descriptivist when he himself rejects the thesis of descriptivism and calls himself a non-descriptivist who does not believe either in the thesis of subjectivism or in the thesis of objectivism. Hare strongly believes in the dichotomy of fact and value. For him, even though value judgements involve descriptive elements in them, we cannot justify the objectivity of value judgements on the basis of them, because there always remains a logical gap between them. Descriptive elements constitute, in his view, only the criterion of application for a value judgement. But they do not constitute the whole meaning of a value judgement. If we attempt to justify the objectivity of a value judgement on the basis of its descriptive contents, we would be committing a logical fallacy on his view. This is so because, we would be identifying in that case the notion of value with the notion of fact and to muddle them is to commit a logical error since they are conceptually different.

One might argue that although Hare has said that he is not an objectivist still he is an objectivist since he believes in the thesis of the universalisability of a value judgement and the notion of universalisability contains the notion of objectivity in its meaning. Professor Shaida also subscribes to this view. (1979: 454) But I think this line of argument does not have any logical strength. Because Hare's notion of universalisability, in fact, doesn't conceptually involve in its meaning the notion of objectivity in the explained sense of the term. This we can see from Hare's notion of unversalisability itself. For him, to say that value judgements are universalisable is to say that value judgements commit the user to make similar judgements about anything which is alike the subject of the original judgement in the relevant respects. (1989: 44) And to say this is not tantamount to saying that anyone who uses them commits himself to the view that they refer to some objective facts; nor does it tantamount to saying that what he universalises is also subscribed to or recognised by all other individuals of the society who come under its jurisdiction. It is logically quite possible that what we universalise may or may not be subscribed to or recognised by other individuals of the society to which we belong.

Because of these reasons we cannot logically deduce the objectivity of any value judgement from its feature of universalizability. If we do it, Hare would say that we are committing a logical mistake. But from this, it does not follow, Hare would consider that value judgements are bereft of rationality. What follows from this, he would say is that they are bereft of objectivity. According to him, value judgements always rest on universal prescriptive principles. They are deductively derived from them and universal prescriptive principles ultimately rest on our decision (1989: 30) and not on any subjective or objective fact. But to say this is not to say that they are relative to our mind. It only means that it is we who ultimately accept or reject them on the basis of our thinking. If it were the case, Hare would not have propounded the thesis of universalisability because the thesis of universalisability goes against the thesis of relativity. When we universalise our judgements on the basis of the descriptive elements involved in them, he says, we do it on the basis of logic and not on the basis of fact. And to uphold this view is not to admit that the notion of rationality logically rests on the notion of the objectivity of fact. The value judgements no doubt are supervenient in character. But from this it does also not logically follow, that the objectivity of fact entails the objectivity of value judgement. If it were the case, Hare would not have maintained the dichotomy between fact and value, which he does.

There could be another line of argument. One might say on the ground that the very fact that Hare believes in the view that value judgements do contradict one another, that he is an objectivist, because no two value judgements can contradict one another if they are not objective judgements. There is no doubt that Hare believes in this view that we cannot logically say that one and the same action is both right and wrong; one of them has to be wrong. But from this it does not follow that they are objective judgements; nor does it follow that there pre-exits, pre-determined principle or rule which determines which of them is wrong. I might think for long time and then decide which one is wrong. And when I do it, I do it no doubt on the basis of some principle or rule which I accept on my own. But to say this is not to say that the principle or the rule which I use in deciding the rightness or the wrongness of any contradictory value judgement exists independently of my decision. What in fact follows from the two contradictory value judgements is this that both of them cannot be true or false at the same time on the basis of logic; one or the other has to be false. And to say this is not to say that they are objective. Above all, when any two value judgments contradict one another, they contradict because of their *phrastic* elements and the *phrastic* elements according to Hare, do not determine by themselves the rightness or the wrongness of any contradictory judgments in the question. What is determined by the *phrastic* element of a value judgment is its criterion of application and the criterion of application of a value judgment does not entail its rightness or wrongness. The notion of universalisability Hare connects with the *phrastic* and not with the *neustic* elements of a value judgment. Since on his view there always remains a logical gap between the *phrastic* and the *neustic* elements of a value judgment, we cannot logically justify the objectivity of value judgment on the basis of its *phrastic* elements alone. If we do it, Hare would say we are muddling the notion of value with the notion of fact which are conceptually different and distinct.

To conclude, for Hare the feature of universalisability of ethical judgments does include in its meaning rationally justified nature of ethical judgements. But it does not include in its meaning objectively justified nature of ethical judgements. And to say this is not to say that ethical judgements for him are subjective. Hare doesn't uphold the thesis of subjectivism. For him, ethical judgements do not abnegate presence of rationality and impartiality. What they abnegate is presence of feelings, emotions and objectivity in the sense explained above.

References

Brown, H.I., 1987, *Observation and Objectivity*, Oxford University Press, New York.

Hare, R.M., 1952, *The Language of Morals*, Clarendon Press, Oxford,

———, 1965, *Freedom and Reason*, Oxford University Press, Oxford.

———, .1981, *Moral Thinking: Its Levels, Method, and Point,* Clarenden Press, Oxford.

———, 1989, *Essays in Ethical Theory*, Clarendon Press, Oxford.

Shaida, S. A., 1979, "Nature of Ethical Statements", *Indian Philosophical Quarterly*, vol. VI, No.3.

———, 1989, "Moral Scepticism", *Indian Philosophical Quarterly,* Vol. XVI, No. 3.

16

Can Values be Derived from Facts?

Vanlalnghak

I

In most of the recent ethical theories the focal point of interest has been the alleged unbridgable gap between 'fact' and 'value' or between natural and non-natural terms. Since the publication of Moore's *Principia Ethica* (1903), this problem has become the crucial test for the validity of an ethical theory. Any theory that tried to bypass this limitation has been summarily dismissed either as fallacious or devoid of any significance. Similarly, mutually exclusive stands are taken on the question of the subjectivity and objectivity of moral terms and moral judgements. Theories are generally divided on this issue. The followers of Moore and the protagonists of Logical Positivism have taken unambiguous position in favour of objectivism or subjectivism. Consequently, the relevance of ethical theory to actual performance of actions has been given the least importance. But, in my opinion, a more balanced, conciliatory and synthetic stand on all these points is required for any ethical theory to do justice to the complex nature of moral issues. The question of whether value statements are derivable from factual statements needs to be critically re-examined.

Naturalistic Fallacy

Facts and values seem to be clearly different from one another in that the former is expressed in natural terms and the latter in non-natural terms. Any attempt to identify a natural term with a non-natural term, according to Moore and his followers, commits the 'Naturalisitic Fallacy'.

> It may be true that all things which are good are also something else. . . . But far too many philosophers have thought that when they named those other properties . . . they were actually defining good; that these properties, in fact, were simply not 'other', but absolutely and entirely the same with goodness. This view I propose to call the 'naturalistic fallacy'. (Moore, 1903: 10)

The naturalistic fallacy is, summarily, the fallacy of 'identity', namely the fallacy of identifying one thing with something else, which it is not. Whenever a value-statement is deduced from a factual-statement, the fallacy of identifying a factual-term with a value-term (which is not a factual-term) is committed. This is the naturaslistic fallacy in question.

The question whether the 'naturalistic fallacy' is a fallacy is debatable, for Moore and his followers didn't clarify what is meant by 'natural' and 'non-natural' terms. Hence it is desirable to examine the issue in fresh lights, especially with a view to finding out whether there is some *non-logical* yet quite legitimately meaningful way of deriving values from facts. For, it may be that the alleged fact-value impasse is caused by an unwarranted logical structure of deductive inference — the demand of deductive link between the factual premises and the value conclusion.

II

Ethical Naturalism and Ethical Rationalism

In general, ethical philosophers are divided into two groups: Ethical Naturalism and Ethical Rationalism. Debate between them in the eighteenth century centred on the question: Is ethics a matter of feeling or reason? In the twentieth century greater attention has been paid to the logical features of moral judgements. The old debate continues but it has taken on a new form.

The rationalist theory takes value to be a kind of fact, not a fact known by the experience of sense in feeling, but the fact known by rational understanding. The fact that having your arm amputated is painful is something that we get to know by experience. The fact that pain is bad is, according to the rationalist, something that we get to know by rational understanding. Let us accept, for the sake of the argument, that the proposition 'pain is bad' states a fact. When we have accepted this proposition, we want to conclude that if pain is bad, we ought not to cause pain, and we ought to remove pain when we are able to. But how can we infer that we ought to perform some action from the fact that something is such and such? The inference would be fallacious because it would introduce a term into the conclusion that is not contained in the premises. Compare these two simple syllogisms:

1. All philosophers are crackpots.
   Socrates is a philosopher.
   Therefore, Socrates is a crackpot.

2. All philosophers are crackpots.
   Socrates is a philosopher.
   Therefore, Socrates is a snub-nosed.

In the first syllogism, which is logically valid (although one might doubt the truth of the first premise, and so of the conclusion), both the subject and the predicate of the conclusion are terms which enter also into the premises. In the second syllogism, however, the predicate of the conclusion introduces a term 'snub-nosed' that is not included in either of the premises. This syllogism is therefore logically invalid, although the conclusion happens to be true. Now the same sort of fallacy occurs in an inference in which the copula 'is' (or 'are') in the premises is followed by the different types of copula 'ought' in the conclusion. For example:

> All pain is (or all painful states are) bad.
> Starvation is painful.
> Therefore, starvation ought to be alleviated.

It would have been a valid inference if the conclusion were 'starvation is bad', but to say that something is good or bad is not the same as saying that it ought to be produced or ought to be removed. In implying that *Y* is not the case, or is not a fact now, we are talking about the possibility or the urgency of making something to be the case, to be a fact. And if we say that *Y* ought to be removed, we are talking about the possibility of making the existing fact cease to be one. A call to action cannot be simply a logical consequence of statements of fact.

Prescriptivism

This line of thought leads to a different sort of theory known as prescriptivism (Hare, 1950), which concentrates on the practical character of the language of values. To say, 'You ought to go to bed' is not exactly a command, but it approaches a command. It is an advice, a recommendation, an urging. Value judgements are not statements of what is the case. Nor are they simply expressions of what the speaker feels. They are extortion to the hearer, intended to affect action. The older theories, both subjectivist and straightforward rationalist, compared value-judgements with statements of facts. The expressive theory compares value-judgements with exclamations. The prescriptive theory compares value judgements with commands.

So far as the word 'ought' is concerned, prescriptivism seems plausible enough and is indeed nothing new. Kant, a rationalist of the eighteenth century, talked about moral judgements of 'ought' as 'imperative'; he distinguished between the 'categorical imperative' of morality and the 'hypothetical imperative' of prudence and of skill.

The prescriptive theory, as put forward by Hare, also makes

ample provision for the rational character of moral prescriptions. Hare, again reviving a key element of Kant's theory of ethics has emphasised a feature of universality that, in his view, characterises all moral judgements containing the word 'ought'. Such a moral judgement differs from a command proper, he says precisely because it can be universalised. A command is normally addressed to a particular person or group and applies only to a particular situation. A moral prescription goes further, although it may say directly that a particular person is obliged to do this or that, it implies that anyone or everyone, in an exactly similar situation, would likewise be obliged.

What is implied by Hare is that the acceptance of a moral ought-statement implies being obliged to do what is stated, but this doesn't mean that "moral ought-statements" are derived from "factual-statements". The task we set before us remains unresolved, that is, "Can value be derived from fact?" Perhaps, in the strict, deductive logical sense of inference, 'value' cannot be inferred from 'facts'. This has been recognised by most ethical theories including Kant.

Kant's View on Deduction of Rights from Facts

Kant makes an observation concerning the alleged deduction of 'right' from 'facts' in a relatively unknown passage which occurs in the beginning of the second chapter of 'Transcendental Analytic' in the *Critique of Pure Reason* when he observes:

> Teachers of jurisprudence, when speaking of rights and claims, distinguish in a cause the question of right (*quid juris*) from the question of fact (*quid facti*), and while they demand proof of both, they give to the proof of the former, which goes to establish right or claim in law, the name of Deduction. Now we make use of great number of empirical conceptions without opposition from any one; and consider ourselves, even without any attempt at deduction, justified in attaching to them a sense, and a supposititious signification, because we have always experience at hand to demonstrate their objective reality.

> There exist also, however, usurped conceptions, such as fortune, fate, which circulate with almost universal indulgence, and yet are occasionally challenged by the question, *quid juris*? In such cases, we have great difficulty in discovering any deduction for these terms, in as much as we cannot produce any manifest ground of right, either from experience or from reason, on which the claim to employ them can be founded.
> (Kant, 1934: 85-6)

What Kant denies is not that we use words like 'ought' or 'right' on the strength of certain facts, but that there is a deduction or inferential movement from facts to obligation or rightness. What is a perplexity to Kant is the alleged deduction from the one to the other. This perplexity can only be removed if we get rid of 'deduction' or inference (in strict logical sense) and connect the two in some other way.

III

R.B. Perry's Definition of Value

It seems that R.B. Perry exemplifies this other way when he tries to connect 'value' with 'interest'. In ordinary parlance 'interest' belongs to the category of natural terms and 'value' belongs to that of non-natural terms. Perry proposes to define value in terms of interest. He writes:

> According to the definition of value here proposed a thing — anything — has value, or is valuable, in the original and generic sense when it is the object of an interest — any interest. Or, whatever is object of interest is *ipso facto* valuable. (Perry 1954: 2-3)

This means that the definition of value has been rendered in terms of 'interests.' Perry writes:

> Interest is a train of events determined by expectation of its outcome. Or, a thing is an object of interest when

> its being expected induces actions looking to its realisation or non-realisation. Thus peace is an object of interest when acts believed to be conducive to peace, or preventive of peace, are performed on that account, or when events are selected or rejected because peace is expected of them. (Perry 1954: 3)

Thus the word 'interest' points to attitudes for and against, or what are sometimes called motor-effective attitudes. It is a name for a certain class of acts or states that have the common characteristic of being for and against.

Perry's attempted definition of value in terms of 'interests' should not be understood in the strict logical sense of definition according to which there invariably is the relation or synonymity between the two. In that strict logical sense every statement of a definition becomes a tautology and, hence, insignificant. But for Perry, the definitional statement in question is very significant. In *General Theory of Value* (1926) he clearly says that definitional statement is the 'fundamental synthetic judgement of value'. He also takes it as 'the criterion of judging value.' (Chapters XX-XXII) It is not Perry's intention to claim that to assert that a thing has value when it is an object of an interest. Rather it is to assert a denotational identity between 'value' and 'interest.' The language of the proposed definition is quite clear on this.

One may, however, object that Perry's use of the word 'definition' in this context is misleading. This may be so. But what is more important is to understand the real import of his contention. This brings us to the question whether interest is a purely naturalistic concept. In common parlance interest obviously imply attention, concern or advantage. This feature of interest comes out more clearly in certain derivatives from interest, for example, 'interested' and 'interesting'. Perry indicated the peculiar role and functions of interest in our motor-affective-life when he says that a thing is an object of interest when its being expected induces actions looking to its realisation or non-realisation. When we expect the occurrence or non-occurrence of something or when such expectations induce corresponding actions, the element of import, significance or concern get attached to interest as its features. In one of the sense of 'interest' it comes very close to profit, benefit or advantage. Thus, to insist upon the so-called 'naturalistic' or purely factual nature of interest is to misunderstand the meaning or use of the term 'interest.' Like 'desire' interest (at least in the generic sense in which Perry is initially interested and in the context of which he proposes his 'definition' of 'value' and 'interest') is also obviously a value-impregnated concept.

Value is Real and Existence

Now let us come to the main point, that is, how can values be said to be placed within reality or existence? By relating value with interest, Perry obviously wants to find the locus of value within the motor-effective-life of human beings. Value is not used by Perry in the sense in which it is used in religion or ideology, where divorcing value from the domain of fact is an essential characteristic of value consciousness. Perry seems first to suggest that the cognition of value is possible through the perception or discovery of some interest either in oneself or in others. And then, he tries to suggest that interest function as the criterion of value. Perry says:

> In discussing the definition of value, we shall be dealing constantly with the motor-effective life; that is to say, with interest, desire, feeling, will and all their family of states, acts and attitudes. (1926: 27)

And he then hastens to add that interest is the term that comprehensively embraces all that is characteristic of this strain in life and mind.

Viewed in this perspective, the apparent dichotomy of fact and value presupposes a certain scientific view of the world within which the world is purely value-neutral. But when values enter on the scene, they do so only because there are sentient being or beings with rational consciousness for whom things are valuable. On the other, the values, essentially are related to objects, events or situation which are said to be valuable when they have any actual or possible effect on human beings. At the same time, it is also essential to note that value always refers to some objective characteristics of objects. The question of reality and existence of value cannot be properly answered without considering both these aspects embedded in our concept of value. If values are invariably related to or refer to or reveal certain features and aspects of objects, they are very much real — at least in the sense in which the significance of a thing can be called real.

One may object here that what is real is the feature (characteristic or the set of features/characteristics) that are termed valuable, but not the value itself. But this would be true if the relation between value and objects (or their features) were contingent. What is contingent is the relation between value and a particular object. In other words, it is not necessary for any specific thing to be valuable. But it is necessary that in order to be valuable there must always be something without which the term value has no application. Apart from informing us about certain objective characteristics or features of certain object, values themselves become objectively real as features of objects which are themselves real. Moreover, as Philipa Foot in her article 'Moral Beliefs' (1958) has pointed out that there are certain properties or characteristics which are referred to in and through terms which are both descriptive and evaluative at the same time, e.g., 'dangerous', 'cruel', 'kind', 'notorious' and a host of similar words which have their natural (depending on the nature of man) and associates and cognates.

Looking from another point of view, if values are relates to desires, wants, wishes, or wills of human beings and values arise only within this framework, values are as real human desires, wants and wills. We can even say that values, apart from being 'subjective' in the Kantian sense, are the objective co-relates of our psychological attitudes and states.

Perry in his moral theory emphasises the question "What

ought I to do?" rather than "What is good?". Since to claim that action or states of affairs are good is to have reason to act positively; this kind of reason is implied by harmonious happiness. Perry holds that harmonious happiness is the first principle of ethics upon which all other moral conceptions depend. Perry writes:

> When men differ as to the specific application of moral opinion it is to the standard of harmonious happiness that they look for common ground. And it is by this standard that men criticise and justify their major social institutions. (1954: 135)

Since the harmonious happiness is the very good ground of peaceful co-existence or social harmony, it is (in principle) in some sense harmonious with the interest of all persons. And in the event of disagreement about moral issues, one has to fall back upon the notion of harmonious happiness in order to find out satisfactory answers to various moral problems. Harmonious happiness supplies the criterion in terms of which moral solutions can be determined. This is done only when the conflicting parties are brought into agreement, or only when they are prepared to positively co-operate with one another.

IV

Fact-Value Connection

As it has been earlier maintained, in the strict logical sense of inference, 'value' cannot be inferred from 'facts' as they are not conceptually homogeneous. Nevertheless, there is a sense in which these two concepts can be related. Let us consider the performatory aspects of the speech acts. The performatory aspect is neither simply reducible to some 'is-propositions' nor to 'ought-propositions'. What we call performatory aspect of the speech depends upon the context, situation, human desires, needs, his understanding and so many variables. Reference to 'want' or 'desire' is perhaps the most important feature which may facilitate the movement from 'is' to 'ought' or 'fact' to 'value'. The factual content of want or desire apart, what can actually influence our will and action in a moral context would be evaluative of the want or desire itself. May be, the evaluative element is already contained in the very process of wanting or desiring.

One can indeed say in the strict logical sense a deduction from 'is' to 'ought' or 'fact' to 'value' is not possible. But since morality is not mere logic, there is in fact a passage from 'is' to 'ought' or 'fact' to 'value' because matter of facts are not entirely irrelevant to morals. Moral judgements are not passed on the basis of certain facts. The transition from 'is' to 'ought', 'fact' to 'value' is made by arguments concerning matter of fact, and man's purposes, desires, aspirations, wants, sentiments, etc. It is in the light of these various factors that a new way of bridging the gap between fact and value can perhaps be conceived.

Fact-value or is-ought statements are indeed of a different logical order and in employing them we have to pass frequently from one order relations and concepts to a different order of relations and concepts. But though this distinction can be maintained at purely logical plain, it is generally neither possible nor fruitful to over emphasise it in ordinary language and ordinary life, the purpose of which the former subserves. Morality and moral-judgements are essentially related to our practical life and to our nature as a whole. Hence, any theory which doesn't do full justice to this intimate relationship does prove pointless, misguiding and may be termed, as is called the 'Vulgar System of Morality'. Moral judgements are indeed neither self-evident propositions nor mere factual ones. They operate different levels and use concepts of different orders. Thus even if we implicitly can endorse the logical distinction presupposed in Moore's argument, we cannot really engage in normative moral discourse with the watertight compartmentalisation of terms into the exclusive categories of the factual and the evaluative. Moral reasoning is not a species of deductive reasoning because we can never logically deduce an ethical conclusion from non-ethical (factual) statements. But at the same time it appears that we do 'infer' a moral statement because there are some facts that is why people feel intrigued when they find that there is an inference without there being any obvious ground for this. Those philosophers who are for inferring an 'ought' from an 'is', 'values' from 'facts' wrongly employed a *tour de force* procedure of presenting a sentence containing a descriptive-cum-evaluative word like 'promising' as merely a descriptive or factual statement. Then showing that one ought to do something can be derived from such a statement. One can also maintain that 'One ought to keep one's promise' analytically follows from the very concept of definition of 'promise'. The 'performative force' of 'I promise' as shown by Austin is also a significant point. Taking this course seems to suggest that 'deduction' presupposes some 'entailment' between the two.

One may, however, look at this problem from a different point of view and give up the presupposition that in ethics there are only deductive inferences. This may enable us to attempt at some different solution of the vexed problem. Moral reasoning is based on a number of institutions and 'self-evident' (i.e., incapable of proof) moral principle which serves as models on the basis of which we do pass moral judgements. It is a case of anological reasoning wherein we pass from some facts to some moral conclusions on the strength of certain similarities between our moral standards and the fact under consideration. In anological reasoning we pass from fact to fact and draw some moral conclusions because of the similarities between an idealised and abstract form of good or right actions or persons and the facts of the case whether a given action or person does possess those features which are contained in the former. Our moral standards do arise as a result of idealisation and example of living persons. The difference between 'is' and 'ought', 'fact' and 'value' is a difference between concrete and abstract, particular and universal, individual and general and these belong to two different 'categories' or logical types. Hence, no deduction from the former to the latter without committing the "naturalistic fallacy" or the "category mistake". But we can indeed pass from the one to the other noting the criteria of good and features of obligation in the fact on which value is to be imposed. For some, the connecting link has been desires and sentiments.

References

Foot, Philipa, 1958, 'Moral Beliefs', in *Proceedings of Aristotelian Society,* Vol. 59, pp. 83-104.

Hare, R.M., 1950, *Language of Morals*, Clarendon Press, Oxford.

Kant, Immanual, 1934, *Critique of Pure Reason*, tr. by J.M.D. Meikle John, Guernsey Press, London.

Moore, G.E., 1903, *Principia Ethica*, Cambridge University Press, Cambridge.

Perry, R.B., 1926, *General Theory of Value*, Longmans, New York.

———, 1954, *Realm of Value*, Harvard University Press, Cambridge.

17

Lebenswelt and the Welter of Values
Towards an Overview of Phenomenology of Values

V.T. Sebastian

PHENOMENOLOGY of values, as it has appeared within the contemporary phenomenological movement, is an inchoate discipline, labouring to articulate its own methods and subject-matter. It is said to be an uncharted philosophical terrain concealing significant autochthonous issues that deserve to be mapped. This article attempts to explain:

i) that in keeping with phenomenological notions of intentionality, *Lebenswelt* and existential surpassing, value is not something 'here' as a subjective modification of the mind, but something "over there", not over there in itself, but over there in its-place, relative to a context of significance;

ii) that value is a whole of meaning that is positively or negatively required in its place within a life-world context;

iii) that which is prior in the realm of values, is not any sort of formal absolute but an individual meaning's structural possibilities open to life-world context and significance.

Man's life-world includes many realms of experience, such as the ideal, the imaginary, the cultural, social, historical and the World of perception. Each realm is distinct with a peculiar meaning and value structures. In the following pages, we shall attempt to tease out certain important aspects concerning the nature and modes of relatedness of a value situation/experience. Before taking up this task, however, I feel that a few general remarks are in order concerning the philosophical techniques wielded by a phenomenological account of values.

Phenomenology: Subject-Matter and Methods

Phenomenology, of course, is not merely a name for whatever Husserl himself has wrought. Certainly those who stand, wholly or primarily, within his philosophical shadow are no less to be accounted phenomenologists. And, although perhaps with somewhat less appropriateness, we may legitimately agree to deem 'phenomenological' even those philosophies that were developed chronologically prior to Husserl's but nonetheless fall within a certain recognisable dimension of philosophical concern and practise continuous with that of the contemporary phenomenological movement. For example, Kant referred to his pre-critical work as 'phenomenology'. Fichte's thought provided phenomenological inspiration even for Husserl. Hegel's conceptual edifice is profoundly phenomenological. But certainly phenomenology or "protophenomenology" did not begin with Kant. Further, there are reasons to welcome Buddha and the 'old master' Lao-tzu as phenomenologists for their meditative insights regarding the nature of egological 'causality'. St. Augustine's writings are, in part, brilliantly phenomenological. And Plotinus' transformation of meditation into philosophical technique is no less so.

Phenomenology to be truthful to both Husserl's ancestors and his progeny, is specified in terms of two coordinates, its subject-matter and its method. Phenomenology applies itself to "phenomena" and does so through reflection. But disagreement is evident among the practitioners of phenomenology concerning the nature of phenomena and of the reflective method. For Kant, phenomena are generated by the 'noumena' that they occlude. For Husserl, there is nothing of the proto-etiology posited by Kant spanning noumena and phenomena. A phenomenon is rather an object (a thing-in-itself) as it appears. The 'thing itself' is revealed in the appearance of it. For Kant, phenomena are appearances to a deduced transcendental ego, but are not, except in the proto-etiological sense, appearances — of the objects they conceal. In Sartre's vision of the egoless impersonality of consciousness, phenomena, while decidedly *appearances of* are not *appearances to*. And for Husserl, an appearance is necessarily endowed with both genitive and dative references, i.e., *appearances of* and *appearances to*. For Husserl, the reflective method of phenomenology is transcendental, involving a suspension of our natural doxastic positing of the world. For Heidegger, Sartre and Merleau-Ponty, our very being in the world precludes the possibility of a 'complete' reduction.

Although there is no unanimity regarding subject-matter and method among those whom we would classify as phenomenologists, yet they enable us to isolate a certain range of philosophical views as decidedly phenomenological by virtue of the following two distinctions:

1. Philosophies either take phenomena as their subject-matter or they do not;
2. Philosophies are either reflectively achieved or they are not. (Laycock and Hart, 1995) If we apply this suggested alternatives in philosophy to our present interest of the phenomenological account of values, thus is generated the following fourfold schema of permutations in value theory:

   (i) Value theories that take phenomena as their subject-matter and that are reflectively achieved.

   (ii) Value theories that take phenomena as their subject-matter and that are not reflectively achieved.

   (iii) Value theories that do not take phenomena as their subject-matter but that are reflectively achieved.

(iv) Value theories that do not take phenomena as their subject-matter and are not reflectively achieved.

Evidently, value theories falling under category (i) are phenomenological, and value theories falling under category (iv) are not. But categories (ii) and (iii) may well give us pause.

If we expand our conception of the subject-matter of phenomenology to include not only phenomena but also anything essentially connected with phenomena, and our conception of phenomenological method to include eidetic and conceptual techniques which, while pre-supposing reflection, the value schema, thus, generated embraces meanings that have a certain distinctive positive or negative requiredness about the phenomena too. Some such distinctive positive requiredness are a beautiful song, a lovely face, a magnificent sunset, a courageous action, someone we love, a good meal, a valid line of reasoning, etc. Some such distinctive negative requiredness are an approaching hurricane, a garbage-strewn lawn, a cold blooded murder, a hostile act, a fallacious argument, a job poorly done, etc. Meanings such as these (and are value experiences) are characterised by their place in the referential totality of the World. That is to say that the examples that we have cited above seem to possess an essentially self-sufficient external requiredness with internal requiredness that renders them the meaning and the values they are. Values thus, never can be considered solely in terms of their internal requiredness. They are rather co-determined by their everyday life-world context. What is distinctive about values is their status as wholes of meaning required for what they are in their place in the fullness of their life-world dimensionality. The term value here specifies a meaning's external requiredness with a meaning's internal signification.

Value, by the present hermeneutic account, then, is a whole of meaning brought close in the requiredness of its life-world place, so to say, an internal requiredness within its context of external requiredness. The law of requiredness essentially is a law of value. The task before phenomenology is to treat genetic questions regarding the foundations of meaning which constitute the framework of a value experience and the internal meaning. Phenomenology is not ready to stop with the main acceptance of the reality of things but proposes to probe into the roots of objectivity, i.e., into the respective 'essences' constituting the meaning of the objects in view. Be that as it may, it is clear that distinctively phenomenological account of values — in contradistinction to other theories of value — seeks to discover its subject-matter in that web of intuitively articulable necessities in which phenomena are caught and seeks to do so by means of the reductive-eidetic-reconstructive techniques characteristic of phenomenology. Thus, a phenomenology of values could be "investigated on the basis of pure subjectivity with attention directed to essential structures and relations". (Faber, 1967: 185)

Modern Theories of Values

Modern theories of values and indeed many classical ones are psychologically based but they differ from one another in the psychological phenomena they select as the ground of values. The hedonistic theories such as classical utilitarianism select the spectrum of pleasures and pains as the totality of contingent values, positive and negative. Such theories have largely been either displaced or supplemented by two other forms of value theory, the conative and the conceptual. Conative value-theories focus on motivations and attitudes as the indicators or basic determiners of value. One thinks of Plato's conception of eros by which worldly creatures participate to limited degrees and in contingent ways in goodness by virtue of the fact the striving which animates them has as its proper objective the eternal good.

Modern versions of conative value theory, such as R.B. Perry's interest theory (Perry, 1954), are more inclined to emphasise conation as the creator of value than as a response to it. Taking an interest in something makes it to be valuable just because it has become the object of the interest taken in it. The emotivist theories of the positivists, the preference based theories of the economists, and the accounts of freely generated projects of the existentialists are at variants of conative theories of value. Also, there are several conceptualistic and linguistic theories of value. Karl Aschenbrenner (1971) calls attention to a vast array of evaluatively charged words in our ordinary vocabulary such that our social descriptions of friendly, ugly, cruel, efficient, etc. Persons and objects are also at the same time evaluative. Robert S. Hartmann states as his paradigm value judgement '*X* is a good *Y*' interpreted to mean that the object denoted by '*X*' well fulfills the properties of the concept of a '*Y*' that is, the '*X*' is a good specimen of a '*Y*' and well exemplifies the concept. Nicholas Rescher (1969) offers as an interpretation of sociological concepts of value that they are slogans for the rationalisation of action. What is common to all these accounts is that they appear to the human capacity to conceptualise norms by which the world we confront, and we ourselves, are measured. According to these theories, values, at least in their contingent worldly embodiments, are mentally dependent phenomena requiring desires, feelings or conceptualisations.

There are numerous examples of metaphysically grounded distortions of ethical and value-theories in the history of thought. The Platonic form of good is coupled with an ethical elitism in which philosopher king or knowledgeable statesman discern what ought to be and thus direct an obedient populace at large, which is incapable of such insights. Classical Christian theology, on the metaphysical or ontological premises of an everlasting life and a providential rectification of injustice in this life or the next, counselled an acceptance of the temporal powers that was ordained by a God and a patience with injustice suffered. The Hegelian "World Spirit" expressed itself in a *Zeitgeist* controlling the ethical norms of an age from which an individual was powerless to diverge. The existentialist ontologies of freedom offer little purchase for any virtue other than authenticity. The general psycho-centrism of most post-cartesian value theories unduly constructs the range of instrinsic values to qualities and phases or relations to conscious life.

The Question of the Human Subject

After having explained a general theoretical understanding of phenomenology, its subject-matter and method, let us turn our attention toward the question of the 'human subject' in order to bring to fore the issue of the scope of phenomenological inquiry.

It is always an assumption of the phenomenological school that there exists a world of people, whose distinguishing characteristics include the possession of individual conciousness. There exists a world of numerous subjective unities of experience called selves or persons, and persons have, besides organic and other defining characteristics, the paramount defining characteristic of being unities of consciousness. Brentano implies such an ontology of persons when he discusses the concept of self in his prospective psychology. He affirms that a subject, the self, underlies the 'totality of our psychic life' at any given moment. He outlined an ontological primacy of a concept of person in his works. This shift to anthropomorphic, man-centred ontology, as developed by later writers, is a defining feature of the phenomenological school.

Persons are held to be intentional entities in as much as they can think and do what they want. In this formulation of phenomenology, intentionality involves the concepts of thought and action. To attribute intentionality to an entity means attributing thought and action to it. Thus a person is an entity which can formulate plans, project and purposes concerning the future and which can act to implement them.

These considerations suggest that phenomenological description has nothing to do with the mere registration of empirical matters of fact, nor does it involve the framing of empirical generalisations. But it has something to do with the phenomenological ontology of the human subject. Phenomenologically the human subject is an experiencing subject who knows, experiences and realises his value situations. This principium of knowledge and existence, we wish to suggest, is the basis of a phenomenological inquiry into a value-theory; that is to say that the human subject may be given a special ontological standing as a subject who grounds the experiences of himself and realises values in his situations. The domain of values is centred around the human beings and their conduct. There are no value realisations which are context-free and man-free. Now when phenomenology contends that "true morality is the embodied morality" (Merleau-Ponty, 1963: 8) it gives importance to values as always context dependent. It does not advocate the conception of values in the sense of categorical imperative of Kant which says that 'Moral Law' holds true whatever the case or situation may be. (Kant, 1952: 8) To the question "What is good?" Kant's disciples answered "Good is what you ought to do". The concept of duty was thus the root of their whole ethical system. But if man is a creature who can in principle act rightly but will not in practice easily do so, then a series of consequences are bound to follow. Man cannot then be a unitary being; he must have two warring natures — one sensible, the other, supersensible; there must be a phenomenal and noumenal man. It will confront man as someone independent of his experiences. In other words, the ethical teachings of the Kantian school was an abstract and formal doctrine of 'duty' and not a concrete and material catalogue of values.

The above contention suggest that the question of the realisation of values be brought within the conditions of the human subject and his *Lebenswelt* — Life World. Consequently, the phenomenological treatment of values is indebted to the concrete realities of the human subject and his social experience in the *Lebenswelt*.

Lebenswelt **and the Human Subject**

From the Husserlian point of view, the notion of life-world and whatever it comprises pertain to perceptual consciousness in both its orignal and derivative moods. It is understood by Husserl strictly as the 'human' world, i.e., as a sphere characterised by its specific spritual and cultural character; it is the human world of human experience as interpreted by man which is continuously in the process of becoming in the course of history. As early as 1913, Husserl in *Ideen Zu Einer Reinen Phenomenologie und Phenomenologischen Philosophie* designated a descriptive and analytical study of the world of common experience or as it has come to be denoted in the terminology of his later writings the 'Life-world' (*Lebenswelt*) as an urgent desideratum. What is meant is, the world as encountered in everyday life and given in direct and immediate experience, especially perceptual experience and its derivatives such as memory, expectation and the like, independently of, and prior to scientific interpretation. Man's *Lebenswelt* includes many realms of experience, such as the ideal, the imaginery, the cultural and the historical as well as the world of perception. Each realm is distinct with a peculiar meaning and value structure of its own.

The human subject exists in the world means that he is involved in it. Thus, to approach the study of values means considering man in the full concreteness of his existence in the life-world. That is to say that following existentialism and philosophical anthropology, we are led to consider consciousness and its sets; acts through which the life-world presents itself to us and is interpreted in the sense it has for the socio-historical group to which we belong and conceive of ourselves as mundant existent. (Husserl, 1941:8) Acts of consciousness are in play in our conduct, doings, involvements, value judgements, perception, commitments, hopes, wishes, fears, actions, projects and so on.

Human existence, taken in full concretness, further comprises a socio-historical aspect. Man is born into a certain cultural group whose language he speaks and whose interpretation of and outlook upon the world has been conveyed to him, and is accepted by him as a matter of course. He lives in a certain society at a given period of its history. In this society, he occupies a certain place, either assigned to him by birth as in a class society of rigid social stratification, or defined by his profession, his function, his wealth, influence, etc. What is in question is not social or historical facts and the connections between them as they are but as they appear to and enter the consciousness of those whose historical and social conditions they define and determine and who are involved in that situation. A world is thus recognised, known and realised in terms of a host of meanings through which the things of the world are discriminated and characterised all in a pre-scientific way. (Husserl, 1960: 38)

The life-world as understood above, is a horizon of meaning which in some particular version, is always found with men. It includes all the persons, events and things which we do or can encounter. In other words, the life-world is that world in which, from the first constitutive level, that of passive genesis, meanings are thematised and predicatively expressed by higher level activity (active genesis), so that the world pre-predicatively grasped at the first level, becomes known as the world of our everyday perceptual experience. This world of meaning encompassed all that we can know by feeling, imagination, etc. What lies beyond this world of objects is a reference to what transcends our experiences in the widest sense of this word. Any person, event or thing in the world presupposes this background of meaning and value-realisation.

Thus, our awareness of the horizon of meaning and the differences in it enter into everything that we do and say and enable us to consider them as isolated islands. But this is a mistaken view of what is known as relativism. It arises from a failure to understand the perspectival character of human awareness. I can never see or grasp, for example, the whole of the table for me, except in a partial perspective from the left or right, from above or below. But this does not mean that I cannot see the whole table in this way. I look at the table from the above and in front, I can see the bottom of a rear leg, and also the table top that keeps me from being the rest. In this and other ways, each perspective leads beyond itself of other parts that it sees itself not to see. Hence, a single perspective remains open to other perspectives revealing other parts of the object without interference. Thus, in and through a partial perspective or through a number of perspectives, I can grasp the style and pattern of the whole. This is the case with the human world of meaning too. We must recognise that there is no world in itself apart from our human versions.

The above line of argument obviates the necessity to consider that value is something. We are 'at', something that we are not, non-mental meaning "over there" in the life-world. Values are requiredness in their place, not merely ideas inside our heads. What is important in the realm of value, then, is not any sort of formal absolute, but an individual meaning's structural necessity. Nevertheless, values are seen to cluster together in terms of the particularity of their life-world place as use values or as person, knowledge or morality values.

We have stated earlier that a certain distinctive positive or negative requiredness renders value realisation and accordingly the law of requiredness essentially is a law of value. In other words, the life-world and the manifold experiences constitute a demand made upon the human subject. This demand character of value, as something to be accepted, welcomed, appreciated and respected because of something's positive requiredness. Or something to be loathed, pushed away, neglected and looked down upon because of something's negative requiredness. A thing of beauty for example, already is experienced in its very positive requiredness, as a meaning to be accepted for the meaning it is. Meaning, in its very origin as a positive value, is experienced in the "to be accepted" of its beauty, or goodness or truth or usefulness. To experience something's positive requiredness, then, is to find ourselves already obliged to it. All in all, then demand character is inherent in the experience of value for what it first is as a meaning, that is as a positive or negative life-world requiredness. This demand character of value, in Kohler's words, is 'the ought' or requiredness in it. The experience of a value is therefore is the experience of the "to be accepted" of its "ought to be" (positive requiredness), the experience of the "to be rejected" of its "ought not to be" (negative requiredness).

Life-World as a Value-World

The value-world is primarily the world of everyday life as lived appreciated and interpreted by the human subject carrying on the cognitive and emotive traffic of daily life. Although an object exhibits its "value" as a property pertaining to it and essentially determining and defining it, an abstraction if possible by means of which value-realisation comes to be regarded. By virtue of this abstraction, an "absent presence" is made as the presence that is absent. In this regard, Husserl's emphasis of the cultural sense of an instrument, a utensil, a world of art, is applicable to the value-realisation of objects. In other words, the phenomenological account of value takes its departure from the thing world and traverses the same path as the abstraction indicated above. In a word, value experience may be regarded essentially toward making the object 'meaningful' as they appear in perceptual experience. A painting of slum, for example, has not only a shape and colour, but also perceived as something 'good' or 'bad'. It means that our perception reveals a structure which gives perceptual objects their value-significance. We are confronted with our value-world which is our life-world, a world of objects and events apperceived, apprehended and interpreted in a specific way.

The above contention suggests that, phenomenological account of values, has its inception in the reflective conversion of consciousness, estabilishing a dimension of intuitive access to pre-reflective act-life when human subject is accessible through the phenomenological technique which is intimately connected with reflection. In a similar characterisation, it may be said that the phenomenological account of values is an experience of a value situation as positively or negatively related to the human subject in the life-world. But the things and events encountered in the life-world are not adequately and completely characterised, when they are described only in terms of their primary and secondary qualities. The chair has not only a certain shape and colour, but is also perceived as something to sit in. Things present themselves as suitable and serviceable for certain purposes; in a word, with reference to actions to be performed or performable upon them. Hence, the things and events perceived present themselves as defined by the purpose they serve, the use that can be made of them, the manner in which they are to be handled and so on, briefly, as determined by schemes of apprehension and evaluation. In a phenomenological theory of ethics, value-reference, therefore, is a self-evident fact of experience and phenomenologically nothing is 'revealed' as a value which is not itself a consciousness. It is disclosed through a description of consciousness in its lived intersubjectivity.

The Life-World as a Social and Cultural World

The human subject is born into a world of others, in a world of people which contribute the social reality for men living within it. This world is from the outset not merely physical but a socio-historical and cultural one also. The world of my daily life — my *lebenswelt* — is by no means strictly a private world, but is an inter-subjective one shared with my fellow men, experienced and interpreted by others, in brief, it is a world common to a "we". Thus, the human subject finds himself always within an historically given world which is a social world, so to say, the world 'belongs' not only for me but also for my fellow-men. These fellow-men are elements of my situations as I am of theirs and experience a common world in the same dimensions and directions of space and time and particularly an historically given world of nature, society and culture. Sociality is, therefore, constituted by communicative acts in which the 'I' turns to the 'thou' and 'I' and 'thou' joined together as 'we' become the originator of all social and cultural values. These are the possibilities that must be present if the world is to be meaningful as an inter-subjective world.

Moreover, the life-world does not consist of mere corporeal objects. On the contrary, it is a world interpreted, apperceived and apprehended in a specific way; in a word, it is a cultual world, more precisely, the cultural world of certain socio-historical group. Husserl emphasised that the cultural sense of an instrument, an utensil, a machine, a work of art, a literary piece, is not externally attached to or associated as a corporeal thing. Rather, its meaning is incorporated and impressed in the cultural object and thus proves to be a character proper to that object. To be sure, all cultural objects are defined by the meaning embodied and embedded in them refer to mental life of a certain society or certain culture, their plans, project, designs, intentions and aspirations.

A cultural object experienced in an especially pronounced manner when we realise the meaning of that object recognising in it something special and ideal. It requires, however, adopting a point of view beyond one's one life-world situations. A value-experience of a cultural object, therefore, does not occur in isolation. It is always in context having retrospective as well as prospective connections and being inter-woven with the social and the cultural setting in the community in which we live. It is this context of experience which provides the basis for our value-judgements such as 'better' or 'best' which is meaningful to our experiences. All in all, then, some cultural objects are beautiful because its meaning is especially pure and excellent. They are meanings that are outstanding in the beauty of their goodness. A scientific theory can be beautiful. A well-designed Buddha statue is beautiful; a truly moral action is beautiful; a Raj Kapoor movie is beautiful; a Mohd. Raffi music can be *beautifully harrowing*. All such meanings, to name a few, are intrinsically beautiful for just what they are in their place, in their life-world social context. Thus, the social world into which the human subject is born and within which his historical life unfolds is experienced by him as a tight knit web of values, its social relationships, systems of signs and symbols with their particular meaning structures.

Conclusion

Whereas many psychologies reduce value to a psychological process, phenomenology insists that value is a realisation, an experience, in a life-world context. Although value, thus, is no subjective opinion, neither does phenomenology find it to be an objective something ready-made and in-itself. Value in every case is in a circular relationship with the human subject realising it, so to say, value is an event of meaning for the human subject. The search for goodness as value, is a structural invariant of events of the presence of meaning. As Farber says:

> . . . the more complete description of value-experience is based upon the description of existence and its conditions, which include existent individuals and social groups in a historical process of development (1967: 195)

The present article has attempted to disclose and delineate the phenomenology of value rooted in human existence in its life-world experiences. Experience, as understood here, may not be taken in the sense of mental factuality corresponding to which physical facts and mental events can be discovered. The objects of value-realisation we contend, are not the actual contents of mind but the ideal objectivities to which consciousness is related by the way of its referentiality. (Mohanty, 1970: 219) Toward that objective, the present article has taken the liberty of approaching the issue from a critical-creative perspective with a view to the promotion of continuing scholarship in phenomenology and the advancement of reflection which my teacher, well-wisher and mentor, Prof. S.A. Shaida always stood for.

References

Aschenbrenner, Karl, 1971, *The Concepts of Value: Foundations of Value Theory,* Dordrecht, Holland, D. Reidel Publishing Company.

Farber, Marvin, 1967, *Phenomenology and Existence: Toward a Philosophy within Nature,* New York, Harper Row Publishers.

Husserl, Edmund, 1960, *Cartesian Meditations: An Introduction to Phenomenology*, tr. by Dorion Cairns, New York, Humanities Press.

Husserl, Edmund, 1962, *Ideas: General Introduction to Pure Phenomenology,*

Tr. by W.B. Boyce Gibson, New York, Macmillan, Pub. by N.Y. Collier (ed.).

Kant, Immanuel. 1952, *Fundamental Principles of the Metaphysics of Morals,* tr. by Thomas Kingsmill Abbott, in The Great Books of the Western World, *Encyclopaedia Britannica*, Inc.

Laycock, Steven W., and James G. Hart (eds.), 1995, *Essays in Phenomenological Theology*, New York, State University of New York Press.

Merleau-Ponty, Maurice, 1962, *Phenomenology of Perception,* tr. by C. Smith, London, Routledge and Kegan Paul.

———, 1963, *The Structure of Behaviour,* tr. by Alden Fisher, Boston, Beacon Press.

Mohanty, J.N., 1970, *Edmund Husserl's Theory of Meaning,* Hague, Martinus Nijhoff.

Perry, R.B., 1954, *Realms of Value*, Cambridge, Harvard University Press.

Rescher, Nicholas, 1969, *Introduction to Value Theory,* New Jersey, Prentice-Hall Inc.

18

Justice as a State of the Soul
Plato and Gandhi

*Pabitrakumar Roy**

I

ETHICAL theories can be distinguished into two types: *act-centred* and *agent-centred*. Act-centred theories focus on the notion of the *right act*.[1] The primary question is taken to be: 'What is the right thing to do?' The primary notions are taken to be those of *duty*, *moral obligation*, and *morally ought*. Act-centred theories are the kind most familiar in recent traditions of moral philosophy.

---

* I have always admired Prof. Shaida for his kindness, courtesy and civility, and no less for his scholarship and insights. When his paper on "Moral Scepticism" was published in the *Indian Philosophical Quarterly*, I asked my students to study it. I cherish the memory of the days I spent with him at Pune. The memory is, however, coloured with gloom as our host, Prof. Sundara Rajan is no more there. This is a grief which Prof. Shaida and I am left to share.

I am very happy indeed to join Prof. Shaida's friends, admirers and pupils in felicitating him on his completing a long and remarkable academic innings. I offer him snatches of my ideas on a problem of ethics, a subject that has been dear to him. May Prof. Shaida enjoy his return to the pavilion.

1. The distinction between act-centred and agent-centred theories of ethics, a propose of my article, is a reflex of conceptual imagination. What has concerned me is a *possibility*, not that there are ethical theories of such descriptions.

We identify the good person as the person who can be relied on to do his or her duty, and their virtue lies in conscientiousness about doing the right thing.

In contrast, an agent-centred theory focuses on the notion of the *good agent* or *good person*. It takes the primary question to be: 'What kind of person should I be?', 'What is the good life?', 'What kind of life is admirable?', We find out what is the right thing to do, by asking what kind of thing the good person would do in these circumstances. The right thing to do is identified as the kind of thing done by the good person. For the agent-centred approach the primary notions are not duty and obligation, but *goodness* and *virtue*.

Of course, most moral theories have something to say about both actions and agents. What distinguishes the two kinds is not that the one deals only with acts and the other only with agents, but that for the one sort acts come first as moral subjects, and for the other, agents do. Both Kantians and Utilitarians are act-centred theorists, because, although they talk about moral appraisal of agents, they make it secondary to that of the appraisal of acts, which is thought of as the fundamental moral problem.

II

It is possible to undertake a comparative study of the ethical ideas of Plato and Gandhi in the light of the distinction between act-centred and agent-centred moral theories. It may seem curious, and even exasperating to club Plato and Gandhi together. But they come closer to each other in their business with the soul of man. Both of them were utopian thinkers, irrespective of their mode or manner of thinking. The Biblical saying that simple, or for that matter, just souls issue from the hands of God apply equally to Plato's and Gandhi's account of justice. Their engagement with the problem of justice does bring them together.

In Books 2-4 of *Republic*, through the extended soul-state

comparison, Plato has concentrated on the individual's soul, goodness and virtues. The whole development of the argument summed up vividly at 443C-D, where Plato says that the sphere of justice is not external actions but a person's own inward self. He has made the just *agent* primary, and not the questions of just *actions* (which dominated the concerns of Thrasymachus, and of Glaucon and Adeimantus). This is something which Gandhi (1948, 1959) could be said to have argued.

We have to have some *independent* way of saying what the good person is like. It is unhelpful to say that just acts are those the just person would do, if all you can say then about the just person is that he or she is the kind of person who would be likely to do just acts. You have to be able to say independently what kind of person the just person is. Plato's moral psychology, his theory of the parts and virtues of the soul, aims to do precisely this. Plato says, and Gandhi would agree, that the just person is the person who is integrated and morally healthy. This account, for both Plato and Gandhi, makes, no appeal at all to just acts. They tell us what a just person is without reference to the way he or she acts. Both Plato and Gandhi hold that education of character, not academic accomplishments, will produce good people. Their doing so is an important basis for the claim that justice is something that is worth having for the agent. Gandhi was fond of quoting the scripture: "For what shall it profit a man if he shall gain the whole world, and lose his own soul?"

If just acts are to be specified by what the just agent will do, then we cannot lay down *in advance* what acts are just acts. If we take seriously the primacy of being a certain kind of person, we cannot draw up lists of rules and maxims which will settle the question of which actions are just ones.

III

Will doing actions recognised as ordinarily just make you a Platonically or Gandhian just agent? The answer is no, for the question of what acts are ordinarily just, what duties one ought to do, is settled by society's moral consensus quite apart from considerations of what makes an agent just in the Platonic or Gandhian sense. Not only does following society's rules not suffice to make you a just agent, it might turn you into a cramped and rigid person incapable of the freely chosen and reasoned life, which is the just person's life. Not only does conscientiousness not guarantee virtue, it might fail to promote virtue, since, as both Plato and Gandhi have argued, virtue requires harmony and appropriate development of all the soul's parts. That might well be stunted by a rigid adherence to rules and or strong sense of their importance.

Does commonplace judgements of what is ordinarily just are met by Platonic or Gandhian justice? Ordinary justice provides only a constraint, rather of a negative kind at that. Common beliefs are appealed to only on what is absolutely ruled out, not on what is either permissible or desirable. Our intuitions may be trusted only on clear-cut cases of what the just person will *never* do. Ordinary justice not only is not sufficient for Platonic or Gândhian justice, but is not a good positive guide to its content, only a negative check on what the boundaries are.

Does not the agent-centred moral theory of the Platonic or Gandhian sort accept the implication that there is *no* kind of action that is ruled out from being the right thing to do if the good person sees reason to do it? Stoic moral theory is of this kind. There must be some constraints on an agent-centred theory. We would feel lost if we thought that any kind of act what-so-ever could be the right thing to do. Is it really unjust to commit adultery merely because most people feel strongly that it is?

Neither Plato nor Gandhi give us help here. They seem to assume that this example of moral consensus is all right to build on. But we may interpret their intentions in the following way: The idea which they do use, though not articulate, is this: when constructing a moral theory about justice we have to begin with the most central judgements of the moral consensus we have grown up to accept; otherwise we have no ground to stand on. This may have been the insight at the back of Kant in proposing the "Transition from the common rational knowledge of morality to the philosophical." Morality is a matter of practical judgement, and a moral theory is not an abstract structure like a mathematical proof. It rests on people's acceptance of certain beliefs and their capacity to live with certain attitudes. Of course, a moral theory must not only end up justifying what we thought already, only that it cannot ignore our most central intuitions on important topics.

IV

If Plato and Gandhi suggest an agent-centred moral theory of justice, such that the virtue is something worth having for itself, then what are we to say about its consequences? The notion of happiness does not figure in Plato's argument in the Book 4. Justice is not presented as a state which is good to have because it will produce happiness, but simply as a state which is good to have. And Gandhi extolled the capacity to take infinite pain in course of *satyāgraha*. Plato images justice as health. Health is worth having whether you are happy or not. Justice brings happiness, but its value to the agent is not dependent on this. This claim may sound strange to us, because we are used to utilitarian theories that try to make plausible the idea that people cannot but want their own happiness as their only final end, so that any condition, like that of being just, can only be of value to the agent as a means to his or her happiness. It is hard to shake off the assumption that if something is valuable to an agent, the agent's happiness must have something to do with it.

Is it possible to show that justice is valuable to the agent without reference to the agent's happiness? The problem vexed Kant no less, and he solved it with a kind of religio-metaphysical hypothesis, namely, eschew the desire for happiness, but be such as to deserve happiness. I consider it to be a significant insight. It is less familiar to us from modern moral theories than from certain religions, which claim that it is valuable for an agent, not just to do or believe certain things, but to be a certain kind of person, and that this state has a kind of value, spiritual value, which is independent of agent's happiness. Such a state may be supposed to have good consequences, for example, in leading to eternal happiness, but these consequences are not what makes the state valuable to the agent. Gandhi would happily endorse this defense of justice. For him, as per the Hindu tradition, the word *nyāya* is equivocal, it connotes both justice and truth. The Vedic *ṛta* is at once the cosmic moral order and constitutive of the nature of things.

V

For neither Plato nor Gandhi, happiness figures as it might do for a consequentialist. They argue that justice is worth having both because it is in itself a worthwhile condition and because it makes the agent happy. But the happiness brought by being just is not something that merely *happens* to be a consequence of justice, and could as well be sought some other way. It is a natural consequence of being just, something one can only get from actually being just and not any other way. Although the just person's happiness is something over and above the state of being just, still it is happiness that can only come to the just, not to the unjust.

The utilitarian thesis that our reason for being just lies in the fact that this will maximise happiness does not give us a reliable reason. Thrasymachus would argue that more happiness would be forthcoming if justice were not respected. If happiness is something that can equally be attained by just and unjust alike, then the thesis that someone seeking happiness has reason to be just is bound to be a fragile one. Plato and Gandhi would say that happiness is something you get if you are just, but you only get it by really being just. This is a profound way of looking at ethics. It matters, and matters morally, what kind of person you are. We are persuaded to change the ways we think of justice, and of happiness, in significant respects. The appeal to justice is in no way egoistic. For to want justice merely as a means to one's own well-being is precisely not to see it as desirable in itself. Only the person who wants justice for itself is just, and therefore made happy by being just.

We should not assimilate either Plato or Gandhi to a deontological claim that justice is good, and worth having, whether it makes me happy or not. Nor can we assimilate them to a consequentialist claim that justice is good only to the extent that it produces happiness. Neither Plato nor Gandhi think of pleasure or happiness as utilitarians do, that is, definable independently of how it is attained, something attainable by any kind of life, noble or degraded. The just person's happiness can be got only by being just, with no short cut. Experiments with truth is, therefore, called for. But in appealing to happiness Plato and Gandhi don't make an appeal to egoism or selfishness. Happiness may be a prize for the just, but it is no incentive to anyone who does not want to be just anyway. No immoral or potentially immoral reason for being moral is admissible.

VI

The agent-centred view is at once both interesting and fruitful as a moral answer to the question 'why should I be just?' Justice is an intelligible demand on human nature, something in accordance with our potentialities for living creative and fulfilling lives, and not spent following an arbitrary set of external demands. At this point, ethics and economics meet in Gandhi.

Why justice should make me respect the rights of others? Why should the best realisation of my nature be constrained by the needs and interests of other people also trying to realise their own individual projects as best they can? Justice demands that the agent refrain from taking from others more than is his or her due. In other words, justice implies the treatment of others.

If we remember that there is a concept of reason in Gandhi, then we shall see that for him, as it has been for Plato, that the demands of justice are recognised by a reason and that they apply impersonally to all. Justice is part of the bringing about of what is unqualified and completely good, not good in a way relative to particular interests. Perhaps I should qualify the term 'impersonal' to suit Gandhi's case. One way of looking at the needs and interests of others is from a point of view which Gandhi would call *impartial* view-point. Plato would, of course, retain the term 'impersonal'. However, the impartial viewpoint is one from which one can see other people as agents with desires, interests and attainments like one's own. One has a special relation to one's own desires, and commitments that cannot be transferred to others; but one can view others as having the same relation to their interests as one has to one's own. One regards the other person not just as a means to one's ends, or a nuisance to one's plan, but as a person like oneself. Gandhi's equivalence of Truth, non-violence and love rules out certain attitudes and actions, like manipulating or exploitating others, for one knows that they will feel what one would feel oneself; one sees that there is no difference of kind between, say, his doing it to me, and my doing it to him. To make this point Gandhi quotes from the *Mahābhārata:*

> *na tat pareṣu kurbuīt jnānanna priyamātmana*A

The impartial viewpoint excludes selfishness — my giving myself and my concerns a special place and treating others as means to what I do; it makes me regard myself as just one among others. But it is not impersonal in the sense of abstracting altogether from the personal view-point. I am an individual, with particular concerns and so are others; their concerns matter to them just as mine do to me. Regarding others, I can still regard them as persons impartially, with all the attitudes to their concerns that I have to mine.

VII

Since the notion of 'love' in the Christian sense of the term is absent in Plato's *Republic*, the Guardians are led to take the impersonal view-point, one which demands that they abstract from any personal concern at all, for themselves or others. The Guardians identify themselves with their reason, and reject as alien to them any concerns that involve the world of particular actions and people. Their final moral perspective is inhuman, because from it no real importance attaches to anything personal either in their own case or in that of others. Political proposals advanced from such a view-point are expectedly ruthless. When the Guardians advance to philosophical understanding, it is said to be an advance from darkness into light. But the light bleaches out of the picture all the agent's concerns that made justice appealing, all the facts of human nature that the definition of justice as psychic harmony built on.

Gandhi's version of justice in terms of his impartial[2] agent-centred moral philosophy, by contrast, has no such implications. It allows us to see people as individual sources of value, without measuring or judging this value on a single scale. The impartial viewpoint stresses what is common between people, the facts about human nature that makes each person one among others, without losing awareness of the personal dimension: the fact that each person has a special viewpoint on his or her life, one that cannot justifiably be ignored or replaced by a calculations of his or her contribution to some end or the extent to which he or she embodies rationality. Plato has no real notion of rights as Gandhi has. This is not surprising. Theories of right seem to rely on the impartial viewpoint rather than the impersonal one. They stress that each person has a unique and irreplaceable value, Gandhi's moral argument is that justice needs to be supplemented by some considerations of others, and the best way to do this would be to recommend the adoption of a viewpoint that is impartial, and in accordance with one's theory of human nature. Morality, for Gandhi, requires us to become so alienated from

2. I have sought to substitute the alleged 'impersonality' of the just man by 'impartiality.' The just man remains a person, he does not impersonate himself. It is proper to speak of natural laws as impersonal, moral laws and *impartial.* The figure of impartiality that I have in mind is that of *bodhisattva*, who apercieves ontological void, and fills the moral-field with compassion and love. In moral terminology the concept of void may be taken to imply that the *bodhisattva* does not take the existence of any person, for a special consideration, and yet radiates loving concern for all, and is even prepared to lay down his own life to save any.

our own personal concerns as to regard them with indifference as means to the end of achieving some overall good.

References

Gandhi, M.K., 1948, *Selections from Gandhi*, ed. by N.K. Bose, Ahmedabad, Navjivan Publications.

———, 1959, *All Men are Brothers*, ed. by K. Kripalani, Paris, UNESCO.

Kenny, A., 1973, "Mental Health in Plato's *Republic*" in A. Kenny (ed.), *The Anatomy of the Soul*, Oxford, Oxford University Press.

Plato, 1963, *The Republic*, tr. by J. Adams, Cambridge, Cambridge University Press.

Part IV

ETHICS APPLIED TO RELIGION

19

Religion and Ethics

Asghar Ali Engineer

RELIGION and ethics are integral to each other and yet religion conveys to us less of it than dogmas and rituals. Religion is seem to be a set of meaningless rituals and a few dogmas which are to be followed unquestioningly and unhesitatingly. And it is precisely on this ground that religion comes under attack from rationalists and free thinkers. Before we set out to discuss religion and ethics, I would like to throw some light as to why dogmas and rituals tend to dominate any religion almost without exception? It would be interesting to examine this in some detail.

First of all it should be noted that religion provides humankind with a sense of sacred. Secondly, it gives human life a meaning both here on earth and in metaphysical sense. Thirdly, it provides us with a sense of certainty. This is true not only of developed religions such as Hinduism, Buddhism, Christianity and Islam but also of primitive tribal religions. Religion in this sense has always been a part of human life and psyche. Normally all of us as humans are in search of certainties as nagging doubts always troubles us mentally and make our life less comfortable. It is this search for certainty — though often it may disguise itself as a search for truth — that leads to formulation of dogmas and dogmas once formulated perpetuate themselves as along with uncertainty, human beings resist change. Change induces in us a sense of uncertainty and hence dreaded.

Search for certainty and truth makes it necessary to have faith which becomes another integral component of religion. All of us think — and perhaps rightly so — that there can be no religion without faith — be it faith in some dogma or in truth. This faith becomes a source of great solace to us and it comforts our troubled mind. Without faith life of common human beings would become full of anguish and distress. In fact, in many cases life devoid of faith would be impossible to live. Even mutual relationship would be dogged. Not only this — the very foundation of our society would be shaken.

Here, it is also necessary to point out the distinction between faith and superstition. Often this distinction is not made. Rationalists often mount attack on religion on the grounds that it promotes blind faith and superstition. However, faith is necessary even for the most enlightened person though superstition is a mere product of ignorance. The great rationalists such as Bertrand Russell well understood the distinction between faith and superstition. What Russell attacked was superstition, not faith. Some kind of faith and belief is necessary for our day-to-day existence. William James, who propounded Pragmatist philosophy also stresses importance of belief. James argues that as practical men, we cannot remain in doubt on these issues if we are to survive. We must assume, for instance, that the sort of food which has nourished us in the past will not poison us in the future. Of course some-times we are mistaken and die. But it is exception rather than a rule.

It should also be noted that human knowledge is after all, based on certain postulates. Human knowledge cannot develop without these postulates and belief in these postulates is necessary. Without something like the postulates, we cannot believe in the broad general truth of science, and nobody seriously doubts it. Finally if our belief in the postulates was wrong, the human race wouldn't have survived. Thus, Alan Wood, in his book *Bertrand Russell: The Passionate Skeptic* points out that:

> when we climb a ladder, we assume that its rungs will have enough 'quasi-permanence' not to dissolve suddenly into thin air, if we are wrong, we would fall and break our necks. If we had been mistaken in believing in 'quasi-

> permanence' and induction, the human race would by now have died out and been replaced by other beings with more accurate beliefs about the nature of reality. In fact, our beliefs have probably arisen as a result of biological adaptation to environment; we think that way because the world is made that way.

What I am arguing here is that faith and belief is essential even for development of science and human knowledge. Faith and belief is not integral only to religion as commonly thought; it is essential to very existence of human race. Passionate commitment to any cause, secular or religious, is not possible without profound faith in that cause. Russell was passionately committed to the cause of peace and he opposed war with all the strength at his command. On being asked that he being rationalist and dispassionate thinker why he gets so passionate for the cause of peace (he was arrested during first world war opposing war efforts of his own country), he replied that he exerts himself utmost to understand a phenomenon as objectively as possible but once he is convinced of its truth, he commits to it passionately and stands by it by any cost.

We should also understand that faith and belief are psychological and not merely religious categories. They are more integral to human existence, as pointed out above, than to religion. A non-believer in religion also has her/his set of beliefs and passionately defends them like any religious believer. All those revolutionaries who said no to the existing system believed in another system for establishment of which they made supreme sacrifices. The sentiment to sacrifice one's dearest life is truly religious sentiment and is integral part of ethics.

I would also like to make it clear that I am not defending religious orthodoxy at all. I am only trying to say that faith is essential part of human life and so it is of religion. Secondly, I would also like to point out that faith is as healthy as skepticism. In fact blind faith could be very harmful — in religious as well as secular matters. There cannot be meaningful progress unless there is faith with skepticism — and a healthy blend of the two. One may call it human dilemma, and dilemma it is. There cannot be life without dilemmas. Human being can do neither without faith nor without skepticism. Eric Fromm, a noted psychoanalyst in his book *Psychoanalysis and Religion* puts it this way:

> The question is not *religion* or *not* but *which kind of religion*, whether it is one furthering man's development, the unfolding of his specifically human powers, or one paralysing them. (*emphasis* on the original) (1972: 26)

It is blind faith which mars human development and it is healthy faith which unfolds his powers. A streak of skepticism is always helpful to save one's faith from degenerating into orthodoxy. But there is yet another dilemma which we humans often face. We are always in search of psychological certainties rather than truth. No wonder that today's revolutionaries become tomorrow's conservatives. Even Russian revolutionaries who questioned every prevailing dogma of their time became conservatives in time to come. Thus, Nigel Harris points out in his *Beliefs in Society*,

> that Marxist-Leninism (Marxism-Leninism? in Russia provides an excellent foil, since it is "a group of beliefs which began as radical, profoundly opposed to the existing *status quo*, . . . but ended as [medium for] conservatives. (1968, p. 131)

Further on Harris also points out that:

> Marxism had become less a philosophy of revolutionary action, and rather more a temporal ideological system based upon faith in certain doctrinal postulates, called necessary and natural laws.

Marx himself had detected this tendency. The belief that Marxism was part of a temporal and deterministic science was already emerging in the latter writings of Engels. Further, Marx himself detected the same tendency amongst some of his followers when he declared that he was not a `Marxist'. His work, he said, was only,

> an historical philosophic theory of the *march generale* imposed by fate upon every people, whatever the historic circumstances in which it finds itself.

The founders of all major religions were rebels and revolutionaries of their time. They questioned the prevailing dogmas and orthodoxies as they became hurdles for further human development. They revolutionised moral and ethical concepts and broke through narrow boundaries of established thought system. Be it Buddha or Moses, Jesus or Muhammad, Nanak or Kabir, they relentlessly attacked orthodox traditions of their time and gave a new universalistic outlook, a fresh vision and a revolutionary morality. But now it is a matter of history that soon these religions became part of ruling establishments and lost their revolutionary potential. They were reduced to new orthodoxies not to be questioned, let alone to be challenged. At best a lip service was paid to what were their revolutionary doctrine. Their ethical and moral concepts were de-emphasised by over-emphasising their formal and ritualistic aspects. Their value-systems were pushed to the background and thought systems which were dated were elevated as dogmas eternally valid.

These dogmas served as eternal source of solace as well as certainties in the face of trials and tribulations of life. The priests and ideologists, to serve their interests, further reduced them to mere superstitions to demand total submission. When things degenerated beyond tolerable limits a revolutionary thinker such as Vivekananda had to proclaim:

> I would rather see everyone of you rank atheists than superstitious fools, for the atheist is alive, and you can make something of him. But if superstition enters, the brain is gone, the brain is softening, degradation has siezed upon the life. . . . Mystery-mongering and superstitions are always signs of weakness.
> (1994.Vol. III: 278-9)

We have thrown light on the concept of religion, faith and belief as one cannot think of ethics and morality without understanding their true nature. If a religious faith begins to degenerate, ethics associated with it follows the same trajectory. Objective conditions are never static and religious faith as well as ethics must take cognisance of these changes. It would be necessary to elaborate this point further. There is, in every religion what can be termed as normative and what can be called as contextual. What is normative is transcendental and has eternal validity. The contextual must be seen in the context in which it evolved and not having transcendental validity.

Also, what is loosely termed as religions often doesn't belong to its core values and is confused mixture of primordial experience of its founder, traditions antedating this experience and traditions and institutions which are assimilated later from other regions to which the religion spreads in the course of time. What is termed as religion assumes a very different shape and hardly conforms to the primordial experience or the original vision of its founder. On being closely examined all the major religions like Buddhism, Judaism, Christianity, Islam, Sikhism, etc. will be found to have undergone this transformation. The latter accretions are often referred to as little traditions and its original version as great tradition. Not that little traditions should be rejected they reflect the contextual elements and assimilation of these contextual elements serves useful purpose. It also leads to variety and pluralism of experiences.

It is necessary to understand all these as the concept of ethics also vary from situation and it also has the normative as well as contextual elements. What we term as religion is also assemblage of four different categories. The value-system, the thought-system, the institutional-system and the ritual-system. As far as ethics is concerned it is integral part of value-system of religion but subsequently gets defused over the other three categories as well. But it must be understood by students of ethics and ethical concepts that it forms essential part of the value-system. As a rule the value-system is the core of religion, whereas thought and institutional systems form its flesh and bone, whereas ritual system provides cover to it.

The value-systems which form the bed-rock of ethics, though differ from religion to religion (as the original vision of the founder occurs in certain concrete circumstances) they not only don't conflict with each other but, to the contrary, complement and supplement each other. For example, Hinduism stresses non-violence as a value while Buddhism emphasises compassion. Christianity lays stress on love and Islam brings justice, egalitarianism and brotherhood of mankind into focus. Now it can be seen that all these values compliment and supplement each other. While non-violence cannot be thought of without compassion, one can't think of love without justice and equality of humankind.

Each religion, as pointed out above, came to emphasis one or the other value in certain concrete circumstances, it didn't negate other values but rather implied them. One can hardly argue that there is no place for compassion in Hinduism or for justice in Christianity. Similarly it cannot be argued that there is no place for non-violence in Islam. Or that Hinduism perpetuates inequality. Here I think it would be necessary to throw some detailed light as it is believed, more often than not, that Islam encourages violence and Hinduism inequality. Any assertion to the contrary is either dismissed as untenable or at best looked upon rather unconvincingly. No attempt is made to shift normative from contextual aspects of these injunctions.

I would like to tackle here at some length with Islam and concept of violence as violence cannot form part of any ethical system, much less of any ethical system inspired by religion. There is undoubtedly the concept of Jihad in Islam and it is even considered one of the pillars of Islam. It is also true that early Muslims were forced to fight many battles right under the leadership of the Prophet himself. There are also verses in the *Holy Quran* urging on the Muslims to fight. Also, after the death of the Prophet Muslims were involved in several wars with other imperialist power specially those of Byzantium and Sassanids.

No wonder than even many Muslims, let alone non-Muslims, came to believe that violence forms essential part of Islam and that its spread also was quite violent. Thus, violence came to be integrally associated with Islam.

Here we have to make a distinction between what is normative and what is contextual, what is part of the Quranic ethics and what happened in the then historical context. As far as preaching of religion is concerned the *Quran* makes it abundantly clear that it has to be through persuasive and not coercive means. The *Quran* says,

> Call unto the way of thy *Lord with wisdom and goodly exhortation, and reason with them with what is best way*. (16:125)

The Quran also is not in favour of retaliatory violence though it may be used where inevitable:

> If yea punish, then punish with the like of that wherewith yea were afflicted. *But if yea endure patiently, verily it is better to be patient*. (*emphasis* on both verses added) (16:126)

The *Quran* also says:

> *La ikraha fi al-ddin* (there is no compulsion in religion). It is clearly a matter of inner faith and inner feeling. The opening verses of the second chapter, "The Cow" say, "Who believe in the unseen, and establish worship, and spend of that we have bestowed upon them. And who believe in that which is revealed unto thee (Muhammad) and that which was revealed before thee, and are certain of the hereafter. They are on rightly guided path from their Lord. They are those who will be successful. (23.5)

These verses make it very clear that religion is a matter of inner conviction called *I'man* (which literally means a conviction with which one's heart feels secure, secure from uncertainty and doubt). Such a feeling of being secure can come only through inner conviction in the revealed truth. In these verses the *Quran* stresses some essential ingredients of true faith: belief in the unseen (*ghayb* — future potentialities of Allah's creative power, developmental potentialities yet to be experienced by sense organs), establishing prayer (to purify one's soul, to avoid all that is evil that retards potentialities of human development), spending (on the needy and for eradication of poverty) from what God has bestowed on His servants, to believe in what was revealed to earlier prophets and what is to come in the hereinafter (it implies belief in rewards and punishments for what one has done in one's life here on earth).

It is obvious from these essential ingredients of Islamic faith that coercion in preaching them cannot help at all. Moreover, the *Quran* admits that the truth brought by the prophets earlier is equally valid and Muhammad has come to confirm the truth already revealed to other prophets (*musaddiqan li ma bayna yadayhi*, i.e. confirming the truth already before him). It clearly shows that the prophet of Islam, through the revelation from high on, has come to affirm the truth revealed before him. Islam thus doesn't declare other religions as false but accepts their truth. There was therefore, no question of converting their followers through violent means. The *Quran* even gives option to choose between the truth and falsehood (2: 256). Of course those who choose falsehood and goes with *thought* (one who rejects truth) will pay for it following evil is bound to have evil consequences.

Does *Quran* then not talk about compulsion and violence? It does but not in a sense generally understood. The *Quran* primarily plays the role of warner, not that of coerser. It says God doesn't punish without prior warning. To punish anyone without prior warning would be unjust. "We never punish", the *Quran* declares "until we have sent a messenger" (17:15). Thus, there is compulsion of sorts in punishing but only after due warning. An evil doer must be punished but only after proper warning. As for violence either it can be permitted for establishing justice and removing oppression or for self defence. Violence cannot be permitted for aggression and oppression. "And fight them", the *Quran* declares,

> until there is no more tumult or oppression and there prevails justice and faith in god (2:193)

Further it continues,

> But if they cease, let there be no hostility except to those who practice oppression.

Thus, in the later part of the above verse, defensive nature of violence comes out clearly. "If they cease, let their be no hostility" but this will not apply to tyrants and oppressors. This is more eloquently declared in the following verse in which it says,

> And so for all things prohibited there is the law of equality. If then any one transgresses the prohibition against you transgress ye likewise against him. But fear God, and know that God is with those who restrain themselves. (2:194)

Thus even fighting those who transgress prohibited limits, one must restraint oneself and not commit excesses. Thus excessive violence even against oppressor, according to the *Quran*, is unethical. The oppressed also must restrain themselves in use of violence, if Islamic ethics is to be followed strictly.

The *Quran* doesn't permit aggression and use of violence except when inevitable in the service of just cause. It says,

> Fight in the way of Allah against those who fight against you, *but begin not hostilities.* Lo Allah loveth not aggressors (2:190) (emphasis added).

The following verse seems to be rather offensive and seems to permit aggression. "And slay them", it goes unto say,

> wherever yea find them, *and drive them out of the places whence they drove you out, for persecution is worse than slaughter.* And fight not with them at the inviolable

> place of Worship until they attack you there but if they attack you (there) then slay them such is the reward of disbelievers. (2.191)

In this verse too, which seems more aggressive certain ethical concepts are explicitly stated as the underlined portion of the verse shows. The fight is to drive them out of those places from where early Muslims were driven out unjustly and by way of persecution and it is for this reason the verse states that "persecution is worse than slaughter". This fact that war within certain limits is permitted only for the sake of oppressed and persecuted becomes still more clear from the following verse:

> And why should yea not fight in the cause of God and of those who, being weak, are ill-treated (and oppressed)? Men, women and children who cry is: Our Lord! Rescue us from this town, whose people are oppressors; and raise for us from Thee one who will protect, and raise for us from Thee one who will help. (4:75).

Thus one can see that the *Quran* permits violence within certain ethical framework. For this ethical framework justice and fight against oppression and persecution of the weak is quite central and violence can be permitted to protect the interests of the oppressed.

What happened in Islamic History is of course a different story. No one can deny that unscrupulous rulers often legitimised use of violence for political ends by invoking the slogan of *jihad* (holy war). A close and careful study of life of the Prophet will clearly show that he never used *jihad* for expansionist ends and he strictly adhered to the ethical framework laid down by the *Quran* for use of violence. Even those Quranic injunctions which permit violence must be seen in the then prevailing sociological conditions in Arabia. Fierce tribal warfare was normal state of affairs and Bedouins were ferocious people. Those living in urban areas such as Meccā and Medinā also had inherited these traits. The Quranic revelations couldn't but reflect this societal context though it tried to contain violence in a rigorous ethical framework.

Also, with the Umayyads installed in power, all pre-Islamic traditions which Islam had taught to outlaw, came back with vengeance. All Islamic ethical norms were openly violated and open expansionist wars were undertaken. The Umayyad governor of Iraq Yusuf bin Hajjaj was a great tyrant and the whole Arab world shook with terror at the drop of his name. The Umayyad are also indulged in all conceivable luxury though the Quranic ethics had strongly condemned *Israf* (needless expenditure) and had encouraged *Infaq* (Spending in the way of Allah) instead. Islam discourages consumerism and bans use of gold and silken clothes (items of luxury at that time) for men. An egalitarian order could be built only by declaring consumerism unethical and immoral. Yet even the two early dynasties, not far from the period of the Prophets, i.e., the Umayyads and the Abbasids violated all the ethical norms laid down by Islam. They indulged in expansionist wars and built in highly inegaliterian society. They were far removed from the Quranic ethics in every respect.

As Islam has come to be associated with violence in popular image. Hinduism has been thought to be highly inegaliterian religion which sanctions caste and *varṇa* system. The caste hierarchy is considered to be its weakest point. Such hierarchy naturally violates human dignity widely accepted ethical concepts. Again it is the question of shifting normative from contextual and ideological from empirical. No religion can sanction such undignified behaviour with a large section of humanity as we see in practised Hinduism with the dalits, shudras and atishudras.

The religion which produces Upanishads cannot admit of such treatment to a large section of humanity. About Upanishads Nehru writes in his *Discovery of India.*

> The Upanishads are instincts with a spirit of inquiry, of mental adventure, of a passion for finding out the truth about things. The search for this truth is, of course, not by the objective methods of modern science, yet there is an element of the scientific method in the approach.

> No dogma is allowed to come in the way. (1982: 89)

Rajaji in an eloquent passage writes of the Upanishads:

> The spacious imagination, the majestic sweep of thought, and the almost reckless spirit of exploration with which, urged by the compelling theist for truth, the Upanishad teachers and pupils dig into the open secret of the universe, make this most ancient of the world's holy books still the most modern and most satisfying. (in Iyer, 1991: 12)

If what is stated of the Upanishads above is true, and undoubtedly it is, then it would be hard to explain how such noble enterprise of thought could sanction such contemptuous behaviour with so called shudras? Obviously there is big gap between the ideal and the real. Something went wrong somewhere later which brought about such dismal reality. Many great Hindu thinkers were quite aware of such distortions. This decline and fall is mentioned with distress by Aurobindo:

> If an ancient Indian of the time of Upanishad, of the Buddha, or the latter classical age were to be set down in modern India . . . he would see his race clinging forms and shells and the rags of the past and missing nine-tenths of its nobler meaning . . . he would be amazed by the extent of the mental poverty, the immobility, the static repetition, the cessation of science, the long sterility of art, the comparative feebleness of the creative intuition.— (in Nehru 1982: 96)

Swami Vivekananda was also acutely aware of this degeneration of Hinduism and curse of untouchability which came to be associated with it. He put it very eloquently:

> In the words of the Christians — you cannot serve God and Mammon at the sametime. . . . Throw away everything, even your own salvation, and go and help others. . . . The nation is sinking, the curse of unnumbered

> millions is on our heads — those to whom we have been giving ditch-water to drink when they have been dying of thirst and while the perennial river of water was flowing past, the unnumbered millions whom we have allowed to starve in sight of plenty; the unnumbered millions to whom we have talked of Advaita and whom we have hated with all our strength, . . . Wipe off this blot "Arise and awake." — (in 1994, Vol. III : 431)

Untouchability, a highly unethical practice, should not be seen as an integral part of Hinduism. It has no scriptural sanction. All great reformers of nineteenth century Hinduism felt so. Even an advocate of *Hinduttva* such as Veer Savarkar was of this view. Where from then this untouchability and such contemptuous treatment of shudras? In my humble opinion rather than associating it with sublime Hindu thought, it should be seen in the then social context. It is not normative Hinduism but contextual Hinduism which sanctions such an unethical and condemnable practice. It was sheer arrogance of the conquering race and contemptuous treatment of the vanquished dravidians, a different and internalised form of slavery. As the Quranic ethics of egalitarian was unabashedly violated by the violent Umayyad and Abbasid rulers, the Upanishadic and Vedāntic ethics was violated by arrogant Aryan in their zest for conquest and lust for power.

The founder of Arya Samaj, Swamy Dayananda Saraswati also thought it necessary to re-read the scriptures to fight against many evils which had crept into Hindu society. He gave a fresh vision and new ethics in keeping with the changing times and found sanction for it in the scriptures, in his case Vedas. Raja Rammohun Roy too reinterpreted these scriptures to fight against the practice of *satī* and his advocacy of widow remarriage. Rammohun Roy tried to show that *satī* had no sanction in Vedas. Hinduism acquired rather than invented it. According to him, the earliest Indo-Aryan religious literature contains no direct reference to it. The one verse in the *Ṛgveda* which has been invoked as justification is of doubtful authenticity; Max Müller even declared it to be "perhaps the most flagrant instance of what can be done by an unscrupulous priesthood".

No religion has escaped such later accretion when the social context demanded it. No primordial experience of a founder of any religion can admit of inhuman or inegaliterian practices. Nothing that permits degradation of human person, of however lowly origin, can be taken as truly religious experience. Religious experience is a part of one's inner-most being. One has to descend into one's innermost depths so as to emerge with a religious vision. After having had such an experience one cannot advocate ethics violative of human dignity. Or cannot make pronouncements leading to an unjust society. No wonder that most of the reformers drew abundantly from the original scriptures which contained religious vision of the founder. Like Raja Rammohun Roy and Swami Dayananda, the Muslim reformer like Sir Sayed Ahmad Khan, Nawab Muhsinual Mulk, Maulvi Khuda Bakhsh and others drew from the *Quran* and authentic *hadith* (Prophetic tradition) in support of their reform movements.

Religion Ethics and Social Context

One more dimension must be kept in mind if we have to understand the relationship between religion and ethics. A founder of a religion gives certain norms and a humanistic vision emphasising justice, compassion, love, truthfulness, etc. These values are transcendental and must be understood as such. However, in their application in immediate social context, problems or even contradiction might arise and implementation of religious vision can hardly ignore the immediate social context. The potential of the original vision can better be realised with the passage of time and advancement of knowledge, enlightenment, respect for humanity and progressive outlook.

Many example can be given. The holy *Quran* talks of justice and lays great emphasis on it. It also talks of equality of all human beings and also equality of sexes. As for the former it proclaims,

> O mankind! Lo! We have created you male and female, and have made you nations and tribes that yea may know one another. *Lo! The noblest of you, in the sight of Allah, is the best in conduct.* (*Emphasis* supplied) (49:13)

Thus the only criteria to be most honoured in the sight of Allah is to have best conduct, not any particular nationhood, race, ethnicity or social status. As for the latter (i.e., sexual equality) the *Quran* says,

> and they (women) have rights similar to those (of men) over them in kindness. . . . (2:228)

The concept of equality of all human beings propounded by the *Quran* required that slavery be abolished right away. If the then social structure had not intervened the ultimate potential of this Quranic vision could have been realised immediately, not only slavery but all other distinctions would have been abolished. However, it didn't happen. The Prophet had to permit slavery, however reluctantly though making it clear that it is best not to have slavery. He himself manumitted slaves and made them free. But slavery persisted in Islam for centuries until it was abolished in nineteenth century after spread of progressive knowledge and scientific enlightenment and a new social structure came into existence.

Similarly, despite the *Quran*'s proclamation of equality of sexes, sexual inequality persisted in the Islamic world and it persists even today. When Islam spread to feudal society it could hardly improve her status in view of well entrenched sexual hierarchy in it. However, now one can see the significance of the Quranic vision and its potential for sexual equality. The traditional theologians are still not prepared to accede equal status to women. But the progressive reformers saw the potential of that pronouncement and argued on its basis that sexual equality must be established and she should not be assigned traditional roles. Thus, we can see that the humanistic ethics contained within the original religious vision can be implemented only when society is ripe for it.

The religious community imbibes traditions from the existing social structure which are even contrary to the religious vision but these traditions not only come to stay but they are seen as integral part of religion and traditional intellectual and religious leaders defend them in the name of religion not only as part of their inner conviction but for the interest they acquire in perpetuating those traditions. Be it caste system or be it *satī*, be it child marriage or male superiority, they are sought to be defended as part of religion. A reformer who fights against these well entrenched traditions either has to reject religion and its traditional ethics or has to draw inspiration from the original vision of its founder contained in the scripture and actualise its potential in the changed social context. Atheists and left wing intellectuals resort to former option whereas those who have religious belief to latter option.

Misuse of Religion by Vested Interests

Powerful vested interests, those representing political interests deliberately violate religious ethics to achieve their aim. The traditional intellectuals and theologians at least have some basic convictions and their defence of so-called religious traditions may be based on these inner conviction, at least partly if not wholly, but these vested interests have no such inner convictions at all and they violate religious ethics much more flagrantly and hence are more condemnable. In a backward Indian society where religion more communitarian than individual matter; potential of such unscrupulous exploitation of religion for political interest is much higher than in other societies.

May it be Shah Bano controversy or Ram-Janmabhumi-Babari Masjid controversy, it should be seen in this light. These movements basically launched by politicians serve only political purpose and cannot be construed even as semi-religious movements. However, it is true that they seek to exploit the religious sentiments of unwary people. Such movements, needless to say, are grossly violative of ethics propagated by the concerned religion. Ram-Janmabhumi movement has been launched, like its predecessor the Shah Bano movement, purely for political objective and has nothing to do with devotion to Lord Ram. It is also baseless to claim that it would promote national integration. Nothing can be farther than truth. It has, on the contrary, alienated the minority from the majority community.

Many devout Hindus have pointed out that Lord Ram does not need a grand temple for devotion and Ram being incarnation of Vishnu, doesn't need any specific place for worship. This is aptly evoked by Rabindranath Tagore in *Gitanjali*:

> Leave this chanting and singing and telling of beads! Whom dost thou worship in this lonely dark corner of a temple with doors all shut? Open thine eyes and see thy God is not before thee!
>
> He is where the tiller is tilling the hard ground and where the pathmaker is braking stones. He is with them in sun and shower, and his garment is covered with dust. Put off thy holy mantle and even like come down on the dusty soil.
>
> Come out of thy meditation and live aside thy flowers and thy incense! What harm is there if thy clothes become tattered and stained? Meet him and stand by him in toil and in sweat of thy brow.

What Tagore has said is in keeping with true religious ethics. If one is truly religious, she or he will be more concerned with the poor and the oppressed. The Buddhist tradition also shows more concern with *duḥkha* (Suffering) than with other worldly realities. The prophet of Islam also is reported to have said that feeding a widow and an orphan is more meritorious than thousand nights spent in *'ibādat'*(praying). The *Quran* also says that those who pray but neglect the small needs of fellow human beings are only showing off. This is the core of religious ethics. Devotion and prayer is an outward expression of religiosity which often tends to become hypocrisy.

Ram-Janmabhumi movement being primarily a political movement lacks totally religious ethics of tolerance, non-violence and respect for other religions. The Hindu religious ethics can never approve of demolition of other religious place in order to build its own temple. Much more so when idol-worship is not be all and end all of Hindu religion. It is at best, only one form, among many of its expression and lowest form of expression, according to some. The BJP and VHP also claim that they are true patriots and nationalists, and those who oppose construction of Ram-Janmabhumi are not. Let us listen to Vivekānanda on patriotism. Vivekānanda who was imbued with true spirit of Hinduism says:

> They talk of patriotism, I believe in patriotism, and I also have my own ideal of patriotism. Three things are necessary for great achievements. First, feel from the heart. . . . Feel, therefore, my would-be reformers, my would-be patriots!. . . . Do you feel that millions and millions of the descendants of gods and of sages have become next-door neighbours to brutes?. . . . Does it make you restless? Does it make you sleepless?. . . . That is the first step to become a patriot, the very first step. — (1994, Vol. III : 225-6)

If we judge our politicians on the touch-stone of patriotism given to us by Vivekānanda, all of them will be proved more hypocrites. These politicians who incite innocent people in the name of their faith, are weakest of human beings of among us all. They represent either their own interest or those of their community elite. They are devoid of ordinary human decency much less being true representatives of religious ethics and religious tradition they claim to represent. It is they who have promoted communal hatred and religious bigotry and pushed the country to precipice of communal division and probable disintegration. Whether we believe in religious humanism or atheistic humanism - humanism is our common denominator — we must come together and fight the monster of communalism, it is worst than religious bigotry. It is enemy of sublime religious morality. It is antithetical to humanist ideology and is totally opposed to patriotism.

As we have to fight communalism, we also must fight against religious authoritarianism. In fact religion cannot lead to religious authoritarianism. Religion — if we take it in its real sense — cannot be at ease with authoritarianism. It makes one humane and humble, true servant of God and his creatures. A religious person depends more on his own spiritual powers, his own inner experience than on any external authority. Let us dependent on our potential, our own reason, our own spiritual capacities and harness all our energies to promote good. Religious authoritarianism has sapped all our inner strength, our inner potential for growth, religious dogmas have destroyed our intellectual potential, our powers of sublimation besides making us totally dependent on others, on religious authorities.

A Zen Buddhist, in order to warm himself in a cold night, threw wooden statue of Buddha in fire. Another faithful watching this act was aghast and asked the monk, how can you throw Buddha image into fire? Pat came the reply so that I can revive Buddha within myself.

Let us all revive our own spiritual powers to come out of bondage of all dogmas and be truly human, a true creature of God, true servant of humanity, a seeker after truth and we will be truly religious and perfectly ethical.

References

Fromm, Eric, 1972, *Psychoanalysis and Religion*, London, Bantom Books.

Nigel, Harris, 1968, *Beliefs in Society*, Penguine Books Ltd.

Iyer, Krishna V.R., 1991, *Religion and Politics*, Delhi, Konark Publishers.

Nehru, Jawaharlal, 1982, *Discovery of India*, Delhi, Oxford University Press.

Vivekananda, Swamy, 1994, *The Complete Works of Swamy Vivekananda,* Vols. I to VIII, Calcutta, Advaita Ashram.

20

Reflections on the Diversity of Religious Life*

Syed Vahiduddin

IT is always difficult to describe or analyse the situations or experiences with which we are most familiar. Familiarity breeds ignorance. This is as true of the religious situation as of any other phenomenon of human culture. We are brought up in some religion or other and grow up in an atmosphere which is surcharged with religious emotions. But soon we become aware that the peculiar variety of our religious life is not the only possible one. History shows us a striking diversity of religious outlooks and attitudes. Religious beliefs seem not only to differ but also to exclude one another. Hence, if our first feeling was to identify religion with its historical and factual manifestation in our immediate environment, our encounter with conflicting religious outlooks completely perplexes us.

With reflection doubts begin to prevail. What is religion after all? Is it to be identified with the rites and rituals in which it often expresses itself or with the beliefs about man and his destiny with which it is associated? Religion also seems to be fused with aesthetic activity. Music, dance, painting, architecture, sculpture — in fact there is hardly an aesthetic expression in which religious motives and moments are not involved. Even the words which play such a dominant role in scriptural religions have as much aesthetic as religious

* Originally published in *The Aryan Path*, February, 1971.

significance. Is religious consciousness then nothing but our awareness of the beauty and rhythm of life?

A glance at primitive religion shows its strong ties with social communication and association and as we proceed to the developed religions of history the social character of religion does not seem to undergo a radical change. Is religion nothing but a social phenomenon, a product of social forces? Yet however we may emphasise the social function of religion, we cannot ignore the individual, without whom there cannot be any religion. But is then the individual himself a product of social causes? Can we understand Gautama the Buddha without any reference to the history and conditions of the society in which he was born? And, finally, it is only natural to identify religion with morality. If religion is more than superstition, it should express itself in a good life, in moral attitudes and obligations. Indeed no less a thinker than Kant considered religion only a consciousness of moral obligations as divine commands. But anyone genuinely religious can see that religion is not morality and that moral and religious elements often blend in religious life.

The clarification of the issues that we have raised depends on our answer to the basic question about the nature of religion. If our answer is not to remain arbitrary it has to take into account the multiplicity of religious life and experience. It must include primitive religions with their animistic beliefs and practices, with their fetishes and taboos; make room for the developed religions for which the idea of a transcendent or immanent God is central; and also accommodate religions in which the idea of an all-pervasive order is substituted for Godhead. If, on the contrary we define religion from one particular angle or in a particular perspective we will do wrong to the rich variety of religious life.

No wonder then that the definitions of religion are legion, though none is comprehensive enough to include all levels and stages of religious life. One of the best is the one offered by the great German theologian Schleiermacher, for whom religion is the feeling of absolute dependence. But neither religion nor art can be defined in terms of feelings only. It must also refer to the objects which arouse feelings. Hence, a reference to an infinite to provoke religious feelings are considered necessary. Now the feeling for the infinite seems primary, and the feeling of dependence seems to be its consequence. It must, however, be understood clearly that the infinite to which religious consciousness refers is not another name for the indefinite. It is richly suggestive, though indefinable in concepts, indescribable in words, and inexhaustible in any particular experience. In all religious experience there lurks a conviction of something which is not accessible to science or rational understanding and stands above the triviality and superficiality of daily existence. That reality is beyond flux of time and still constitutes the nucleus of our existence seems to be the dominant note of religious consciousness. The English poet Francis Thompson has well put the polarity of religious life, the consciousness of a Beyond which is present, in memorable lines:

O World invisible, we view thee,
O World intangible, we touch thee,
O World unknowable, we know thee,
Inaprehensible, we clutch thee.

Perhaps now we are better able to see the relative importance of the individual and the social elements in the development of religious consciousness. French social anthropologists have seen in religion a pre-logical state of mind with its own way of thinking and indifferent to logical categories. The primitive individual participates in the collective life of society, and his thoughts, emotions, and will are just a reflection of society. The function of religion is only to absorb him in his group. As against this attempt to reduce religion to its social function, we have the powerful voice of Alfred North Whitehead for whom religion is what a man does with his solitariness. Hence, for Whitehead, the most eloquent expression of religious consciousness is to be found in the last words of Jesus Christ: "My God, my God, why hast thou forsaken me?" Religion, however, is not so much a product of loneliness as a reaction against it. It is often a dialogue and a communion. Nevertheless, the contention that the main-spring of religion is not society but the individual with his personal experience is legitimate. There are two elements which seem central in every form of religious experience and they are, in the language of Prof. Clement Webb, the elements of intimacy and ultimacy. Religious consciousness is sustained by a sense of the ultimate with which one is intimately involved.

Misunderstandings about the nature of religion are often due to the confusion of religion as a personal commitment and experience with its manifestation as a historical and social phenomenon. In fact historical religions cannot be understood without the experiences on the basis of which their characteristic beliefs have grown. Religious faith is based on trust, trust in the experience to which it owes its origin. But if we ask what the object of religious faith is, there cannot be one answer. The moment we try to find the common denominator of all religious belief we may perhaps agree with Hoffding that it is the affirmation of the conservation of values, the conviction that values do not meet with annihilation but are conserved somehow. Justice, love, kindness, and all those values which in fact impart meaning to life may appear to be totally submerged in the dark moments of collective and individual life. Religious consciousness, however, can never accept defeat and is sustained by the conviction that values cannot vanish for good but only require acute sensitivity to discover them in times of cultural chaos. Negatively, religious consciousness is the rejection of the view that the material world is all that matters and sense-data are the only instances of reference.

It is most interesting to see the way in which aesthetic and religious moments blend in human consciousness. If the religious situation is marked by the revelation of a depth dimension in human experience, as Paul Tillich has remarked, it is natural to expect any experience, be it of love or beauty, to assume a religious character at a certain stage of its development. We can easily appreciate the profound remark of a French critic that great poetry is a form of prayer. But, in spite of the fact that our consciousness of beauty is apt to be saturated with a religious moment, it is different. Moral, religious, and aesthetic forms of consciousness are autonomous in their own right.

It is of course true that in the world of culture there cannot be any hard and fast divisions; yet there are fundamental distinctions which cannot be overlooked by any means. Moral consciousness is our awareness of an "ought", of duties and obligations which we have to fulfil. The "ought" remains indifferent to the fruits of our actions; what is to be done is to be done at all costs. Moral consciousness demands the sacrifice of pleasures and pleasure, and the renunciation of all inclination, and as such it has found its finest literary expression in the *Gītā* and in the ethical philosophy of Kant. The consciousness of beauty too, as Kant has rightly seen, must be disinterested if it is to remain pure. Hedonistic aesthetics is as fallacious as hedonistic ethics. The joy that we get in the disinterested contemplation of the beautiful is not just a pleasure of the senses or a simple affection of the soul. The delight that we derive from tragedy shows that our feelings are mixed. Even the delights of comedy are sustained by our awareness of fundamental discrepancies in life. Some forms of aesthetic consciousness stand closer to religious consciousness than others. The consciousness of the tragic and the sublime may be specially fused with religious pathos. But even comic situations created by the artist may be motivated by a tragic sense of life. It was said of Gogol, the great Russian satirist, that there were tears in his laughter. It is equally apt to remark that the amusement we get from the master-piece of Spanish literature, *Don Quixote,* is sustained by the tragedy of ideals, ideals that are ineffective in life. Thus, the variety of aesthetic consciousness is expressed in the variety of works of art.

Finally, aesthetic consciousness is distinguished from both moral and religious consciousness. While moral consciousness reveals tension and renunciation there is an element of spontaneity and freedom in aesthetic consciousness. But the moment tension makes an encroachment on aesthetic consciousness the aesthetic object becomes sublime and assumes moral solemnity. This is seen in our experience of tragedies. The religious consciousness, however, does not allow the tragic to become an end in itself; in it the tragic is experienced as transitional.

Now we may appreciate the plurality of faiths not as a curse but as a necessity born of the human situation. In his search for values man is becoming more and more aware of the fact that neither in their ideality nor in their reflection in our experience can values be reduced to a single pattern. Values are many and corresponding to them our experiences vary. Every great religion in history represents certain values and has discovered for man a new perspective of reality. *Karma* or *bhakti*, action or contemplation, renunciation or integration — each is expressible in some form of religious life and a one-sided emphasis on any one aspect of value will lead to blindness to other aspects. In religion this one-sidedness leads to fanaticism, and the claim to exclusiveness may at times even assert itself through violence. Hence the plurality of religions is not to be bewailed; for it creates for man the possibility of satisfying his inner needs according to his own option and commitment and makes allowance for the differences of human temperament and the diversity of historical traditions. Even when the encounter of one religious tradition with another, of one system of beliefs with another, or of one pattern of experience with another has force men to opt for one of the alternative, the choice of one has not remained unaffected by the other. The dialectic of the religious life does not allow the simple rejection of any of the alternatives without letting the impact of what is seemingly rejected be felt positively. The history or religions bears eloquent testimony to this.

Only a superficial view can see in the encounter of religions irreconcilable hostility. Already this encounter has contributed much to the enrichment of human culture. Our own country has been a meeting-ground of great religions and this impact of one religion on another has given rise to novel experiments in culture and to new developments in spiritual life. Many a reform movement within the fold of Hinduism and some characteristic developments of Sūfī orders in India bear eloquent testimony to the fruitfulness of inter-religious penetrations. Man labours, alas! Under the tragic illusion that sees in the conflict of ideas and in the diversity of patterns of life an antagonism which should end, and ignores the dynamic power which moves history and works for the promotion of human culture through complexity and variety. In a world torn with strife and threatened with the immediate danger of total annihilation, the consciousness of the holy with all its multiplicity of expression can still serve as an antidote to man's lust for power and bring home the truth that our little systems built on political ideologies "have their day and cease to be" but that what really matters, endures.

21

Inter-Religious Dialogue

A Study of D.Z. Phillips, John Hick and Maurice Friedman

Goutam Biswas

I

DIALOGUE, either interreligious or intra-religious, is a conscious attempt of divergent religious belief-systems to understand each other both discursively by attending the respective discourses and doctrines, and non-discursively by a silent contemplation on the forms of religious lives and practices leading towards some emancipatory goal. While the former tries to grasp the logic of religious discourses, the latter involves an existential sharing of religious concern. Without sharing this concern, it is difficult, almost impossible, to achieve the former goal as it is this concern which determines the logic of religious discourse. The relation between the two is like that of tacit awareness of something and its explicit formulation. Understanding religious discourse at the discursive level alone is inadequate and if it is parasitic upon sharing of religious concern, then the question arises: 'how is such sharing possible'? This is tantamount to asking 'how is inter-religious or intra-religious dialogue possible'? In what follows I shall discuss three view-points as potent to give an answer to this question namely (i) the Wittgensteinian view-point adopted by D.Z. Philips, — the view-point which considers religious beliefs as constitutive of distinct language game(s) and analyses the nature of religious language-game;

(ii) the epistemological view-point of John Hick which, in a Kantian fashion, grounds religious experience on a general theory of experience implying the possibility of understanding religious discourses and inter-faith dialogue with reference to this theory; and (iii) finally I shall present the dialogical Philosophy of Religion proposed by Maurice Friedman following my critique of (i) and (ii).

Any theory concerning inter-religious dialogue is not possible without an explication of the concept of dialogue. Further, so long as the rationale of any such theory bears an overt or clandestine relation to power and capital, it defies the existential concern of religion, i.e., the basic human urge for an emancipatory fulfilment beyond any system, an urge which is expressed in the Phenomenon of religiosity as distinguished from any religion in its institutionalised form. This distinction will be discussed in the context of my thesis. To substantiate my idea I shall bank upon Maurice Friedman's concept of "touchstones of reality", and present an addendum to John Hick's insightful thesis by incorporating my earlier contention that dialogue is not only conceptual and trans-conceptual but also pre-conceptual. (Goutam Biswas, 1995: 4-5) But this alternative proposal will follow in conjunction with and as a continuation of Maurice Friedman's contention in his book (1982), *The Human Way: A Dialogic Approach to Religion and Human Experience.*

II

One road to inter-religious dialogue can be anchored by analysing the very nature of religious language-game. D.Z. Phillips' Wittgensteinian approach to the problem of understanding different belief-system implies this possibility. (1971: 121-42) While Phillips retains the uniqueness of religious beliefs expressed through religious language-games with reference to the internality of such beliefs, he does not accept any incomprehensibility in religious beliefs as religious language games. For him religious beliefs are important, but if their importance is legitimatised with reference to some external factors making such beliefs relative, the very nature of values involved in these beliefs will be distorted. Phillips adopts Wittgenstein's point of view according to which the non-believer contradicts the believer when he says that he does not believe what the believer believes and in such a case both the believer and the non-believer share a common understanding and play the same game. Wittgenstein held that the contradiction between the believer and the non-believer is not like the case of two people disagreeing about the existence of unicorns. For him God's reality is not one of a kind and he is not a being among beings, and this makes the difference between these two games. God is not a thing. Hence, the claim that the so-called logical peculiarities of religious discourse are nothing but deviations from and distortions of non-religious way of speaking with which we are familiar, and the reality of God can be made subject to a wider criterion of intelligibility is rooted in a prejudice for generality. According to this prejudice what constitutes something as intelligible in one context may serve in other contexts as well.

As Phillips contends, the thesis that religious beliefs constitute distinctive language games does not mean to introduce any incomprehensibility in them. For him,

> within religious practices there will be criteria for what can and cannot be said. (1971: 132)

But the internal consistency of rules does not satisfy the critics. They might argue that such consistency may consist in some pointless rules. The possibility of such pointlessness is argued for with reference to games prevailing in other modes of social life. This kind of criticism, according to Phillips, is due to a strained analogy between religious beliefs and other social games. These other games are easily understandable and their rules are comprehensible because of the possibility of a common participation. This strained analogy again is due to the misgiving that the conception of religious beliefs as constitutive of distinctive language-games makes religious language-games inaccessible and esoteric for those who do not belong to the belief-system concerned; the distinction between religion and other modes of public life is thereby thought to be a major clue for understanding the importance of religion. But if religion takes the world seriously it cannot be completely cut off from other modes of social life. For example, the force of the contrast between a religious teaching and worldliness depends logically on both parts of the contrast. While it is true that "religious reactions to various situations cannot be assessed according to some external criteria of adequacy", Phillips contends that "the connections between religious beliefs and such situations must not be fantastic".(1971: 135)

In a Wittgensteinian fashion Phillips contends that the purpose of the Philosophy of Religion is not to interfere with or pass judgement on religious beliefs or practices but to understand them by studying the behaviour of the concepts within the context of religious forms of life. But the question remains: Is such understanding possible on the part of a non-participant and detached observer or analyst? Also, if a minimum level of participation is required for such understanding what would be its limit so that one can retain one's identity either as a secular non-religious person or as one belonging to a specific or different religious belief-system?

If the thesis of religious language-games does not propose any incomprehensibility of religious beliefs, such participation in religious forms of life is possible on the part of believers of diverse religious groups as well as non-believers. This participation would lead to an interreligious dialogue. But this participation has to be a *participation with distance* or else it would succumb to sheer conformism. Hence the question remains 'how is such participation possible' ? Conformism dissolves *otherness*, but sharing a concern, presupposes and confirms 'otherness'; it is a response to some 'call'.

John Hick's epistemological view-point can be regarded as a serious attempt to solve the problem of inter-religions and intra-religious dialogue in terms of a synthesis of the experiential and discursive aspects of religion within a knowledge-situation of Kantian type. But this needs further examination and evaluation with a point of reference to certain stages in forms of life praxis that are unspoken and the silent bequests of religiosity to human culture.

III

Religious pluralism does not necessarily imply an inter-religious dialogue. Religious institutions can, in principle, exist like unrelated, windowless monads. In this sense, the concept of religious pluralism is descriptive of the co-existence of several religious belief-systems without disturbing each other and without any interaction among themselves. Such a co-existence does not signify anything. The co-existence becomes significant and meaningful as contributive to the culture and human existence as such when a religious ecology develops out of a respectful and dialogical interaction among themselves. This is the positive aspect of religious pluralism. The negative aspect is manifest when there is a mutual defiance among religious belief-systems. The positive connotation of religious ecology is perhaps extremely relevant to our understanding and evaluation of the situations in Indian subcontinent in view of its multi-cultural and multi-religious configuration. This aspect was brought about in theory and practice by mystics such as Kabīr and Ramakrishna and thinkers such as Vivekananda and Rabindranath Tagore. Hick's attempts to highlight the equal status of all religions as human responses to the divine within a common epistemological framework is definitely valuable, but it upholds its discursive and conceptual level alone with an indication of further "inter-faith dialogue". Besides that, such a framework without an inclusion of the tacit dimension of knowledge conspicuously derides the personal involvement of the individual in the religious situation.

Hick rightly points out that problem concerning religious pluralism arises when one particular religion is considered or claimed to be the valid response to the divine, 'a response embodying true beliefs concerning the nature of reality' amidst many other such responses and claims. Religion, for him, is "range of responses to reality". Philosophy of religion cannot afford to choose one among them on the basis of any implicit or explicit conformity with one particular institution claiming final validity. According to Hick, human response to reality in its religious sense too is possible in terms of cognitive input "which can be expressed in different modes and which can be transformed from one mode to another"(1982: 101) This is a general theory of experience in terms of which he attempts to articulate the nature of religious experience. I elaborate his theory of experience in the following fashion:

> All our consciousness of objects and of situations is our experience of them as having a certain character, such that it is appropriate to behave in relation to them, or within them, in this rather than that way. Such awareness represents a fusion between, on the one hand, the information reaching us from our environment and, on the other hand, the system of concepts in terms of which that information comes to consciousness as organised and meaningful experience. (Hick, 1982: 102)

This fusion, for Hick, transform the sensory informations into actual consciousness of the world. For him, there is a "preconscious interpretative process" leading to this transformation, but this process is guided by the 'system of concepts' mentioned above. Thus, according to Hick's general theory of experience, experience is essentially concept-bound in a Kantian sense. Our practical response to the world depends on this transformation and a constitution of the meaning of the world following it. Hick says:

> To say that the perceived world has meaning to us is to say that it is a world which we can inhabit by acting and reacting in accordance with its perceived character, for meaning, in this sense, is meaning for someone; it is the difference which awareness of the presence of this particular thing, or of being in this particular environing situation makes to the perceiver's dispositional stance.

> Thus, to be conscious that the object which I am now holding in my hand is a pen is to be in a distinctive dispositional state in relation to it, such that I expect it to make marks in ink but not to bite or talk . . . (1982: 102).

Religious experience as such is to be understood in terms of this framework. Hick extends this general theory of experience in Kantian light towards our experience of God,

> in a manner analogous to that in which, according to Kant, we experience the world — namely by informational input from external reality being interpreted by the mind in terms of its own categorical system and thus coming to consciousness as meaningful phenomenal experience. (1982: 105)

The positive implications of this approach are obvious and appreciable: (i) it involves religious experience in a wider perspective of information network relating to history, society and environment; (ii) religious world-views come in proximal terms with the secular ones for the background of Hick's general epistemology; (iii) inter-religious and/or intra-religious dialogue becomes an unconstrained task with the acceptability of this epistemology. But Hick's basic theoretical premise that experience is essentially concept-bound keeps the understandability of religious experience and beliefs confined to discursive parameter alone, and the meaning of dialogue is also narrowed down to dialogue as essentially mediated by language. In the chapter "Christian Belief and Interfaith Dialogue" of his book, Hick says,

> I shall be concerned here primarily with discursive dialogue, though with the understanding that this may pass naturally into the deeper interior dialogue . . . (1982: 116).

Discursive dialogue would consist in verbal contemplation upon what is already 'said'; it is a thought-centred method which may pass into a deeper level. But such level would in that case simply be an output of the preceding discursive communication. Is it then possible to devise a dialogical method which would incorporate religious concern in its experiential, non-verbal, existential and prejudicative sense?

IV

D.Z. Phillips arguments for understandability of religious beliefs of diverse systems are based on an idea of semantic overlapping of religious concepts from one system to another, i.e. from one religious language-game to another (and ultimately from religious to public or secular language game) and *vice-versa* through their uses in concrete situations of religious forms of life, and a dispassionate observation and description of the behaviour of such concepts. But it does not state the possibility of inter-faith dialogue through an experiential sharing of religious concern before and after its canonisation. John Hick's most valuable and original epistemology of religious experience takes notice of a 'deeper and interior inter-faith dialogue' only at a later stage, i.e. at a point of transmutation of discursive and conceptual understanding of the religious into a deeper and internal dialectic in the individual psyche exploring an universal epistemic pattern for different systems and beliefs. This pattern would perhaps corroborate Hick's religious epistemology. But the meaning of 'dialogue' remains incomplete in such a case too because dialogue is more than discursive, and it does not consist in sheer transmission of beliefs.

In my book *Art as Dialogue : Essays in Phenomenology of Aesthetic Experience*, I made a distinction between 'dialogue in language' and 'dialogue preceding and over passing language'. (Biswas, 1995: 4-5) With the former the scope of understanding is limited because it cannot break through the conceptual barrier of language as a mediating factor. When language becomes a definite social institution with conceptual, semantic, and syntactic constraints involved in it, it can hardly be generous to an experimental concern wherein a suspension of the commoner's mode of cognising the reality and silence play a major role.

'Dialogue preceding and over passing language' starts from experience, proceeds through the language, and reaches beyond language. This is a broader notion of dialogue encompassing pre-linguistic, linguistic and trans-linguistic framework of the relation between human and reality. 'Dialogue' in this second sense includes the first sense but not the *vice-versa*. The distinction between the two senses of the notion of dialogue corresponds to the distinction between Gadamar's concept of dialogue as a fusion of two horizons through the mediation of language, and the concept of dialogue as explicated by Martin Buber and Maurice Friedman. For Buber and Friedman meaning of linguistic expressions is originally parasitic upon our *meeting* the reality. In his book *Martin Buber : The Life of Dialogue*, Friedman writes:

> Only I-thou gives meaning to the world of it, for I-thou is an end which is not reached in time but is there from the start, originating and carrying — through. (1960: 67)

The world of objects, i.e., the world of *It* does not have any vital force in itself. In Buber's words,

> . . . again and again that which has the status of object must blaze up into presentness and enter the elemental state from which it came, to be looked on and lived in the present by men. (1958: 40)

This is *meeting* the reality or *dialogue* in a broader sense which triggers the human experiential realm back to its primordial and non-propositional state of I-thou relationship, and at the same time carries it beyond the given language structure. Such a relationship consists in self disclosure and there is no question of interiorising the self in this regard. Hence, in a dialogical context, meaning is always meaning in and through meeting the reality. The essence of religion, according to Buber, consists in "the certainty that the meaning of existence is open and accessible in the actual lived concrete, not above the struggle with reality, but in it" (Martin Buber in Friedman, 1991: 312) Religious meaning lies in "the unseduced immediacy of the moment" (Buber, 1991: 312)

Inter-religious dialogue, in the true sense of the term, is possible in a more viable fashion with reference to this explication of the notion of dialogue. Significance of the Buberian standpoint in this regard is enriched further in Friedman's coinage of the notion of 'touchstone of reality' and its analysis.

"Religion", as Friedman suggests,

> is neither an objective philosophy nor a subjective experience. It is a lived reality that is ontologically prior to its expression in creed, ritual, and group. At the same time it is inseparable from these expressions and cannot be distilled out and objectified. The *religious* at this deepest level might be discussed as a basic *attitude* or relationship arising in the encounter with the whole reality directly given to one in one's existence. (1982: 2)

Unlike Phillips, Maurice Friedman views the task of philosophy of religion as a 'conceptual clarification' together with a 'metaphorical pointing to the religious reality' that is known within the realm of the 'between' or I-thou relationship

> but without abstracting from that meeting detached statements about the nature and attributes of God and without doing injustice to the typical and the unique apprehended in the phenomenological study of the history of the religions. (1982: 4)

Friedman's own philosophy of religion is appropriately contained in his concept of "touchstones of reality". This concept, as Friedman himself elaborates, does not imply any prior definition of reality nor any metaphysical absolute. It signifies a basic trust in "the contact with *otherness*". In Friedman's words,

> There is no *touch* independent of contact with *otherness*, an otherness that transcends subjectivity even though

> it cannot be known without it. The coloration of the *Zeitgeist* that seals us within our cultural subjectivity is not a touchstone of reality but a fool's gold. Touchstones of reality must be made true ever again by testing them in each new situation — bringing the life-stance they have produced into a moment of present reality. Unlike scientific generalisations, touchstones of reality provide valid insights confirmable in some situations but not all. Touchstones of reality are closer to events than insights. They provide no secure purchase above the stream of living. We are left with the problem of when to move in the direction of insight and abstraction and when to move back into the living waters. (1982: 7)

The approach of touchstones of reality, for Friedman, is best suited to our understanding of religion. Each religion, for him, is unique by holding a commitment, a life-stance. He says:

> Our dialogue with religions is not a search for *the* truth, accordingly — either Plato's absolute or the one true religion or the perennial Philosophy.

Each religion speaks of its uniqueness, and each says something to us about our life as humankind and as the unique persons we are. The answer to the dilemma of religious particularism versus religious universalism, consequently, is the *mutually confirming pluralism of touchstones of reality*. (1982: 7)

V

The very concept of 'touchstone' bears a magical view of reality, — reality and truth about it to be revealed in a sudden flash of vision in a dialogic situation. The situation is a lived, concrete one where other truths are looked at in a spirit of partnership. In case of religion, such a spirit of partnership demands a wholeness in which no aspect of human existence is excluded or set aside. If any transformation of being takes place in that situation, the transformation would be that of the whole and experiential and concrete in nature. While this is the prejudgemental and experiential level of religion for which no didactic lesson is required and human beings come close to reality in this manner for a basic emancipatory urge to be with the whole, the respect and confirmation of being encountered in that state is also not artificial and it is taken as a 'Thou' within the dialogical space. This is very much consistent with the demand for wholeness.

But religion being a way that one walks and a life-stance, it expresses itself in various doctrinal forms such as myth, creed, theology, and metaphysics. This is what I call 'recording the moments of religiousity', — a recording which generally leads to canonisation and institutionalisation. When understanding other religion means understanding it through certain doctrinal form without referring it to its experiential state or unreduced moments of religiousity there is a fundamental split between experience and expression, existence and thought. With this split, the possibility of interreligious dialogue remains confined to arguments and contemplation centering thought or expression alone as dissociated from its lived situation. The sanctity of the word is thereby lost in verbalism, and the true practice is converted into habit.

Dialogue which incorporates the pre-conceptual or pre-linguistic level too can catch the "unreduced moment of immediacy" in religious experience, and then relate it to the discursive and institutional aspect of it. In this process authenticity in interreligious dialogue becomes confirmed. Interfaith dialogue in a deeper sense as mentioned by Hick is possible when dialogue is understood in an all-encompassing sense, i.e., 'dialogue as preceding and overpassing language'. The deeper inter-faith dialogue of Hick's kind is meditative in nature which dwells upon an antecedent discursive understanding of religious experience. This deeper and interior dialogue mentioned by Hick seems to signify the overpassing of language or trans-linguistic stage of dialogue. But the possibility of perfection in it is much less if it loses its root, i.e., the pre-linguistic and pre-judgemental dialogue.

The space of inter-religious dialogue can be created only with a Thou-orientation towards the 'other' religion as a 'touchstone'. For Friedman,

> touchstones of reality point to a 'narrow ridge' between an objective reality existing outside of us and a subjective truth minus mutual contact with real otherness. Like our images of the human, touchstones of the reality are the way in which the past is brought into the present and made present anew. Both touchstones of reality and the image of the human are a product of meeting and a way of entering and a way of entering new meetings. Both provide a link between the past and the present without fixing the present in the past. . . . Our touchstones of reality are themselves the bond between the absolute and the particular, the embodiment of symbol in the lived life of actual persons. The meaning of the religious symbol is found not in its universality but in the fact that it points to a concrete event that witnesses just as it is, in all its concreteness, transitoriness, and uniqueness, to the relation of the absolute. The symbol becomes abstract, to be sure, when it is detached from a concrete event, when 'the finger pointing at the moon is taken for the moon itself'. (1982: 45)

Hence the 'other' religion as a 'touchstone' refers to the original, primordial meeting, and thereby it presents itself as something with life and not as a dead past sunk in the pages of some holy scripture or routine rituals.

If the discursive dialogue that Hick talkes about is not linked with this primordial and original dialogue unmediated by language, then dialogue becomes not only narrow but also unauthentic in the sense that the understanding it would produce thereof will be invalid. The language-game paradigm offered by D.Z. Phillips for understanding of and access to religious concepts is within strict linguisticality or domains of behavioural patterns expressed by and inter-mingled with such concepts.

Going back to the moments of religiousity, therefore, is essential. Thou-orientation to religions of others as 'touchstones' point to pure, experiential level which cannot be styled as either empirical or rational. Understanding of them is developed and construed further at a discursive level which may incorporate institutionalised approaches. It receives further maturity and a sense of finality when the entire dialogical space becomes meditative for a full assimilation and comprehension of religious beliefs and experiences. A synthesis of these three levels of interreligious understanding conveys a sense of completeness and particularly in an Indian context it helps us in understanding religious pluralism as religious ecology through a lived, concrete dialogue with varieties of religious beliefs and systems.

References

Biswas, Goutam, 1995, *Art as Dialogue : Essays in Phenomenology of Aesthetic Experience,* Indira Gandhi National Centre for the Arts, and D.K. Printworld, New Delhi.

Buber, Martin, 1958, *I and Thou*, tr. by R.G. Smith, T & T. Clark, Edinburgh.

———, 1991, *Eclipse of God,* inter alia, *The Worlds of Existentialism* ed. by Maurice Friedman, Humanities Press International, New Jersey and London.

Friedman, Maurice, 1960, *Martin Buber: The Life of Dialogue,* Harper and Row, New York.

———, 1982, *The Human Way : A Dialogical Approach to Religion and Human Experience,* Anima Books, Pennsylvania.

Hick, John, 1982, *God Has Many Names,* Macmillan, London

Phillips, D.Z., 1971, "Religious Beliefs and Language-Games", in Basil Mitchel (ed.), *The Philosophy of Religion,* Oxford University Press, London.

Notes on Contributors

Margaret Chatterjee is presently a visiting WEXLER Professor in Philosophy at Bryn Mawr, U.S.A. Earlier she was Professor of Philosophy at Delhi University, Director of Indian Institute of Advanced Study, Shimla (1986-89).

Author of several books which include: *Contemporary Indian Philosophy* (London, Allen and Unwin, 1974), *Gandhi's Religious Thought* (London, Macmillan, 1983), *The Language of Philosophy* (Martinus Nijhoff and Allied Publishers, 1981).

Her papers are published in *Religious Studies*, (London), *Kant-Studien*, *Journal of Aesthetics and Art Criticism*, *Philosophy of Phenomenological Research*, *Journal of Polish Academy of Science*, *Topoi*, *JICPR*.

Amitabha Das Gupta is Head, Department of Philosophy, University of Hyderabad. He is an author of a book, *The Second Linguistic Turn*: *Chomsky and the Philosophy of Language*, Peter Lang, Frankfortan, Main, 1996. His papers are published in journals such as, *International Philosophical Quarterly* (New York); *Philosophy of Social Sciences* (Sage Publications); *Economic and Political Weekly, JICPR, Indian Philosophical Quarterly.*

Bhargavi V. Davar is a Ph.D., from IIT, Bombay. Her book (with P.R. Bhat) entitled, *Psychoanalysis as a Human Science: Beyond Foundationalism*, is published by Sage Publications, 1995. Her papers are published in journals which include, *Economic and Political Weekly*, *JICPR*, *Current Literature of Science on Science, Radical Journal of Health.*

Sasheej Hedge teaches sociology at University of Hyderabad. His papers are published in *Third Text, Contribution to Indian Sociology, Journal of Arts and Ideas, Social Scientist*. He has contributed papers to edited volumes.

A. Raghuramaraju teaches philosophy at University of Hyderabad. His papers are published in *AI & Society* (Springer-Verlag, London), *Economic and Political Weekly, JICPR, Studies in Humanities and Social Sciences* (IIAS, Shimla), *Indian Philosophical Quarterly, and he has contributed papers to edited volumes.*

Ahmed Nizar teaches philosophy in the School of Social Sciences, M.G.University, Kottayam. He is a Ph.D. from IIT, Kanpur, and a well-known social and cultural critic of Malayalam literature.

Prasenjit Biswas is a Jawaharlal Nehru Scholar attached to the Department of Philosophy, North-Eastern Hill University, Shillong. He is presently working on his book, *The Other and the Community: Towards a Revisionary Ethics.*

Bijoy H. Boruah teaches philosophy at IIT, Kanpur. He has an M.Litt. from Oxford, Ph.D. from University of Guelph, Canada. He has been a Fellow at IIAS, Shimla. His book *Fiction and Emotion* is published by Oxford University Press, New Delhi and Clarendon. He has published articles in many journals.

Rekha Jhanji is Professor of Philosophy at Panjab University, Chandigarh, Fellow of IIAS, Shimla. She has authored several books which include: *Communication and Art* (Ajanta Publications, New Delhi, 1980), *Aesthetic Communication: The Indian Perspective* (Munshiram Manoharlal, New Delhi, 1985). In addition she has contributed papers to national and international journals.

B.N. Patnaik is Professor of Linguistics and English at IIT, Kanpur. He is a well-known linguist, has contributed several research papers to professional journals.

S.S. Barlingay was the founder editor of *Indian Philosophical Quarterly*, worked as Professor of Philosophy at Delhi University, retired from University of Poona. He authored several books in philosophy, contributed papers to the national and international journals. He was President of the Indian Philosophical Congress, UGC Professor in Philosophy, and represented India in several international conferences.

Hasna Begum is Professor of Philosophy at Dhaka University, Bangladesh. She is author of *Moore's Ethics: Theory and Practice.*

P.R. Bhat teaches philosophy at IIT, Bombay, author of (with Bhargavi V. Davar) *Psychoanalysis as a Human Science: Beyond Foundationalism*, Sage Publications. He has published papers in *JICPR and Indian Philosophical Quarterly.*

Satya P. Gautam is presently at University of Liverpool on a teaching assignment. He teaches philosophy at Panjab University, and has been a Fellow of IIAS, Shimla. He is author of a book entitled, *Reasons for Action: A Praxiological Approach to philosophy of Social Sciences*, Ajanta Publishers, New Delhi.

Jagat Pal teaches philosophy at NEHU, Shillong, he is Ph.D. from IIT, Kanpur. He has contributed papers in *Indian Philosophical Quarterly.*

Vanlalnghak teaches philosophy at Manipur University. He is a Ph.D. from IIT, Kanpur.

V.T. Sebastian teaches philosophy at Panjab University. He published papers in *JICPR*, *Indian Philosophical Quarterly*, and in *The Centre for Research in Value and Philosophy*, Washington.

Pabitrakumar Roy teaches philosophy at North Bengal University. He was awarded a Commonwealth Fellowship. He authored *David Hume: A Critical Introduction to His Theory of Knowledge*. His book entitled, *Hume and Kant: Two Studies in Linkages*, was published by Commonwealth Fellowship of Philosophers, London, 1986. He has publications in many other journals.

Asghar Ali Engineer is Chairman of Centre for the Study of Secularism and Society, Mumbai. He is a well-known scholar on Islam, a social activist, journalist and author of several books and papers.

Syed Vahiduddin retired as Professor of Philosophy from Delhi University. He was President, Indian Philosophical Congress during 1988. His published books include, *Religion at the Crossroads* (New Delhi), *The Islamic Experience in Contemporary Thought* (New Delhi). He has contributed several papers to national and international journals.

Goutam Biswas is Head, Department of Philosophy at Assam University, and has been a Fellow of IIAS, Shimla. His book *Art as Dialogue: Essays in Phenomenology of Aesthetic Experience*, is published by Indira Gandhi National Centre for Arts, New Delhi. He has contributed papers in *JICPR, Indian Philosophical Quarterly* and other journals.

Index